It's Enough to Make You Sick

It's Enough to Make You Sick

The Failure of American Health Care
and a Prescription for the Cure

Jeffrey M. Lobosky, M.D.

ROWMAN & LITTLEFIELD PUBLISHERS, INC.
Lanham • Boulder • New York • Toronto • Plymouth, UK

Published by Rowman & Littlefield Publishers, Inc.
A wholly owned subsidiary of The Rowman & Littlefield Publishing Group, Inc.
4501 Forbes Boulevard, Suite 200, Lanham, Maryland 20706
http://www.rowmanlittlefield.com

Estover Road, Plymouth PL6 7PY, United Kingdom

Distributed by National Book Network

British Library Cataloguing in Publication Information Available

Library of Congress Cataloging-in-Publication Data

Lobosky, Jeffrey M., 1951–
  It's enough to make you sick : the failure of American health care and a prescription for the cure / Jeffrey M. Lobosky.
    p. ; cm.
  Includes bibliographical references and index.
  ISBN 978-1-4422-1462-0 (cloth : alk. paper) —
  ISBN 978-1-4422-1464-4 (electronic)
  I. Title.
  [DNLM: 1. Delivery of Health Care—United States. 2. Health Care Reform—United States. W 84 AA1]
  LC classification not assigned
  362.10973—dc23   2011043768

∞™ The paper used in this publication meets the minimum requirements of American National Standard for Information Sciences—Permanence of Paper for Printed Library Materials, ANSI/NISO Z39.48-1992.

Printed in the United States of America

For Diana:

My inspiration, my conscience, my most candid critic, my staunchest supporter—and the love of my life.

Contents

Prologue

$\mathcal{O}$ur health, without a doubt, is life's most precious commodity. But the word "commodity" really should not apply to our health, for it implies that our well-being is something that can be traded, like Microsoft stock or pork futures. Our health is much more than a mere asset on our financial statement. It is a measure of the quality of our lives, and its preservation and cultivation significantly affect our longevity, our earning capacity, and above all, our happiness. Being blessed with good health enables us to enjoy the fruits of our democracy, to rear our children, to spoil our grandchildren, to attain our dreams, and to grow old with the ones we most love. Lose it and the results can be devastating—physically, emotionally, and with increasing frequency, financially. All life is indeed precious, but a healthy life is cherished even more.

Americans appear to understand this concept and we do indeed value our health, so much so that many have come to view health care as an inalienable right for all of our citizens regardless of their socioeconomic status. Which of life's other necessities are treated the same? Is every American entitled to the same home? Of course not, but we do consider shelter a basic need. Try going into your local supermarket and demanding the same cut of filet mignon that the wealthy shopper just purchased even though you have no money. That won't work, yet we consider food a basic need as well. But go into the emergency room of your local hospital, again without sufficient funds, and you will receive the same care and attention as any patient who crosses that threshold. Or at least you should, for we have laws that mandate it.[1]

With pride, we trumpet our system as the best in the world. Yet, as a nation, we have been poor stewards of the resources available to us to maintain the level of well-being that we have all come to expect. We drink too much, we smoke too much, we eat too much, we exercise too little, and we expect

1

the system to compensate for our shortcomings. As a society, we choose our priorities, and for many of us, our health and the system that supports it have been low on the list. We have come to take our well-being and the institutions that minister to it for granted.

Organized medicine has changed dramatically in the United States over the past 150 years. Gone are the days when country doctors would make house calls on mules or horses, bartering their limited medical skills for a few chickens or a bag of grain. Thankfully, our system has evolved exponentially since those pioneering days. We now have remarkable technologies such as MRI scans and minimally invasive surgical tools. We have at our disposal a plethora of wonder drugs that can eradicate infectious diseases and even cure many cancers. Gene therapies, still in their infancy, hold great promise for eliminating many of the maladies that have plagued mankind since our beginning.

But medical care is not technology nor pharmacology nor research. Medical care and the healing that ensues are the product of a sacred relationship between a patient and his or her physician, a relationship steeped in the tradition of the Hippocratic Oath, by its very nature intimate as well as emotional, infused with trust on the part of the patient and sincere caring on the part of the physician. As patients, we share privileged information with our doctors that may be known to no one else and we have faith that they will use that information to make us whole. Often we literally put our lives in the hands of our physicians.

In return, physicians are expected to treat their patients with compassion and with respect. As doctors, my colleagues and I should be fastidious guardians of the trust placed in us and utilize all our skill and knowledge to keep our patients healthy and relieve their suffering when possible. In order to fulfill that relationship, physicians need to be available to patients, sometimes at inconvenient hours. We need to craft treatment options that best fit the needs of each particular patient while taking into account his or her unique individuality. But above all, we need to listen to and communicate with our patients. The result can be one of the most rewarding personal and professional bonds that either individual experiences.

But times have changed. Although we can celebrate our evolution from pioneer medicine, we can also mourn the progressive erosion of the traditional doctor-patient relationship. With increasing frequency, physicians and their patients are becoming estranged as more and more layers separate us from each other. We become adversaries rather than advocates, and we thrust greater responsibilities for the care of our patients onto nurse practitioners, physician assistants, hospitalists, and the already overcrowded emergency rooms. As a result, we lose that intimacy that is so necessary in maintaining trust and that unique bond between patient and healer becomes frayed.

It seems that every decade or so, public interest in health care is piqued and we hear our politicians debate the issues, offer new and innovative solutions, and demand change. But change never comes. The powerful lobbyists from the insurance industry, the pharmaceutical companies, the American Hospital Association, the trial lawyers, as well as the American Medical Association make certain the status quo is maintained. Our politicians are quick to realize how their bread is buttered, and as long as their campaigns are financed by these special interests, those are the masters they will serve. As a result, the numbers of uninsured will increase, the numbers of underinsured will expand, and the quality of care provided to the average American will continue to decline.

Each decade we will also see books like this one that decry the current state of affairs and offer their own solutions to the crisis. But the majority of these books are written by nonphysicians, usually academic-based free-market economists, Ivy League health care policy experts, nationally renowned social scientists, investigational journalists, or the dreaded left-wing "bleeding-heart liberals" or right-wing "conservative whack jobs." But these "experts" have never had to come into the emergency room at 2:00 a.m. to manage the care of a victim of a drive-by shooting, or tell a distraught parent they were unable to revive his or her overdosed daughter, or experience the frustration of having their request for an MRI scan denied by a nurse working for an insurance company hundreds of miles away. This criticism certainly is not intended to demean the contribution these authors make to the public debate (with the exception of the last two groups), but it points to the limitations when one separates an academic treatise from the reality in the trenches.

Even when the author is a doctor, his or her own prejudices can permeate the discussion as well as the conclusions. Often, physicians write these books out of frustration and anger over a particular experience they have encountered. They focus on a specific "bad guy," usually the insurance companies or malpractice lawyers, and suggest that the pervasive problems inherent in the system would disappear if these villains were held in check. But it becomes easy in such situations to develop a blind spot to the vast array of other mitigating factors that exert a profound effect on the problems at hand.

The issues that contribute to our current crisis in American health care are as numerous and complex as they are diverse. In the chapters that follow, I hope to illuminate some of the causes and to foster a better understanding of just how we got to this point. Of course, these discussions will, by necessity, be infused with my own prejudices, the very same biases I disparaged in the preceding paragraph. Rest assured, I will discuss the roles of the insurance industry, the pharmaceutical industry, for-profit hospitals, and malpractice litigation in creating the prevailing mess. But I also hope to point out how the

American business community, our current political system and their leaders, organized medicine, practicing physicians, and patients themselves share culpability for our current state of affairs. No one group is fully to blame and no one group is fully blameless.

I have made a sincere effort not to overwhelm the reader with a barrage of graphs, charts, numbers, references, or obscure facts. After all, as an English professor of mine once said, "a good author never lets the facts interfere with his conclusions." I have included such data when necessary to make my point, and I owe a debt of gratitude to the numerous referenced authors whose own endeavors have enlightened and inspired me.

Throughout this book I will tell you stories about patients I have treated and explain the difficulties they have encountered with the best medicine America can offer. Their names have been changed to assure their anonymity, and some specific details have been altered slightly only to protect that same anonymity. But the facts of these stories remain true and represent my experiences as well as those of my close colleagues.

I'd like to think of this work as a conversation between the two of us, but one where I actually do all the talking. It doesn't matter how many studies suggest that a physician shortage exists or how many suggest the opposite; or how many purport to prove medical care in the United States is the best in the world or how many may prove otherwise. There are plenty of studies to support either side on almost any issue depending on how they are interpreted. What *is* important is the care that I provide as a physician and the care that you as a patient receive. My real intent is to share with you how all of these varied issues affect the practice of medicine in the real world, not the theoretical one.

The fact of the matter remains that our health care system is indeed broken and badly in need of repair. The traditional doctor-patient covenant has been replaced by a system of market-driven initiatives that have resulted in a shredding of that sacred bond. Hopefully, the pages that follow will explain to you just how our current system has become so dysfunctional, why so many of our citizens lack access to the miracles of American medicine, why our seniors are forced to choose between their blood pressure medications and their groceries, and why hardworking men and women stand to lose everything if, God forbid, they develop cancer. And in the end I hope to provide all of us with a rational blueprint for effective and compassionate health care reform. This blueprint will scrutinize the recent attempts to reform the system and try to explain which components are laudable and which are destined to fail. For years, Americans have walked into their physicians' offices, taken an uncomfortable seat, and waited with anticipation for the nurse to announce, "The doctor will see you now." In the following pages I will explain to all of you why, just maybe, the doctor *won't* see you now!

Great, Another Book on America's Health Care System. Don't You Have Better Things to Do, Doctor . . . Like Play Golf?

I was eleven years old when I decided to become a doctor. While playing baseball with my neighborhood buddies, I fell in the street and split open my chin, prompting a visit to the local emergency room near my southern California home. I had been to a hospital before, as a very young child when another accident resulted in a laceration to the back of my throat and an emergency surgery was required to stop the bleeding and repair the cut. I was three at the time, and had little recollection of the event other than the sweet aroma of the anesthetic agent utilized to put me to sleep.

This time it was different. I was fully conscious and keenly aware of my surroundings. Although injured, as an eleven-year-old boy, I wasn't about to betray my fear, so as I concentrated on projecting a brave demeanor, I became fascinated at the milieu into which I was propelled. I remember the bright lights, the rows of gurneys covered in crisp, white sheets. I was intrigued by the myriad of technological wizardry that surrounded me (obviously modest compared to today's standards) with flashing colored lights and beeping alarms.

I was impressed with the gleaming silver trays that supported what seemed to be an endless array of steel instruments that I knew, with some trepidation, would be used to close the gaping wound in the bottom of my chin. I was mesmerized with the bevy of pretty young nurses who whisked in and out of my cubicle in their starched white dresses, white nylons, and uniquely shaped white caps, assuring me that all would be well. Although ten to fifteen years their junior, I was certain that the attention they lavished upon me reflected their recognition that I was remarkably handsome and mature for my age. It never dawned on me that they were just doing their job. Forty-nine years later, it still doesn't.

Yet, what I most vividly remember about that Saturday morning encounter was the emergency room doctor. The forty-nine years since have erased his name and face from my memory, but his impact upon my life and career is etched indelibly. He projected both confidence and authority, but at the same time, a kindness and compassion that allayed my fears and filled me with trust and awe. Within minutes, my chin was repaired and I was sent on my way. In that one instant, I imagined how rewarding it must be to devote one's life to relieving suffering and how gratifying it would be to have patients filled with such admiration as I was that day. I was hooked. I knew then and there that I wanted to be a doctor.

I never wavered from that objective, and that singular goal defined me for years to come. My desire to go to medical school endowed me with the discipline and work ethic necessary to succeed in high school and college and gave me the strength not only to survive, but actually to thrive amid the tremendous challenges, both intellectual and physical, of medical school and a neurosurgical residency.

It is remarkable that the rigors of medical training do not completely extinguish the idealism that characterizes most young physicians. The long hours, the enormous amount of required knowledge, the sometimes sadistic abuse by superiors, the cutthroat competition among peers, the psychological trauma when patients do poorly, and the immeasurable stress on family life all conspire to replace that idealism with cynicism and compassion with indifference. But fortunately, the majority of my classmates and I emerged unscathed, and I entered practice in 1984 ready to live my dream.

I was fortunate to associate with a truly outstanding partner, Dr. Bruce Burke, who for the past twenty-seven years has served as mentor, teacher, role model, and above all, friend. My wife and I were blessed to settle in a community where we could raise our children in a safe and nurturing environment and I could practice state-of-the-art medicine as a member of a progressive and highly talented medical staff. As the years passed, our good fortune at finding this opportunity became increasingly apparent.

Throughout the '80s and early '90s, the practice of medicine for me remained idyllic and I suspect the same could be said for most of my local colleagues. However, there were forces in motion that had the potential to significantly impact the way we practiced our craft, and I began to hear rumblings from friends and colleagues in the larger metropolitan areas about how "managed care" was beginning to infiltrate their medical communities. The result of this new medical model was diminishing reimbursement, increasing paperwork and red tape, and an entirely new competition for patients based not on medical quality but economics.

Insurance companies were awarding contracts to provide care for their clients to the lowest bidder, pitting one physician against another and replacing the traditional referral patterns based on clinical reputation and word of mouth. Soon, physicians of all specialties who were considered among the most talented in their communities saw their patient bases eroded as insurers required clients to see only selected practitioners who agreed to treat patients at a reduced fee. Suddenly, the surgeon or internist who the week before was struggling to maintain his practice because of a less than stellar reputation found his office overflowing with patients, while the pillars of medical quality were forced to either relocate or reduce their fees to unsustainable levels.

As reimbursement for medical services began declining, the only way that physicians could maintain their incomes was by increasing the volume of the patients they saw or the number of procedures they performed. Patients began complaining that they were feeling rushed by physicians who could no longer afford to take the time to listen carefully to their complaints and analyze their problems. Many physician offices began hiring "physician extenders" such as nurse practitioners or physician assistants, who were utilized to significantly increase the volume of individuals seen, further isolating the doctor from his or her well-established patient base.

With the competition for managed care contracts becoming more frenzied, doctors experienced a significant decline in the collegiality that characterized long-established medical staffs, with a resultant loss of civility and cooperation that further diminished the quality of care that was being provided. Physicians began looking for unique ways to succeed in this new environment and began forming multispecialty groups, selling their practices to larger medical conglomerates, and creating Independent Practice Associations (IPAs) so that they could better negotiate with the large insurance carriers. These efforts most often failed as primary care physicians and specialists found themselves at odds over utilization of services and reimbursement.

Experience with these new paradigms expanded, with more and more physicians becoming disgruntled, cynical, and downright angry. Discussions in physician lounges at lunchtime across America took on a distinctly different tone. Debates about the latest treatments extolled in *The New England Journal of Medicine* for hypertension or whether Joe Montana was the greatest quarterback of all time were now superseded by complaints about the dismal reimbursement rates offered by Medicare and Blue Cross, the skyrocketing malpractice insurance premiums, and the overwhelming frustration at having to call a nurse in some distant office in order to receive permission to order an MRI scan on a patient with a suspected brain tumor.

Doctors developed a foreboding sense of impotence in their ability to combat this assault on both their income and autonomy. Antitrust laws prevented them from legally discussing what they extracted from insurance carriers or from collectively bargaining with the carriers outside of a formal IPA or large group organization. Physicians became depressed and despondent, and after realizing they were unable to successfully contend with insurers, they began lashing out at the only entities with whom they still had some influence—their hospitals and their patients.

Over the past decade, primary care physicians have, with an alarming increase in frequency, refused to provide emergency room coverage or inpatient services for their patients and relinquished care to "hospitalists." A hospitalist is a physician who practices full time within the confines of a hospital, admitting and caring for patients whose own doctors no longer provide those services or who are without a primary care physician. Generally a number of hospitalists constitute a given group within the institution and care is handed off among members of the group as their "shift" ends. So, although you have been a patient of Dr. Jones for twenty-three years and he has provided the best of care for you and your family over that period of time, you can kiss those days good-bye. Now when you are sick enough that you require hospitalization, your care will be provided by a group of doctors you don't know and who don't know you. Welcome to twenty-first-century medicine in America.

In addition, many trauma centers across the country have been forced to close as more and more specialists in the critical fields of general surgery, neurosurgery, orthopedics, and anesthesia opt out of emergency room coverage and limit their practice to more lucrative elective care. Many of the hospitals that have been able to maintain their emergency departments have done so by providing "on-call stipends" to physicians, which can range from $25 to $5,000 per day depending on the geographic region and specialty involved.

With the emergence of this model for supplementing income, hospitals and their medical staffs have been placed in adversarial positions. Physicians increasingly expect their hospitals to make up the difference between what they think they should earn and what they actually make. When those demands are not met, physicians are threatening to forgo on-call responsibilities, jeopardizing not only the hospital's continued survival but patient lives as well.

Hospitals respond to these challenges with threats of their own. Oftentimes they try and recruit new physicians to an already saturated market to displace the "troublemakers" whom they perceive as unreasonable. They may restrict the uncooperative physicians' privileges by providing less operating room time for their elective schedule or denying their requests for new equipment or services. Hospitals become desperate and are forced to hire "locums" or temporary physicians to provide services, often at a much higher cost than the original demands and not uncommonly with a reduction in quality of care. A vicious cycle ensues that insures a lose-lose situation for the hospital, the physician, and most importantly, the patient.

Physicians have also responded to this crisis by developing their own freestanding care centers, which compete with their local hospitals for the most desirable and well-insured patients. These facilities may specialize in providing kidney dialysis or chemotherapy infusion. Many offer surgical treatments that may cover a single specialty such as spine surgery or a variety of differing surgical disciplines. Physician "investors" in these centers traditionally send their well-insured patients to these mini-hospitals and reap the economic benefits while they refer the uninsured or underinsured to their community hospital for care. This "cherry-picking" further erodes the financial viability of the community hospital as well as the professional relationships with the physicians. However, with reimbursement declining at such an alarming rate, many physicians are forced to resort to these alternative sources of income to pay the bills.

When physicians turn fifty, inevitably we ask each other how long we plan to keep working. My practice has been wonderfully successful for the past twenty-seven years, at least successful by my definition. I may not earn the most money, have the largest house, or most elaborate toys; I don't define that as success. But throughout my career I have been able to practice my craft in a community with outstanding colleagues who have been as dedicated as I to providing state-of-the-art care to the population we serve. Our hospital has also been committed to the same mission. I have especially enjoyed my patients and the opportunity to relieve their suffering when I could and to assist them in other ways when I could not.

My answer to the "How long do you plan to work?" question has always been, "Until it is no longer fun and rewarding." A few years ago, for the first time in my life, I became fearful that time may be approaching and I began yearning for the bygone days. Yet, I found it difficult to accept the finality of that conclusion and I keep fighting to maintain that flame of idealism, not just in my own practice but in our larger medical community and on a national scale as well. In doing so, I am encouraged by the number of physicians who, like me, are frustrated with the direction medicine has taken but refuse to surrender to the forces that threaten how we practice and, ultimately, the quality of care provided to the American population.

It is easy to assign culpability for the sad state in which we now find ourselves. There are certainly plenty of villains to go around. Managed care programs, HMOs, Medicare, Medicaid, pharmaceutical companies, for-profit hospitals, illegal immigrants, malpractice lawyers, greedy doctors, the uncaring business community, insurance companies, politicians, lobbyists, Democrats, Republicans, Buddhists, Catholics, Muslims . . . the list is endless. Pick one . . . or two . . . or three . . . as long as it isn't you or I.

And therein lies the problem.

Before we are able to effectively address the issues of medical care in the United States, each of us must examine our own contribution to this crisis and accept collective responsibility. Only when the finger pointing and rhetoric subside will we be in a position to collaboratively face this challenge as a nation and craft sustainable solutions that involve, by necessity, all the factions that got us here in the first place.

My colleagues and I have deliberated these matters ad nauseam in the operating room, in the doctors' lounge, at national meetings, and over our own dining room tables. However, we are only one component of the greater debate and only one component of the ultimate solution. It was my wife who suggested I write this book, initially as a catharsis, in hopes that giving a more formal voice to these frustrations would somehow reverse the cynicism she had observed surfacing in me. But more importantly, my goal is to catalyze a national debate where all of us can discuss and understand the complex forces that define and direct the delivery of medical care now and in the future. Hopefully, the interested reader will appreciate that there are no absolute villains nor heroes and that together we just may be able to constructively solve the health care crisis and provide all our citizens with the quality of care and quality of life they so richly deserve.

That is why I wrote this book.

· 2 ·

Health Care in America: The Best
That Money Can Buy . . . Oh, Really?

$\mathcal{M}$an, I love this country! Don't you? After all, we are trained from early childhood to believe in America's superiority in almost any arena. We're taught that we are the wealthiest nation on earth, we are home to the most prestigious universities in the world, we have created the most extraordinary inventions known to mankind, we have walked on the moon, pioneered the most advanced medical treatments, dominated the Olympic Games, and saved the world from tyranny in two World Wars. America has provided the rest of the seven billion inhabitants of this planet with a shining example of democracy and freedom, given millions of downtrodden immigrants a chance to experience the American dream, championed universal human rights, and provided Starbucks, McDonald's, and Coca-Cola to a grateful world.

Now many of you may read the above paragraph and interpret my comments as flippant and cynical of America's place in the world. Let's get this clear—you would be dead wrong. I am deeply sincere about my pride in our country and its contributions to the world. I feel blessed every day that I had the good fortune to be born in America. But one problem with Americans, as I see it, is that we continue to boast about our past accomplishments and trumpet our democratic system without carefully analyzing whether those boasts are still warranted. We have become blind to many of our shortcomings and allow a wide variety of special interest groups to prevent us from honestly and objectively analyzing our democratic system and taking the steps necessary to assure we remain atop the world.

Look at our educational system, for example. We do indeed have the world's greatest universities. We offer free elementary and secondary education to all of our citizens. Yet when you compare American students with others around the world, we are mediocre at best. We continuously score

11

among the lowest of the developed nations in math and science.[1] Increasing numbers of high school graduates are unable to manage even the basic math and English skills required to succeed at those outstanding universities we extol, and many are forced to take remedial classes as college freshmen (almost a third of entering students at last count).[2]

When I was in high school, many of my classmates in the honors program did exceptionally well. We studied rigorously and achieved good grades, but no one in my graduating class had a 4.0 GPA. However, many of us scored extremely well on the SATs and went on to matriculate and succeed at a number of the nation's top universities. Currently, it is not uncommon to find ten or fifteen students in a graduating class with GPAs *exceeding* 4.0 but whose SAT scores are mediocre at best. With the financial resources we expend on education in this country, we should expect more from the system than inflated GPAs and underperforming students unable to compete with their counterparts in Europe and Asia.

But God forbid we criticize the American educational system! The National Education Association would be quick to point out that the problem is not poor teachers but lack of funding. Politicians will rebut that view, cite the lack of accountability, and then try to establish guidelines for teachers and students that they are loath to enforce or to fund. Classroom teachers will bemoan the behavioral problems rampant among their students that create a milieu hardly conducive to learning. And, of course, parents will lay blame on teachers, administrators, and politicians alike.

So we stagnate. We still proclaim America the best while mediocrity reigns.

The same can be said for health care in America. How can we measure it? We must be the best; after all, we have the greatest centers for medical research and teaching that attract students from around the globe. Most major breakthroughs in medical science and medical technology emanate from the United States. Patients with means from around the world come here for innovative treatments. The American health care system is truly outstanding. Who could argue?

I will.

The difficulty one encounters when trying to assess the performance of our health care system is how exactly to measure it. Which standards do you apply? How do you compare the U.S. system with others around the world? There are no easy answers and no matter which benchmark is selected, people who disagree with your conclusions will find fault with the standard you utilize.

The World Health Organization (WHO) is an arm of the United Nations responsible for the directing and coordinating of health among member states. Periodically, the WHO collects data from its 191 members and surveys a wide variety of health-related issues that range from percentage of children who receive immunizations to AIDS-related deaths. Their data bank is enormous and provides a reasonably accurate accounting of the health status of member countries. Every several years, the WHO collates the data and ranks member states on a vast array of health indices. So just how does the outstanding American health system measure up? The answer is, not very well.

Life expectancy is a reasonable place to begin to measure how well we care for our population. It seems only intuitive that if you have the best health care system in the world, your population should be among the healthiest in the world and live the longest. According to the *World Health Report* from 2006, American men can expect to live seventy-five years and American women eighty years.[3] Those figures tie for twenty-ninth and thirtieth in the world, respectively.[4] American men and women have a life expectancy similar to men and women in Cuba, for example, and below Canada, the UK, France, Germany, Italy, Sweden, Switzerland, and twenty-two other countries.[5] But critics will argue that those figures are not an indictment of our health care system but more a reflection of our lifestyle, which is characterized by obesity, lack of exercise, alcohol and tobacco abuse, and so on. There is truth in that criticism, but isn't one of the roles of a progressive health system to promote and encourage healthy lifestyles among its citizens? One look at the growing epidemic of childhood obesity in this country should answer the question of how well we are doing in that regard.

How about a less intuitive issue such as infant mortality, which we usually associate with the third world and underdeveloped countries? Indeed, in sub-Saharan Africa, infant mortality rates can be as high as 100 to 130 deaths per 1,000 live births.[6] We have all come to expect that. In the United States, it's a mere 6 per 1,000, certainly dwarfing Somalia, Chad, and the like.[7] But those numbers tie us for *thirty-third* in the world with Cuba, Croatia, Estonia, and Andorra.[8] Once again, France, Germany, Italy, Canada, the UK, and twenty-eight other countries outperform us. Maternal mortality rates are not much better; the United States is ranked thirtieth in the world behind the same group of developed countries.[9] In the United States, the number of maternal deaths per 1,000 live births is 14.[10] Canada, our neighbor to the north with the so-called horrendous health system we always hear about, loses 5 mothers per 1,000 live births.[11]

Select almost any of the parameters studied by the WHO and the U.S. system falls short in almost every single category: cancer-related deaths (ninety-ninth), deaths from heart disease (twenty-sixth), childhood deaths from pneumonia (twenty-fourth), mortality rates from traumatic injuries (fifty-seventh), and the list goes on.[12] These figures are unsettling, especially in light of the fact that America is home to some of the world's greatest cancer centers, has pioneered almost all technological and pharmaceutical cardiovascular advances, and has a nationwide trauma system designed to care for the victims of trauma.

Wait a minute; this is America! We must be number one in some of these indices. We are; in two, as a matter of fact. The United States ranked number one in the world in total expenditure on health care as a percentage of gross domestic product (GDP) at 15.2 percent.[13] More recent figures for 2008 have been quoted at 16.9 percent.[14] This far exceeds any of those countries who perform better than our own on the WHO survey: Canada (9.9 percent), the UK (8.0 percent), Germany (11.1 percent), Switzerland (11.5 percent), Italy (8.4 percent), and France (10.1 percent) all rank higher than the United States in core health indicators yet spend significantly less to attain those goals.[15] Along the same lines, we also rank number one in per capita total expenditure on health care (in current U.S. dollars), spending an average of over $5,700 per citizen; compared to Canada's $2,669, Japan's $2,662, Germany's $3,204, France's $2,981, the UK's $2,428, and Sweden's $3,149.[16] According to the Centers for Medicare and Medicaid Services, in 2009 the figure rose to $8,086 and represented 17.6 percent of our gross domestic product.[17] Am I the only one who thinks we are spending an extraordinary amount of resources on the health and well-being of our citizens for very modest returns?

In 2000, the WHO published its *World Health Report 2000*, where it incorporated all of the focused indicators and actually ranked health care systems as a whole. The United States finished thirty-seventh.[18] Critics have made a career of using that figure to decry our system and the number "37" has been cited ad nauseam to prove that America's delivery of health care is a colossal failure. However, one must be cautious in relying on that figure alone to indict American health care. The editor-in-chief of that same WHO document, Dr. Phillip Musgrove, actually reiterated that very point in a controversial article published in the British journal *The Lancet* in 2003.[19] When I interviewed Dr. Musgrove, he was quick to agree that the indicators such as life expectancy, infant mortality, and the like were indeed reasonably accurate, but he went on to say that much of the data regarding economic and nonclinical factors was imputed and only 39 percent were actually based on country-level observations. His opinion was that the WHO report was a helpful stimulus to drive improvements in global health care but that the "ranking" of each country's system as a whole from 1 to 191 was a meaningless exercise since the responsiveness indicators were not comparable across countries.[20] In a more recent letter to the editor of *The New England Journal of Medicine*, Musgrove offered four reasons for the continued propagation of the ranking. First, people want to trust the WHO and believe it is accurate. Second, few people are aware of the shortcomings of the WHO report. Next, having a number, any number, confers a sense of precision. Lastly, those people who initially presented the number continue to cite it without question.[21]

The accuracy and relevance of the WHO will most likely continue to be debated for years to come, but if nothing else, the data suggests that we can do better, much better. And just to answer the naysayers regarding the validity of the WHO statistics, be advised that in May of 2010, two studies that looked at progress in childhood mortality and maternal mortality were published in *The Lancet*.[22] They were not funded by the United Nations or the WHO but instead by the Bill and Melinda Gates Foundation. In each of these papers the United States once again had significantly higher mortality rates in both groups than any of the other industrialized nations in Europe or in Canada. The rate of childhood mortality has been declining at an encouraging rate throughout the world except for the United States, the UK, New Zealand, and South Korea, where rates of decline are inexplicably slower than would be expected.

As a nation we must ask ourselves how it can be that the United States has such great centers for medical care and research and spends 17 percent of its gross domestic product on health care, yet is mired below almost every other developed country in the WHO. To me, the answer is quite simple: America does indeed have a wonderful array of medical miracles and outstanding physicians, but a significant portion of the American population has limited or no access to that care. In America, if you are wealthy or well insured, then you are able to take full advantage of the opportunities afforded a nation that spends 17 percent of its GDP on health care. But if you are poor, uninsured, or "underinsured," as many Americans are, that same lifesaving system is not available to you.

In this country, if you look at almost any disease category, survival rates are invariably associated with socioeconomic status. The disappointing outcomes in the indices of life expectancy, maternal or infant mortality, cardiovascular disease, and the like that are detailed in the WHO report are significantly overrepresented among the poor of our country. In a population of more than three hundred million, there are between forty-five and fifty million Americans who are uninsured. In addition, a similar number of our citizens depend on the Medicaid system or private insurance with such high deductibles and limited services that often access to appropriate care is near impossible.

Pundits will argue that Medicaid is our social safety net for the American indigent, allowing them the opportunity to benefit from our advanced medical breakthroughs. As a practicing physician who has always treated

Medicaid patients, I can tell you nothing is further from the truth. A grow-ing number of physicians, in California and elsewhere, refuse to see Med-icaid patients or do so under very limited circumstances, such as one day per month. Thus, those patients with significant chronic diseases and even life-threatening maladies wait months and months to see a doctor (or more likely a nurse practitioner) and then will wait even longer for approval of the necessary tests and specialist referrals, frequently exacerbating the underlying condition to the point that treatment is rendered ineffective or turning a fairly manageable problem into a complex one.

The obvious answer is that we need to hold responsible the greedy, un-caring doctors who refuse to see these patients, right? After all, the indigent are covered by insurance so the doctor *is* getting paid. But few in the general public realize that Medicaid reimbursement to physicians is much less than traditional insurance rates and even much less than Medicare. For example, Medicaid pays the doctors in our group about 25 percent of our usual and customary fees. Thus, when you consider the cost of skyrocketing overhead and medical malpractice insurance, we actually *lose* money on every Medicaid patient we see. That situation is bad enough for physicians in high-income specialties like neurosurgery, but imagine the effect it has on those doctors whose incomes are more modest, like pediatricians and family practitioners. In the past, physicians were able to provide indigent care and offset the losses because of the more generous reimbursements we received from the private insurers, a practice known as cost shifting. But with the advent of managed care, those days are gone and so is timely access to quality medical care for a large part of the American population.

Another fallacy is that individuals with private insurance, usually ob-tained through their employer, are safely matriculated into the system. Yet many of those have policies that severely limit their benefits or have cata-strophically high deductibles. When these individuals get a serious illness or suffer a major injury, the financial results can be devastating. When those crises do occur, patients really have no choice but to seek proper care for their cancer or their son's complex fracture of his femur. But hospitals and physi-cians have bills to pay too, and with reimbursement dwindling, they have a great capacity for sympathy but little for charity. Thus, these unfortunate individuals who are faced with life-threatening situations can easily face fi-nancial ruin as well.

The uninsured, forty-seven million at last count, have it even worse.[23] They have no insurance to offset any of the costs of their treatment, and since they are not aligned with a carrier contracted with the hospital or physician, they are charged *more* than anyone else. These are the so-called usual and customary fees set by doctors and hospitals and always negotiated downward by the insurers. But no one is there to negotiate for these patients; therefore, they are billed at the high end of the spectrum. Does it not seem ironic to you that those with the least capacity to pay are charged the most? The uninsured and underinsured in this country face losing their homes and other assets because they were unfortunate enough to need treatment in the great American health care system.

Ponder this for a moment if you will: the number one cause of bankruptcies across the United States is catastrophic medical debt. Even more revealing is the fact that over 75 percent of people who were forced into bankruptcy as a result of their illnesses actually had health insurance when they first got sick! According to an August 2009 article that appeared in the *American Journal of Medicine*, 62.1 percent of all bankruptcies filed in 2007 were primarily related to medical bills and 78 percent of those who were forced to file bankruptcy had health insurance.[24] But many of those policies had exclusions that resulted in out-of-pocket expenses that overwhelmed the insured, were accompanied by significant deductibles, or had an inadequate limit on benefits in the event of a costly illness or injury. In addition, a significant number of patients lost their jobs as a result of their illnesses and thus lost their health insurance as well. Indeed, it may be a bit of a stretch to conclude that such financial failures were solely the result of the cost of medical care, but certainly most of these cases were pushed over the edge by an unexpected medical expense.

I met Bob Resnick on a Saturday afternoon several years ago. A fifty-seven-year-old farmer from a community near us, Bob owned a small orchard, which he and his wife had managed for over twenty years. The almonds and walnuts did not make the Resnicks wealthy, but they were able to live in a nice but modest home, put away some savings for their eventual retirement, and fund a college education for their two sons. The one thing they were not able to do was afford health insurance since Bob was self-employed and the premiums were beyond their reach. But the Resnicks and their boys had always been healthy, took good care of themselves, and had little reason to suspect they would need a significant amount of medical attention.

That is, until that Saturday morning, when Bob was working in the orchards and began feeling light-headed. He went back into the house and called out for his wife, Liz. When she entered the kitchen, Bob was on the floor, unconscious, with his arms and legs flailing, foam bubbling from his clenched teeth and nose. Bob Resnick was in the throes of a grand mal seizure. Terrified, Liz dialed 911 and within minutes the paramedics arrived. The seizure had stopped; Bob was beginning to arouse and was transported to our facility. In the ER he was quickly given a loading dose of medication to reduce the risks of a subsequent seizure, blood was drawn, and an emergency CT scan of the brain was performed.

The lab work was relatively normal but unfortunately the CT scan was not. Bob Resnick, fifty-seven-year-old farmer, husband, and father of two, had a malignant brain tumor. I was summoned to the ER for a consultation and explained to Bob and Liz the implications of the darkened region in the right parietal lobe of his brain, located above and behind his right ear. We spoke of options and I recommended surgery to remove as much of the mass as possible, explaining that the prognosis for these types of tumors was uniformly poor but that statistics indicated longest survivals for patients undergoing a gross total resection followed by radiation and chemotherapy. Without hesitation, the Resnicks agreed. Bob wanted to fight this invader and we agreed to perform the surgery five days later.

The procedure went smoothly and Bob emerged from anesthesia neurologically intact. A follow-up MRI scan confirmed we were able to remove all of the apparent tumor, but I cautioned them that eventually these cancers return because of the microscopic extension of cells invisible to the eye or the scan. Bob spent two days in the ICU and by five days after surgery was well enough to be discharged to the care of his family. I explained that we would discuss the radiation and chemotherapy when he saw me in the office the following week.

Mr. Resnick made a remarkable recovery and began his radiation treatments two weeks after the surgery. A follow-up scan at six weeks still looked clean and Bob asked about returning to work. I suggested he wait another few weeks to begin working, but Bob was insistent that he had to start soon. When I asked why he was in so much of a hurry to get back to work after such a major procedure, he softly began to cry. Bob told me he had no insurance, made too much money to be eligible for Medicaid, and had just received his bill for the recent hospitalization. My charges were $4,977 and the hospital bill was $109,952! If the Resnicks had Blue Cross or Blue Shield, those charges would have been $3,630 for our services and almost half for the hospital's care. They would have been responsible for only 20 percent of those figures; not great, but manageable.

Instead, Bob's two sons would have to drop out of Chico State University and the Resnicks would have to deplete their retirement savings and sell their home. Only then would their income level allow them to apply for Medicaid. I was deeply moved by Bob's revelations and felt compelled to help. Fortunately, our hospital had a fund to assist needy patients, and I told the hospital CEO that I would be willing to forfeit my surgical fees if the hospital could negotiate down Bob's devastating financial obligation. They agreed. Bob's boys were able to remain in school and Bob's retirement fund was preserved, which was fortuitous because nineteen months later, Bob

Resnick died from his tumor. But his wife was not forced to lose her husband *and* her home in the process.

Bob Resnick was unfortunate. He had a tumor that took his life despite everything American medicine had to offer. But the Resnicks were also lucky. I was sympathetic to their financial plight and had a good relationship with our hospital CEO, so we were able to address their financial crisis and preserve the quality of life for Bob's wife and sons. Other patients aren't always so fortunate and find their modest assets slipping away with their lives.

Still impressed with America's health care system? Still want to tell me how we're the best in the world?

In defense of our system, I constantly hear people denigrate the medical care in other countries, as if blowing out their candles will make ours look brighter. The previously cited WHO statistics deflate that argument, don't you think? Yet people will continue to recite story after story about how patients in Canada, for example, hate their system, die waiting for treatment, and flock in droves to their more capable neighbors to the south so they can finally obtain the care they desperately need but their own system fails to provide them. I picture hordes of individuals in wheelchairs and on gurneys, using canes and crutches, following a Moses-like figure to the Promised Land. It must indeed be a pretty poor system that forces its population to abandon their homeland and travel to foreign shores to obtain proper treatment for their illnesses.

On March 8, 2007, I was driving to the hospital listening to our local National Public Radio affiliate, when Neal Conan did a story on medical tourism, the practice of traveling to foreign countries to obtain medical procedures. I was aware that a number of patients went elsewhere for cosmetic surgical procedures like face-lifts, liposuction, and tummy tucks. They could travel to exotic lands and recuperate in lush hotels, and it was far less expensive to boot. And their friends would never have to know they had surgery. They just went on an "extended" vacation to Mexico or Brazil. But what I heard on *Talk of the Nation* that day was altogether different.[25]

The discussants related how more and more Americans were traveling to countries like India, Thailand, Malaysia, and even—now hold on to your hats—Canada to obtain necessary procedures like hip replacements, spinal fusions, and gynecological surgery. Why? It was because of the costs. The huge population of uninsured and underinsured Americans have been priced out of the American health care system and are forced to go abroad to get the care and treatment they need. Typically, costs for overseas procedures, including flight, hotel, hospital, and physician, are one-fifth to one-third of what the patient could expect to pay in the United States. Hip replacement surgery, for example, typically costs in excess of $45,000 in the United States but approximately $16,000 overseas.[26]

The obvious concerns are quality of care and follow-up for complications, but according to many observers, those issues have not been significant. I interviewed Patrick Marsek, managing director for MedRetreat, which is the largest of the companies offering medical tourism services. He revealed that instances of post-op complications that need to be addressed once patients return home are exceedingly rare. As costs related to surgery have escalated and the number of uninsured and underinsured Americans has risen, Marsek noted that more and more of their clients are now seeking their service for noncosmetic procedures, with orthopedic and gynecologic surgeries leading the way.[27] Mark Tutton, a reporter for CNN, cited a report by the consultancy firm Deloitte that estimated 750,000 Americans traveled abroad for medical procedures in 2008, a number that is growing every day.[28]

More surprising is the interest shown by U.S. insurance carriers in the medical tourism industry. On *Talk of the Nation*, Marsek revealed that his company was in negotiations with several commercial insurers to provide care in foreign facilities. In May of 2007, Dawn Frantangelo did a story on *NBC Nightly News* that actually discussed the possibility of Blue Cross and Blue Shield offering overseas treatments to their clients.[29]

And it's not just for health care that we travel. It's also for drugs, and I don't mean cocaine and marijuana. In America's northern and southern regions, there are regularly scheduled buses that take senior citizens across the borders to Canada and Mexico for the sole purpose of obtaining affordable prescriptions drugs. The pharmaceutical industry has for years successfully lobbied the U.S. Congress to block laws allowing Medicare to collectively negotiate bulk pricing for their recipients, leaving many seniors having to choose between food and blood pressure medicine. So they too go to Canada or to Mexico.[30]

Let's review. America is the best! We have the greatest health care in the world! We're Number One! A 4.73 GPA! Yet a *third* of our population has little or no access to that care, we perform far *worse* on every index of health care than any other of the advanced countries of the world, we spend considerably *more* on that care than any other country, and a growing population of Americans are being forced to seek proper care *outside* of our borders. Any of you who still believe we're the best, please do me a favor . . . bend over and stick your heads even deeper into the sand.

Because you ain't got a clue!

Insuring America's Health

A Lesson in "Mis"Managed Care

$\mathscr{Y}$ou know it really did start out as a good idea, this concept of "insurance," collective risk spread among friends, neighbors, and fellow workers in order to protect each other against the catastrophes of life.

It is fascinating to review the evolution of the insurance industry, but there is general agreement that the origins lie back with the ancient Babylonians around 2100 BCE.[1] Then, as now, trade was the lifeblood of civilization and early merchants transported their wares from kingdom to kingdom by caravans of pack animals across wide expanses of the blistering desert. The scorching sun, seasonal droughts, and devastating wind storms conspired to make the journey as inhospitable as one could imagine. But the climatic elements alone were not the only barriers to the safe delivery of their goods. Inevitable injuries and a variety of diseases also took their toll on the band of travelers as well as their camels, horses, and other livestock. They also faced attack from gangs of roving marauders who robbed and pillaged their way across the desert, a situation not too dissimilar from what merchants in America's inner cities experience even today![2]

To protect themselves from financial ruin in the event of one of these unforeseen calamities, the early traders would each contribute to a pool of funds that would assist in covering their losses if their journey was unsuccessful and their goods failed to reach their market.[3] Sometime later, the Greeks, who relied on the high seas rather than the arid desert for transportation lanes, adopted a comparable system to insure the shipping industry. Not long after, this concept of pooled risk proliferated and became commonplace among the many trade guilds across Europe.[4]

Although most early insurance agreements related to the safe transport of goods, the Romans were the first to actually address social issues and, indirectly, medical issues with insurance. Neighbors in ancient Rome estab-lished "burial clubs" where surviving members would collectively pay for the funeral expenses of the deceased. Although the trade guilds in Europe insured their members primarily against the loss of goods from fire, shipwreck, and the like, a few began providing assistance to families in the event of death or disabling injury. In general, "insurance" was provided by small groups of individuals to protect each other. These individuals knew one another well and shared similar occupations and similar risks. They essentially were "self-insured."[5]

That all changed in the late 1600s when a small group of ship owners, merchants, and businessmen congregated in a popular local establishment on the outskirts of London. They discussed the idea of forming a new company that would offer insurance to a broad range of clients from various industries. What emerged from those deliberations in 1688 was the founding of the first known insurance company. The meeting place where these talks originated was Lloyd's Coffee House, and the insurance company became known as Lloyd's of London, which has insured everything from Betty Grable's shapely legs to the Hope Diamond. Soon, much of British commerce had some form of insurance.[6]

The British introduced the concept of insurance to their American colonies, and after the American Revolution, in 1787, a group of New York businessmen started the first American insurance company to protect against fire.[7] Benjamin Franklin did the same in Philadelphia in the early 1790s.[8] For over a century, the American insurance industry concentrated on protecting against loss of property, but little initiative was taken to protect against the loss of good health.

The reason for this lack of health insurance was twofold. First, Ameri-cans had little need for insuring their health since little was available to minister to it. American medicine was still in its infancy and doctors had few resources to offer ill patients. In addition, most Americans, when ill, were cared for at home rather than in hospitals for the same reason. Thus, the costs related to health care were nominal. Secondly, the insurance industry itself had little motivation to create a product that was not in demand. Even more problematic for established insurers was how to assess actual risks and assign premiums that would make such an endeavor profitable.[9]

But advances in medical knowledge and technology would come and with them an increase in the cost of care. The introduction of antibiotics and the evolution of surgical procedures resulted in more Americans surviving maladies that just a decade before had been uniformly fatal. The American Medical Association made a concerted effort to improve the quality of medi-cal practice by establishing more rigorous standards for licensure and closing a significant number of medical schools that failed to meet those standards, in turn reducing the number of practitioners.[10]

Hospitals began to proliferate as many of the new treatment options required care unavailable in the home. And so with more patients seeing fewer doctors, more technology available to treat disease, and the expanding use of hospitals to provide the care traditionally bestowed by patients' families, costs could go nowhere but up. Sound familiar? As early as the first decade of the 1900s there were calls for some form of national health insurance, but as would happen again in the 1930s and 1940s, opposition by organized medicine and the business community would assure its demise.[11] However, the years immediately following World War I ushered in an era of reasonable prosperity in the United States and the financial burdens to the average citizen associated with the newly found advancements in American medicine were initially well absorbed. But when that same economy began to sputter and the Great Depression descended upon America, those same financial burdens, as well as many others, became overwhelming.

Ironically, it was during those same bleak times that the first genuine movement for health insurance appeared. Its emergence was not born out of a benevolent concern for the health and well-being of economically struggling Americans but instead came as a response to the growing number of struggling hospitals and doctors whose bills were increasingly being left unpaid by a financially devastated patient base.

Like other institutions, Baylor University Hospital was feeling the economic pinch and fighting desperately to stave off insolvency resulting from the mounting bad debt from their collective patient load. Justin Ford Kimball was recruited from the Dallas, Texas, public school system to join the administration of the floundering hospital and soon came up with a novel idea that capitalized on his relationship with the school districts and their teachers. In 1929, Baylor Hospital offered the 1,300 teachers of the Dallas School District twenty-one days of care in their facility in exchange for a nominal monthly fee and the assurance that at least 75 percent of the teachers would participate. This plan set the foundation for what became "Blue Cross" insurance. Soon physicians began to see the wisdom of this approach and created "Blue Shield" insurance to cover doctors' bills.[12]

About the same time, America's first model of managed care in a Health Maintenance Organization (HMO) began to develop. In 1933, Sidney Garfield had recently completed medical school and was struggling to establish a practice. At the time, the influential business mogul Henry Kaiser had formed the Industrial Indemnity Consortium with a number of other industrialists to provide workman's compensation coverage for their many employees. Garfield saw an opportunity and offered to provide care for the five thousand plus workers who were erecting the Colorado River Aqueduct in the Mojave Desert for a prepaid fee. He rehabilitated a local medical clinic, hired several doctors and staff members, and found success.[13]

Several years later when the Grand Coulee Dam Project was undertaken in Washington State, Industrial Indemnity once again turned to Garfield to provide care. It was there that he first met Henry Kaiser and developed a close relationship that would endure for years to come. In the 1940s, Kaiser established a major shipbuilding company in the Oakland area and collaborated with Garfield to establish a permanent medical clinic, not only for the company's employees but their families as well. The Kaiser Permanente system emerged, where injury and illness prevention became as important as treatment.[14]

In the HMO model, patients were managed by primary care doctors who evaluated their complaints and decided if and when they would need specialist referrals. Physicians were salaried, with some incentives, and costs were controlled by encouraging healthy lifestyle choices and limiting specialty care to those whom the primary care doctor deemed appropriate. This newly devised paradigm clashed with the traditional "fee for service" model and was quickly denounced by the AMA as an assault on physician control. As a result organized medicine quickly discouraged their members from embracing the HMO model and promoted the support of the Blue Shield plans.[15]

Until World War II, the majority of Americans who contracted for health insurance continued to do so as individuals or small groups, such as fraternal organizations. Indeed, when Franklin Delano Roosevelt began drafting the Social Security Act as part of his New Deal, the business community, as well as the AMA, made it abundantly clear to the president that if he expected their support for this sweeping social program, mandatory universal health care must be taken out of the equation. Thus the Social Security Act of 1935 did pass, but without a provision for health coverage.[16]

The United States was drawn into World War II after the Japanese bombed Pearl Harbor in 1941. A large population of young American workers enlisted to fight the tyranny spreading throughout Europe and the Pacific theater. The result of this exodus was a relative depletion of able-bodied workers so essential in supporting the war effort here at home. American businesses found themselves competing vigorously for these precious workers and were forced to pay higher and higher wages. With the increasing cost of the workforce, those same companies had to charge higher and higher prices for their manufactured goods as well as their services. Not surprisingly, inflation began to soar.

In an attempt to soften the inevitable competition for scarce employees and stabilize the economy, Congress passed the Wage and Price Stabilization

Act of 1942.[17] This legislation essentially froze the wages of American workers but did allow companies to use fringe benefits, such as health insurance, as the carrot to lure new employees. For the first time, health insurance became enmeshed in the employer-employee relationship, which resulted in much more widespread coverage of the American population.

The post–World War II economy thrived, and although unions routinely demanded health insurance as an integral part of negotiated compensation packages, American businesses were more than happy to oblige since profits were strong and the cost of insurance remained relatively modest. But President Harry Truman foresaw stormier times on the horizon. He recognized that increasing numbers of former American workers were left without health insurance once they retired. In addition, as the U.S. population continued to expand, so too did America's poor, left behind and uninvited to the table of economic bounty.

Truman understood that such circumstances conspired to potentially leave a significant number of citizens without access to decent health care. In 1945, he proposed to Congress the establishment of a National Health Insurance Plan to provide universal coverage to all Americans. Once again the idea was rebuked, with the label of "socialized medicine" playing to the anti-Communist red-baiters prevalent at the time. Truman's plan was derided on both sides of the congressional aisle and was successfully assailed by the AMA and their lobbyists as well as the business community.[18] Sayonara, universal coverage!

Little changed during the Eisenhower years as most American workers remained covered by their employers. By 1960, three-quarters of Americans had some form of health insurance.[19] But the sinister proponents of a national health plan continued to lurk in the shadows and decided that the best strategy would be to initiate such a program incrementally rather than thrusting it all at once on the country. With the election of John F. Kennedy there was a sense that maybe their time had come. The logical starting point was the nation's elderly. After all, who could argue with providing assistance to people who needed health care the most and who were among the least able to afford it. Most retired Americans did not have the benefit of an employer-sponsored insurance plan and the majority subsisted on a modest fixed income.

In 1964, the Democrats retook Congress and Lyndon Johnson wasted little time in constructing his "Great Society." Initially, Medicare was envisioned to provide assistance for the elderly poor, but sufficient support for enactment of the program would only come when coverage was extended to all U.S. citizens sixty-five years of age or older. On July 30, 1965, President Johnson and Vice President Humphrey traveled to Independence, Missouri, to sign Medicare into law and to honor former president Harry Truman as the first enrollee.[20] Almost twenty years after his own failed attempt at national health insurance, Truman finally received at least partial vindication.

But the concept of Medicare, as expected, was still despised by the AMA as another attempt at "socialized medicine" and an effort to wrest control of care from the hands of America's physicians. Congress feared that the AMA would rally the troops and that physicians would refuse to treat Medicare beneficiaries. To encourage their support and squelch the opposition, participation in the Medicare program by physicians was "voluntary" and those who did participate would be reimbursed at their usual and customary fees. The revolt was thus averted.

Medicare Part "A" was a mandatory program into which every American was automatically enrolled upon turning sixty-five. Part A covered hospital charges and was provided at no additional cost to the patient. Medicare Part "B" was voluntary and covered physician charges up to an allowable "reasonable" fee. Patients paid a modest premium of $3 per month for Part B coverage and physicians were free to charge whatever they desired for their services and collect from the patients the difference between what Medicare allowed and what they charged.[21]

I think I like this Medicare stuff. I can charge what I want and the government will actually pay for these poor, elderly uninsured folks to get care. Works for me! Additionally, Medicare provided financial support to hospitals for facility expansion and new technology. How long do you think such a generous system could survive? You're right, not very long. In a few short years, Congress began to see the program hemorrhaging money beyond what anyone had envisioned. The patients were happy, the docs were happy, the hospitals were happy . . . of course, they were. But Congress was beside itself.

In conjunction with Medicare, those subversive national health care promoters managed to attach an additional government program to the bill that had the audacity to provide health care to *poor* people who weren't sixty-five! It was called "Medicaid" and varied in benefits from state to state but, when combined with Medicare, contributed to the exponentially skyrocketing costs. This was *the* pivotal moment in the transformation of American medicine. As expensive medical technology emerged, costs soared and not only for governmental programs, but in the private sector as well. The American business community began feeling the pinch of rising premiums to pay for this newfound expensive care. Something had to be done, so Congress and American businesses turned to organized medicine to help control runaway expenditures. But the AMA and its members were disinclined to address the issue, so Congress and Big Business did.

In the early 1970s, President Richard Nixon began feeling the heat of runaway health care spending from the opposite ends of the political spectrum. The business community, with their political clout and lobbyists' dollars, were livid and demanding that something be done. Senator Ted Kennedy and the liberal left once again gave voice to calls for a national health plan. Nixon was in a tight spot. He became intrigued by plans such as Kaiser Permanente and the other handful of HMOs that appeared to significantly suppress costs while at the same time providing excellent care.[22]

In 1973, Nixon signed into law the HMO Act, which strongly encouraged participation in one of these "managed care" programs with the idea that such a transition would lead to the desired savings.[23] The administration, however, was careful not to alienate the business community or the AMA and again made the program voluntary. They allowed traditional fee-for-service practitioners to contract with HMO entities at reduced fees. The problem was that the relatively scarce number of established HMOs, such as Kaiser Permanente, the Cleveland Clinic, and the Mayo Clinic, had limited capital and resources to absorb a large portion of the U.S. population. Seeing the profit potential of such an arrangement, the commercial for-profit carriers came to the rescue and began offering HMO (managed care) plans of their own.[24] With one tiny difference . . .

Groups such as Kaiser Permanente, the Mayo Clinic, and others were "not-for-profit," meaning that every dollar they generated above expenses went back into patient care. On the other hand, commercial carriers craved profits as they improved their companies' bottom lines and enhanced their appeal to Wall Street and the investing community. The primary concern of the Kaiser Permanentes of the world was patient care at a reasonable cost. The primary concern of the commercial carriers was return on investment to their shareholders. They were in the business to make money and health care was merely a potential money-making commodity. The traditional not-for-profits could not compete with the capital available to the commercial carriers, so they rapidly began to lose market share. In the mid-1970s, over 90 percent of all HMO plans were provided through not-for-profit companies. By the mid to late 1990s, nearly two-thirds of HMO plans were controlled by commercial carriers, and market-based decision making regarding health-related issues became the norm.[25]

And what about the Nixon administration's plan to quiet opposition from organized medicine by allowing rank-and-file practitioners to participate in this grand experiment called managed care? We physicians quickly learned what that participation entailed. For most of us it meant drastic reductions in reimbursement as the commercial carriers let "the market" decide what was a reasonable fee for the services we provided. They began rather benignly offering modest reductions in customary fee schedules in exchange for increased patient volume to both doctors and hospitals. As more and more contracts were signed with managed care groups, the screws began tightening. Reimbursement declined further, and if a physician refused to sign a contract at the lower fee schedule, it was simply offered to the guy next door. Market forces were really nothing more than finding the lowest bidder for medical care. Does anyone really think that was Nixon's original vision, to surrender the care of the American population to a physician or group of physicians based on how little reimbursement they would accept rather than the quality they provided?

The commercial carriers knew exactly what they were doing as they attempted to "divide and conquer." They pitted one physician against another, one physician group against another, and one hospital against another. And ultimately they pitted physicians against their own patients. In a brilliant stroke of economic genius the carriers developed a system of *capitation*. Put simply, this plan reimbursed a given practitioner or medical group a specific amount per patient per month to provide all the necessary care for those patients. At the end of the month what remained unused was profit realized by the doctor or the group.

However, if patients were sicker than anticipated or required more diagnostic procedures or complex care, there was no additional money available to pay for those tests or that care. Mrs. Jones might come into the office complaining of headaches and personality changes and Dr. Doe might rightfully suspect a brain tumor and determine an MRI scan was indicated. But if Dr. Doe or his group had already exhausted the funds available to them for that month, then he or they would have to pay for Mrs. Jones's MRI scan. Maybe we can just watch Mrs. Jones for another month or so, don't you think? If Dr. Doe knows his daughter's college tuition check will be coming due soon, do you think he would be as likely to order that MRI scan knowing he would have to pay for it?

Capitation is the ultimate conflict of interest. It may be a reasonable solution when contracting for janitorial services or even managing a professional sports franchise but it has no business in the delivery of health care. None. I hope I'm clear on that. Most physicians and group practices soon realized this and today most managed care contracts are based on a reduced fee-for-service model rather than a capitated one. That same fee-for-service contract usually goes out to the lowest bidder.

Insurance companies have developed a multitude of innovative ways to hold on to their money even when they have contracts with physicians. One common practice, vehemently denied by the carriers, is simply to reject a claim. Physicians file thousands of claims a year, adding significant cost to their annual overhead. When a claim is denied, it must be resubmitted and redocumented, which takes more time and costs the practitioner more money. Sometimes it is just easier to forget it and the insurance carriers know that. In our own practice, it is not uncommon to have a very clear-cut claim denied by the carrier and immediately approved when resubmitted. If we didn't bother, they wouldn't have to pay. And on and on it goes.

In the managed care model, procedures and tests must be preapproved by the insurance company before they are performed or else the claim can later be denied, placing the burden of payment on the patient or physician. Again, an enormous amount of time and money is expended on obtaining the authorizations. They may be requested in writing or by phone. Most often the individual responsible for approving the request is a nurse who may have absolutely no experience with the test or procedure. He or she simply follows written guidelines as to what is allowed. The following example reveals the frustration that we practitioners go through on a daily basis.

A young woman was referred to me by her primary care doctor with a ruptured disk in her low back. This occurred after she fell carrying a canoe up from a river several months earlier. As a consequence of the injury, a piece of disk, the cushion between adjacent vertebrae, had pushed out of the disk space and was compressing a nerve going down her leg. This resulted in significant pain, numbness, and weakness in her leg. After putting up with it for several weeks, she went to her doctor who placed her on anti-inflammatories as well as pain killers. When this failed to improve her after four additional weeks, she was sent to a physical therapist for twelve treatments of traction, massage, ultrasound, and exercises, all to no avail. Finally, an MRI scan was performed, revealing a large ruptured disk at a level consistent with her symptoms, and she was referred to me for definitive surgical care.

After examining the patient and reviewing her scan, I gave her the option of either a cortisone injection or microsurgical removal of the offending disk fragment. The patient, who had been in abject misery for almost two months, opted for surgery and we called to request authorization from her carrier. It was denied. I then had to get on the phone and speak with the nurse on the other end. She told me that she would approve the surgery if I would order first an electromyogram (EMG) of the patient's leg. This test looks for evidence of nerve and muscle injury by inserting needles into the muscles and passing electrical currents along the course of the nerves. As you can imagine, this is not a very comfortable procedure.

I courteously explained to the nurse that I did not feel the EMG was indicated as the patient already had clinical evidence of nerve damage. I told her that regardless of the results of the EMG, my recommendations would be the same. She told me she could not allow the surgery unless the EMG was done. I then asked to speak with her supervising physician.

He and I talked and once again I explained that the test was unnecessary and would not affect my decision making. I also pointed out that it would actually *save* the insurance company money. He admitted to me that he totally agreed with me and that he would authorize the surgery whether the EMG revealed nerve damage or not. But he would not authorize it without the EMG. I told him I refused to order an unnecessary test. He then called the patient's primary care physician and had him order the EMG before allowing me to provide proper care for this patient.

The commercial carriers have plenty of other ways to reduce spending on health care and increase the profitability of their stock. One simple way is to insure only the healthy. This practice flies in the face of the so-called shared risk principle upon which health insurance was founded. But if your primary concern is profit, then the practice makes perfect sense since premiums come in but less goes out. By denying coverage to individuals with preexisting conditions such as diabetes, hypertension, or other chronic illnesses, the carriers protect themselves from the costs associated with providing such care. Sometimes they do not actually refuse to cover individuals, but the premiums would be so exorbitant as to be unaffordable to most patients. Thus, a significant number of U.S. citizens, many of whom need medical care the most, are left stranded without coverage. These patients are too well off to qualify for Medicaid but not well off enough to afford coverage for the care they require. For these unfortunate many, their only options are to do without the care or deplete their assets to the point that they do become eligible for Medicaid.

Others, who develop a serious illness while under their employer's coverage, find themselves now stuck indefinitely in that job for fear that if they leave for any reason they will lose that insurance and be unable to secure a new policy at a reasonable cost. Insurance slavery has become a fact of life for a growing number of Americans.

There are a myriad of excellent books currently available that relate some of the horror stories associated with denial of care. There are a significant number of patients who die or become permanently disabled because their insurance companies refused care or delayed their care until it was too late. Jonathan Cohn has written a compelling book entitled *Sick: The Untold Story of America's Health Care Crisis and the People Who Pay the Price.*[26] Read this book and you will appreciate how our current system is failing Americans in their access to care.

Another novel method to avoid paying for contracted claims is a practice known as "post claims underwriting." An insurance company will use all its marketing tools to attract a client and have the individual fill out a detailed application, which is then processed and accepted along with the monthly premiums. However, even years later, when that same client files a costly claim, the company will have one of their adjusters go over the claimant's application again to try and find information that may have been omitted or incorrect as a basis for canceling the policy and denying the claim, even if the information in question has nothing to do with the patient's current condition. Thus, individuals who may have been paying thousands of dollars in premiums over many years find themselves abruptly without coverage and facing catastrophic medical and economic hardships.

Fortunately, in December 2007, a California Appellate Court halted this widespread practice and the insurers are now required to demonstrate that they conducted a reasonable investigation prior to issuing the policy to prove that the applicant deliberately lied.[27] In that case, Blue Shield was the defendant but they were certainly not alone. Just one month earlier, California health regulators fined Health Net $1 million for lying to state investigators about paying *bonuses* to employees based on the number of contracts they were able to cancel after the policyholders got sick.[28] This type of activity characterizes the market-based delivery of health care in the United States. Is there anyone out there, other than insurance carrier executives and stockholders, who can honestly say this is a reasonable way to provide insurance?

So if doctors are getting pinched and hospitals are struggling to survive and patients are losing coverage when they most need it, who is winning? If the goal of a market-based endeavor is profit, where is the profit in health care and who benefits from it? Let's take a closer look . . .

Under the current system, Americans spent over $2.5 trillion on health care in 2010, representing in excess of 17 percent of our gross domestic product.[29] At this rate, those figures will increase to over $4 trillion and 20 percent of the GDP by the year 2015. Insurance premiums continue to rise, skyrocket really, despite the promises that market-based managed care would rein in costs. Premiums rose by an average of 11.2 percent from 2003 to 2004; 9.2 percent from 2004 to 2005; and 7.7 percent from 2005 to 2006.[30] Those increases can only mean one thing—the major insurance carriers must be losing their shirts and the only way they can continue to provide that great care and service for which they are known is by raising premiums. They really hate to do it but they have no choice.

Oh, really?

The three largest health care plans in America are United Health Group (UHG), WellPoint, Inc., and Aetna. In 2003, United Health Group posted $29 billion in sales and $1.8 billion in profits and paid their CEO, William McGuire, a salary of over $9 million. In 2006, the "struggling" carrier actually posted over $71 billion in sales and almost $18 billion in profits and rewarded Mr. McGuire with a salary package in excess of $51 million. Maybe UHG was just lucky. WellPoint, Inc. saw their sales jump from $17 billion in 2003 to $57 billion in 2006. Their profits also leapt from just over $775 million to over $15 billion in 2006. Their CEO, Larry Glasscock, got lucky too. Despite these terrible times requiring the companies to raise your premiums, Mr. Glasscock received a salary of over $23 million in 2006. And how about Aetna? They must have been the ones to bear the brunt of this out-of-control health care spending. But surprisingly their sales increased from $18 billion to $25 billion between 2003 and 2006, their profits also *rose* from $934 million to almost $11 billion, and their CEO, Dr. John Rowe (finally a doctor who reaps the benefits of managed care), saw his compensation package improve from $9.6 million to over $24 million.[31] As a matter of fact, the CEOs of the nation's ten largest insurance companies received an average salary of $11.9 million each.[32]

So, from 2003 to 2006, insurance carriers were increasing premiums by over 28 percent, they were denying care to policyholders who were desperate for that care, they were paying bonuses to employees who could find loopholes to cancel policies when they were most needed, they were issuing contracts for delivery of care to the lowest bidders, *and* they were increasing the red tape and paperwork necessary to provide that care. At the same time, their profits rose almost 50 percent and their CEOs found their salaries, already well into the millions, increasing just as fast. Market-based medicine . . . managed care. Where do I sign up? As a preferred provider, of course.

·4·

The U.S. Pharmaceutical Industry

Providing the Right Pill for Whatever Ails You and the Wrong Pill for Whatever Doesn't

The faint halo surrounding the minute particle of mold was really quite small—barely even perceptible to the casual observer. But then again, Alexander Fleming was anything but a casual observer.

Born in Scotland in 1881, Fleming had a voracious appetite for knowledge coupled with a keen intellect that served him well as a young student. Following in his older brother's footsteps, he became an accomplished physician and was recruited into the Bacteriology Department of St. Mary's Hospital in London. Fleming realized early on the profound limitations of the antimicrobial agents that were currently in use, and he began in earnest his quest to discover the elusive key to eradicating the infections that claimed so many lives.[1]

Although intellectually brilliant, Fleming's research laboratories were in constant disarray, most likely earning him a reputation as an absentminded professor. One can only imagine the shelves of soiled and upended glassware, the scattered papers, and half-eaten sandwiches that made up his research milieu. By the late 1920s, he was already busy studying the properties of the staphylococcal bacteria in hopes of finding a weakness in the armor that protected the tiny microbes from the multitude of medicines that attempted with little success to halt their devastating effects.[2]

By his own admission, it was pure serendipity when he returned to his lab after a much needed vacation to find that many of the cultures he was growing had been inadvertently contaminated by a mold, thus forcing him to discard the soiled culture plates en masse into a container of disinfectant. Some days later as he was showing a guest his laboratory and explaining his research, he retrieved one of the culture plates that failed to submerge completely in the cleansing solution and was astonished to find that the staphylococcal organism did not proliferate around the opportunistic mold. Working feverishly, Fleming was able to isolate the contaminant and correctly identify it as a member of the genus *Penicillium*. Thus, penicillin and the modern pharmaceutical industry was born.[3]

The earliest pharmacies originated in ancient Baghdad and soon spread throughout the Islamic Empire.[4] In the Middle Ages they became commonplace in Europe as they dispensed a plethora of concoctions designed to alleviate the maladies of the time. Around the 1800s, a number of entrepreneurial drug stores began forming pharmaceutical companies and took a more systematic approach to the development of drug therapies. The majority of these first companies cropped up in Europe although North America did have a few. Even so, by the early 1930s, there were only a handful of diseases considered amenable to drug therapy. Thus, research and development was limited since the profit potential seemed modest at best.

Gerhard Domagk was a young researcher at the Bayer Laboratories in Hitler's Germany in the 1930s. He searched tirelessly for properties of various substances that could control the growth of the streptococcal bacteria. He noticed that one of his red dyes actually killed the organism in rats and he published his discovery in 1936. Fellow researchers scoffed at his findings, unable to accept that a red dye could kill bacteria. Yet two French scientists discovered that it wasn't actually the red dye but one of the by-products of its metabolic breakdown that held the deadly bacteria in check. The metabolite of the red dye was sulphanilamide, and thus the first sulfa drug, Prontosil, was created.[5]

This important work would have remained relatively unheralded for several years if it were not for the untimely illness of the son of President Franklin Roosevelt. The young boy had developed a bad case of tonsillitis that was refractory to the available treatments of the day. Soon the infection spread to the bloodstream. The resulting bacteremia or "blood poisoning" brought with it the very real possibility of death for the young child. The Roosevelts' personal physician, George Tobey, had read of this new German drug, Prontosil, and in desperation administered it to the boy. Within days he fully recovered and soon word of the miraculous cure spread throughout the country. Newspapers across America heralded the new "wonder drug" and overnight interest in drug development soared.[6]

With the proven efficacy of this new class of drugs and the unprecedented notoriety as a result of young Roosevelt's recovery, soon every pharmaceutical company in the world began producing their own sulfa drug. The era of "me too" or "copycat" medicines had begun in earnest. However, as the market was flooded with a plethora of similar drugs, the price began to drop precipitously and profits began to decline. At the same time, however, the

Roosevelt administration was urging the fledgling American pharmaceutical companies to continue developing more and more antibiotics as World War II engulfed the globe and the need for these lifesaving medicines by American soldiers drastically increased. Streptomycin and Fleming's penicillin soon emerged, but the pharmaceutical companies noted the same pattern of diminishing profits as more and more companies developed their copycat drugs. The companies soon began to balk at pursuing new drug therapies and demanded protection of their investment in research and development, as well as their profits. The U.S. Congress, under pressure from the industry's lobbyists, responded by passing legislation granting long patents, sometimes a decade or more.[7]

In the early years of pharmaceutical development, like in Fleming's experience, a bit of luck and an inquisitive mind combined to result in therapeutic breakthroughs. Consider, for example, the first chemotherapy agent, Mustargen. In World War I, Germany introduced the use of mustard gas, a form of chemical warfare, against British soldiers in Belgium. Although not truly a "gas," the agent was dispersed as an aerosol by a variety of exploding devices and had a devastating effect when inhaled by the advancing troops, blistering their respiratory system and resulting in an agonizing death. After the war, its use was banned and stores of the poisonous agent were supposed to be dismantled. However, during the Second World War the Allies received information suggesting that Hitler still possessed significant stockpiles of mustard gas, and the decision was made by Britain and the United States to amass their own supply of the chemical to use as a deterrent in the event that Hitler decided to unleash the weapon on Allied troops.[8]

On December 2, 1943, the USS *John Harvey* was docked in Bari Harbor off the coast of Italy. The ship, under the shroud of secrecy, had transported over 2,000 bombs armed with mustard gas into the region to be used in the event of a German attack. In the early hours of the evening, the German Luftwaffe carried out a surprise raid on the harbor, sinking seventeen Allied ships and significantly damaging eight others. Unfortunately, one of the causalities of the attack was the *John Harvey*, which exploded in an immense fireball igniting its secret cargo and sending a cloud of the deadly gas over the city of 200,000. Soon after, hundreds died and autopsies revealed that many victims succumbed to a near total depletion of their white blood cells, or leukocytes, which form the backbone of the body's immune system. Army physicians eventually learned of the USS *John Harvey*'s "secret" cargo and began to piece together the puzzle. They subsequently theorized that the same agent in smaller doses could well be effective against certain leukemias that are characterized by an abnormal proliferation of those same white blood cells. Trials were begun and the world soon had its first "chemotherapy."[9]

Even today, unexpected effects of newly designed drugs can reap re-markable financial benefits. Researchers at one of Pfizer's laboratories in England were looking for an agent to dilate the coronary arteries in patients with significant heart disease and high blood pressure. They thought they had a winner in Sildenafil, which causes increased levels of cyclic guanosine monophosphate (cGMP) and leads to smooth muscle relaxation and dilata-tion of blood vessels. Unfortunately, as clinical trials progressed, it became apparent that the drug was not nearly as effective as hoped, and the Pfizer sci-entists abandoned further testing. But an interesting phenomenon occurred. Patients who were enrolled in the failed clinical trial were resistant to giving up the drug despite evidence that it was of little or no benefit in combating their heart disease. Why? Although Sildenafil had only a marginal effect on dilating the coronary arteries, the men who took it noticed that it had a rather dramatic effect upon the blood vessels of another organ . . . their penis. Suddenly men who had been impotent found another "miracle drug" (maybe even more important to them than Prontosil) and Pfizer began to market this new medicine as the "little blue pill," Viagra. Industry figures suggest this blockbuster drug, discovered by accident, results in over $5 billion in annual sales for Pfizer.[10]

As our understanding of the basic pathophysiology of diseases pro-gressed, pharmaceutical companies and medical school researchers relied less on luck and more on the scientific probing of disease. They began crafting drugs that interfered with various processes unique to that disease, and by the 1950s and '60s, the pharmaceutical industry exploded. Drugs to treat high blood pressure, diabetes, and cancer were introduced in addition to more powerful antibiotics, mood elevators (at one time Valium was the most prescribed drug in U.S. history), and contraceptives.[11] By the early '70s, the pharmaceutical boom was in full swing, but no one could have imagined just how successful "Big Pharma" would become.

Pharmaceutical companies began investing significant resources to cre-ate and test a myriad of new drugs. This process became known as "research and development" (R & D) and was a considerable component to any com-pany's budget. The problem was that millions of dollars could be spent in search of the next new wonder drug only to find that it failed to live up to its theoretical promise. Lost with the failed drug were the millions of dollars invested in the research. Yet, the industry's profits continued to expand at an unprecedented level.

Ironically, as Big Pharma's success increased, the cost of prescription drugs across the United States continued to rise. Many Americans, in partic-ular the elderly, began feeling the brunt of such costs and soon found they had to choose between paying for their blood pressure medicines or paying their heating bills. Now if there is one American demographic whose cage you do not want to rattle, it's the elderly. They have plenty of time on their hands, they are not shy about making their concerns known, and most importantly . . . they vote! Congress was soon attuned to the gathering storm and began threatening the pharmaceutical industry with regulations and price controls.

For their part, the pharmaceutical giants continued to recite the mantra that the skyrocketing costs were justified on the basis of the enormous risks associated with "R & D." They told Congress and the lay press that without the high revenues generated by the current market drugs, resources to support further R & D would quickly evaporate, putting an end to the search for cures for diseases such as cancer and diabetes. This thinly veiled threat was enough to frighten Congress and the public into abandoning serious attempts to control the costs of prescription medications.

I will be the first to admit that the development of a new drug is a crapshoot. Now it is a crapshoot engineered by some of the most brilliant and innovative scientists in the world, mind you, but a crapshoot just the same. Modern medicine relies on the steady flow of new drugs to save lives and relieve suffering. America's patients reap tremendous benefits from the efforts of the world's pharmaceutical companies. Their products help control chronic diseases such as hypertension and diabetes and eradicate life-threatening infections that become more virulent each year (because of the overuse of previously developed antibiotics, ironically). They allow us to now cure many cancers that a generation ago were uniformly fatal and to extend the lives of patients with AIDS, while at the same time relieving the terrible suffering of hordes of men with erectile dysfunction, all resulting from the research and development of Big Pharma. But to quote the late, great American icon and radio personality Paul Harvey, "now for the rest of the story."

Former *New England Journal of Medicine* chief editor Dr. Marcia Angell wrote a scathing indictment of the workings inside the giant pharmaceutical companies entitled *The Truth About the Drug Companies: How They Deceive Us and What to Do About It*.[12] I strongly recommend it to anyone who wonders why drug costs are so high in the United States. Her book exposes the myths that have been perpetrated by drug companies at home and abroad and gives the reader an illuminating, albeit somewhat biased, look into the workings of Big Pharma.

In her book, Dr. Angell chronicles the growth of the pharmaceutical industry and exposes the manner in which their extensive network of lobbyists manipulates both Congress and the U.S. public into believing the claims that exorbitant drug costs are justified based upon the considerable investment involved in getting a new medicine to market. In 2001 the industry proclaimed that it cost pharmaceutical companies an average of $802 million to develop a new drug.[13] Further, they claimed that the lion's share of expenditures was on research and development, all without a guarantee that the newly discovered drug would be effective or, more importantly, profitable. Thus, the high prices Americans are forced to pay for medicines are necessary to ensure that the pipeline of lifesaving drugs will remain open. It sounds reasonable to me. These unappreciated pharmaceutical companies work diligently to try and find new therapies to relieve suffering without any assurance their hard work will be fruitful. God bless them for their efforts.

But Dr. Angell found some very interesting information regarding our pharmaceutical crusaders. To begin with she looked a little deeper into the $802 million price tag for each new drug. It so happens that this oft-quoted figure emerged from a press conference held in Philadelphia in 2001 following a symposium of economists sponsored by the Tufts Center for the Study of Drug Development.[14] The figure impressed Washington lawmakers and the lay press who were willing recipients of the information spoon-fed to them by the Pharmaceutical Research and Manufacturers of America (PhRMA), the industry's lobbying arm. But before long, that same astounding figure came under attack from a wide array of consumer groups who decried the study as flawed and biased.

It appears that in arriving at such a mind-boggling figure, this panel of "impartial" economists relied heavily upon confidential documents provided by the pharmaceutical companies themselves, which were not subject to the scrutiny of outside interests. The $802 million calculation was based on only sixty-eight new drugs that came to market over a ten-year window, suggesting a somewhat convenient selection of specific medicines presented to the economists by the pharmaceutical industry. Instead of choosing sixty-eight specific drugs over an entire decade, Dr. Angell used industry figures to simply look at all the drugs in a given year and the costs associated with developing them. In the year 2000, ninety-eight new drugs came on the market with a total R & D budget of $26 billion, $260 million per drug, a far cry from the $802 million constantly touted by PhRMA. When Public Citizen ran the industry-supplied numbers on *all* the drugs created between 1994 and 2000, the cost after taxes totaled approximately $100 million.[15]

In addition, as the pesky consumer watchdog Public Citizen pointed out, the $802 million figure failed to take into account that research and development costs were tax exempt, significantly reducing the actual costs to the pharmaceutical companies and deflating the figure dramatically. Most controversial, however, was the inclusion of the estimated revenue that would have been generated if the monies had been invested in the equity market rather than developing new products—so-called opportunity costs. What if the Ford Motor Company put its capital into the stock market rather than using it to manufacture new cars? Or if Apple invested its profits in mutual funds rather than making new computers? Ford, Apple, and the pharmaceutical industry exist to sell their products. They are not investment brokerages and including such a dubious figure as lost potential equity revenue is creative at best and shamefully misleading at worst.[16]

Whatever figure you choose to believe, the concept that our major pharmaceutical companies are financially disadvantaged by the high costs they invest in developing a constant stream of innovative, lifesaving medicines may be bit overstated. First, oftentimes the cost for "R & D" comes from public sources such as the National Institutes of Health (NIH) or the Centers for Disease Control (CDC), which are supported by taxpayer dollars and distributed to the many great research universities throughout the country. Secondly, the overwhelming majority of "new" drugs coming to market are neither innovative nor lifesaving. Instead most are simply minor revisions of existing drugs that alter a few molecules to circumvent patent infringement laws or extend the life of a drug whose patent has run its course.

In the late '70s and early '80s, pharmaceutical companies, the American public, and eventually the U.S. Congress (thanks, of course, to the industry lobbyists who financed their campaigns) began complaining about the long delays between new drug development and FDA approval for sale. In addition, discoveries emanating from publicly funded research traditionally belonged to the public domain (i.e., the taxpayer), making it economically unattractive for the large private drug companies to produce medicines that resulted from such research. But that all changed on December 12, 1980, when Congress passed the Bayh-Dole Act[17] sponsored by the respected senators from Indiana and Kansas, Birch Bayh and Robert Dole (yes, ladies and gentleman, the same Robert Dole who ran for president against Bill Clinton and soon thereafter starred in television commercials promoting Viagra for erectile dysfunction).[18]

This important piece of legislation allowed U.S. universities to patent discoveries that resulted directly from publicly supported research and then in turn grant licensing rights to private industry in return for a percent of the royalties. The great American research institutions found in this new law an excellent opportunity to bring much needed revenue into their coffers, and the pharmaceutical industry found an entirely new source of research and development paid for in large part by American taxpayers. Academic scientists would secure funding from the federal government through grants awarded by agencies like the NIH, perform the necessary research, develop the new drug, and then sell the rights to market that same drug to a pharmaceutical firm in the private sector. On the surface, it certainly appeared like a win-win situation for everyone involved. And indeed it was, for everyone, that is, except the American public, whose tax dollars paid for the research but who were now being charged exorbitant fees for that same drug.

What the Bayh-Dole Act essentially accomplished was the arranged marriage ('til death do they part) between industry and academia. It also set in motion a system fraught with conflicts of interest. The cozy relationship between the pharmaceutical giants and the facilities where research is being carried out, either in university settings or in private laboratories, is predicated on the almighty dollar, which brings into question the objectivity of such research. Industry is obviously anxious to bring to market new drugs that hopefully benefit the world's many patients but, more importantly, improve the companies' bottom lines and benefit their stockholders. Researchers, on the other hand, are not naïve and realize quite clearly who butters their bread. Therefore, it is not surprising that we are recently seeing a plethora of news articles documenting a variety of unsavory practices.

Research articles published in respected journals downplay serious side effects of new drugs while overstating benefits. Companies pay academic scientists to attach their names to research articles that they had little or nothing to do with, but that were actually "ghostwritten" by company writers. Drug companies distribute lucrative honoraria (speaking fees) to esteemed researchers who fly across the country giving lectures touting the companies' new "breakthrough" drugs, which, in reality, are marginally better than placebos or simply minor variations of older, generically available medicines (but significantly more expensive). Utilizing these industry whores, now joined in holy matrimony by the Bayh-Dole Act, some of our most successful pharmaceutical firms propagate this new form of *objective scientific research* on the American public as well as American physicians.

I certainly do not wish to imply that all pharmaceutical research is sullied or malign the vast majority of academic scientists who pursue innovations yet remain true to their scientific principles. Indeed, it is only through such painstaking scientific research that the wonderful advances in medical care come to fruition. But that same painstaking research can now be compromised when it is the pharmaceutical companies who are pulling the economic strings and significantly affecting the true objectivity of that research. One only needs to look at the Vioxx debacle and the role that pharmaceutical giant Merck & Co. played to understand how those lines of objectivity can be lost.

In 1999, Merck released a new anti-inflammatory drug, Rofecoxib, under the trade name Vioxx. This revolutionary class of drug, the so-called COX 2 inhibitors, was designed to provide the benefits of other nonsteroidal anti-inflammatories without the risk of gastric irritation and ulceration that accompanied many of the other available arthritis medicines. Using a barrage of direct-to-consumer (DTC) advertising on TV and in print ads, Vioxx soon became a "blockbuster" for Merck, and in 2003, just four years after its introduction, it generated a whopping $2.5 billion in sales revenue.[19] Not bad.

But what those successful ads (featuring silver-haired grandmothers that could now rise from their wheelchairs and play middle linebacker for the Pittsburgh Steelers) did not disclose was that an alarming number of Vioxx users were dying from heart attacks and strokes! It was only when the numbers became public that the FDA forced Merck to pull Vioxx from the market. The resulting lawsuits cost the company and its stockholders a cool $4.85 billion. (Can you consider that figure part of the R & D budget?) But Merck's trouble didn't end there.[20]

Two articles that subsequently appeared in the prestigious *Journal of the American Medical Association* (JAMA) reported that Merck had actually paid academic scientists to attach their names and take credit for research articles on Vioxx that were actually compiled and authored by company-hired "ghostwriters." Additionally, these reports contended that Merck willfully downplayed patient deaths in studies utilizing Vioxx to treat patients with Alzheimer's disease. Not surprisingly, Merck vehemently labeled all allegations as "false and misleading" and accused the JAMA authors of bias since five of them were paid consultants who had assisted plaintiffs in their suits against the company. Yet, despite that fact that the claims were all "false and misleading," despite the fact that the patients in the Vioxx studies died from causes "unrelated to Vioxx," and despite the fact that a company spokesman admitted that Merck did "hire outside firms to write only *drafts* of studies that academic scientists were later credited as first authors," Merck decided to cough up $58 million to settle the suit brought by twenty-nine states. This was even though they did nothing wrong, mind you.[21]

But Merck is not the only pharmaceutical company to find themselves in hot water. Eli Lilly's own blockbuster drug, Zyprexa, originally approved by the FDA for the treatment of schizophrenia and *severe* bipolar disorder, generated over $4.8 billion for the company in 2007 alone. How did it become so successful? There must be a boatload of schizophrenics running around the country! Not really. Federal prosecutors charged the pharmaceutical giant with encouraging physicians to prescribe the drug for much more than schizophrenia and severe bipolar disorder, resulting in the medication being utilized for entities such as non-Alzheimer's dementia and depression. It's enough to drive you crazy, isn't it? Well, if it does at least you can take comfort in the fact that Lilly will have Zyprexa there to help. As a result of such practices Lilly, in January 2009, agreed to pay a fine of $1.4 billion and plead guilty to a *misdemeanor*—illegal marketing of a drug for off-label use. Misdemeanor? Imagine what the fine would have been if it were a serious offense. And by the way, this is in addition to the $1.2 billion Lilly already paid to settle some thirty thousand lawsuits related to severe side effects that resulted from use of the drug. I imagine the settlements are worth it, however. After all, as mentioned above, Zyprexa added over $4.8 billion to Lilly's bottom line in 2007 alone. If you do the math, that still leaves $2.2 billion for corporate jets. Well, I'm not being very fair. I'm sure it is going to R & D.[22]

While we're on the subject of marketing, it is instructive to examine just how the pharmaceutical industry gets their new products from the benches in their own laboratories (or maybe the labs of NIH-supported universities) into the hands of the consumer. In earlier times, reports of medical break-throughs were published in rigorously refereed journals, which were then read by physicians who judged whether such medications or procedures were appropriate for their patients. Indeed, when Dr. Tobey was frantically searching for something, anything, that could help President Roosevelt's desperately ill son, he came across an article in a medical journal describing Prontosil and tried it.[23] But times have changed and with the avalanche of medications available for whatever ails you, it is impossible for busy physicians to keep up with all the current options.

As the pharmaceutical industry expanded, they began reaching out to their clients (at that time the doctors who prescribed the drugs) in more innovative ways. Those same journals that carried the scientific studies soon were filled with paid advertisements by a host of pharmaceutical companies who touted the tremendous benefits of their newest medicines, which began to erode the fine line maintaining scientific objectivity. It can become difficult to reject an article that promotes a pharmaceutical company's product when that same pharmaceutical company is providing the journal with much needed advertising revenue. But just as many of us get out of our easy chairs and head to the refrigerator or bathroom when TV commercials appear, many doctors simply paged through the journal ads, and drug marketing departments had to find more effective ways to get their message out. Enter the era of the pharmaceutical salesperson or "drug rep."

Pharmaceutical companies utilize a virtual army of salespeople who come to physician offices to "educate" practitioners on the virtues of the latest and greatest drugs to appear on the market. These "reps" are almost always young, attractive, and charming, and frequently female, improving the chances that the physician will allow them a few minutes of their precious time to pitch their products. Invariably, they bring with them an impressive stack of research articles extolling the irrefutable advantages offered by their innovative new drugs but conspicuously devoid of any significant discussion of side effects or cost effectiveness. They usually leave a handful of patient education pamphlets as well as a liberal supply of free samples to be generously distributed by the doctor to his or her grateful patients. Occasionally, the physicians and their staff will also get a catered lunch provided by the rep as a way of thanking them for taking time out of their busy schedules for the visit. And as an added bonus, the physician will usually get an attractive pen with the drug name etched on the side. I can't begin to tell what a godsend those are!

At last count, U.S. pharmaceutical companies employ a sales force of over 100,000, nearly doubling in size from 1999 to 2003. This number represents nearly one rep for each of the 120,000 prescribers in the country and is a significant portion of the costs involved in the creation and distribution of a new medicine. Companies spend in excess of $5 billion for these "detailers" to make their rounds and another $11 billion or more on free samples.[24] That doesn't include the educational seminars where "select" (read "high volume" prescribers) doctors are flown to luxurious locations, put up in plush hotels, and "educated" by a hired staff of company-paid physicians as to why this new drug is the best thing to come along since sliced bread.

But in 1997, all of that changed dramatically. That was the year the federal government, thanks to extensive lobbying efforts by PhRMA, began to allow direct-to-consumer advertising on television and in mainstream magazines. By 2006, the industry was spending almost $5 billion on such ads, and our airwaves, as well as our latest copies of *People* magazine, were saturated with them.[25] I don't know about you, but I was surely grateful to be able to watch *Everybody Loves Raymond* with my kids and, during commercial breaks, hear about the heartbreak of erectile dysfunction with advice about what to do if an erection lasts more than four hours!

But the effects of such advertising were more sinister than that. The marketing gurus at the major drug manufacturers were shrewd and knew exactly what they were doing. In public they defended DTC advertising by telling us it was the industry's way of "educating the public about diseases such as depression and diabetes and encouraging them to see a doctor," according to Billy Tauzin, PhRMA president.[26] If that were really the case, one wonders why PhRMA didn't just sponsor public service announcements about such disease entities and run those instead. The answer is pretty clear.

With DTC advertising, the industry could successfully bypass those who were best able to scrutinize a medicine's efficacy and cost effectiveness, namely, America's physicians. Up to that point, the pharmaceutical industry had really done a rather admirable job of recruiting physician support through the questionable practices outlined earlier in this chapter. But it was not enough. Now these companies were going directly to the American public, convincing them that their new drug (which was not even a new drug most of the time, but simply a minor variation of a less expensive preexisting drug) was the best one for treating their maladies. Patients then began flocking to their doctors' offices and demanding this "new" wonder drug. Physicians responded by acquiescing since it was much more cost effective to just write the prescription rather than spend the time involved in explaining to the patient why it wasn't any better than the ones available on the market.[27]

Sales soared! Since the introduction of DTC ads, the number of prescriptions written in the United States has increased over 60 percent to 3.4 billion. Sales have more than tripled from $72 billion to over $250 billion and the average cost per prescription has more than doubled from $30 to $68.[28] As a country, are we any healthier because of it? The evidence of such is conspicuously lacking. But the pharmaceutical industry is certainly healthy. In 2001, despite only modest increases in cost, spending on prescription drugs in the United States climbed to $155 billion; by 2006, that number exploded to $289 billion. In addition, the industry continued to secure its position as the most successful on America's Fortune 500 list with a whopping 17 percent rate of profit! This compares with an average of only 5 percent for all other members of the list, including the lucrative banking industry (maybe not so lucrative anymore).[29]

Big Pharma spends a lot on this advertising. In 1997, prior to the government's relaxation of DTC ads, the industry reported an advertising budget of about $788 million. Once the floodgates were opened, that budget exploded to over $2.5 billion by 2002 and $4.8 billion in 2006. But it is worth every penny.[30] Studies show that over 33 percent of Americans who are exposed to pharmaceutical ads on TV actually ask their physicians for the specific drug at their next appointment. Over half of surveyed physicians just relent and prescribe the requested drug. It is interesting to note that as of this writing, New Zealand is the only other country in the world besides the United States that allows DTC pharmaceutical marketing.[31] Makes you wonder why, doesn't it? My guess is that the lobbyists in all these other countries aren't quite as influential as they are here. More about that later . . .

These ads don't really "educate" the American public as Mr. Tauzin would like you to believe. In fact, they convince us that we are actually sick and in desperate need of these expensive remedies. Many of us remember the good old days when after eating a spicy Mexican meal, we would experience the belching and irritation associated with what was termed "heartburn," although the symptoms had nothing to do with the heart. It was caused by the jalapeño peppers and beer that were percolating in the stomach. The solution was simple, and cheap. Mom would reach into her purse, hand us a "Tums," and voilà, problem solved. But not so today, as every acid indigestion has become the dreaded gastro esophageal reflux disease requiring first Tagamet, then Zantac, then Prilosec, then Nexium, and the list goes on. Each of these compounds, of course, cost exponentially more than "Tums." But DTC advertising has convinced the American public it is necessary, to the tune of billions of dollars per year.

In their book *Selling Sickness*, Ray Moynihan and Alan Cassels discuss how the large pharmaceutical companies are redefining mild medical problems as serious illnesses and labeling common complaints as medical conditions.[32] Runny noses become "allergic rhinitis." When your wife gets a bit irritable around her menstrual cycle, she now has "premenstrual dysphoric disorder." In the view of our pharmaceutical "educators," Americans can no longer just have a bad day or go through a spell of the blues. What they suffer from is *depression* and you know what? Big Pharma has just the pill for you. Prozac, Zoloft, and Paxil are now prescribed like Pez candies from white-coated, stethoscope dangling, bobble-headed dispensers. Every woman in America needs treatment for osteoporosis, every man for erectile dysfunction, and every child for attention deficit disorder. Am I saying that there are not patients who may benefit from these therapies? Of course not. But DTC advertising has convinced the nation that all of these new wonder drugs available on the market are here because of the epidemic numbers of people, just like you watching *American Idol*, who are suffering miserably from this multitude of maladies that plague modern society. And AstraZeneca, Pfizer, and Merck are here to help.

While we are on the subject of new wonder drugs, it is instructive to assess just how "new" and just how "wondrous" all these newly minted medicines really are. In her book, Marcia Angell looked at all the drugs approved by the FDA between 1998 and 2002. Of the 415 new medications, less than one-third of them were new drugs and only 58 were given priority review, meaning that their importance to the American public was so essential that they warranted accelerated approval by the FDA.[33] The rest were nothing more than minor alterations in existing compounds that allowed the companies to list them as a "new" drug and begin again their patent cycle. Thus Prilosec, when its patent expired, was replaced by Nexium, and along with this new name (although hardly a new drug) came an aggressive marketing campaign touting it as the latest and greatest treatment for gastro esophageal reflux disease. Company officials and physician spokesmodels were quick to explain the benefits of Nexium over Prilosec, which was now available in the generic form and cost a fraction of what it had while under patent.

Despite their claims that exorbitant medication costs were necessary to ensure adequate R & D budgets so that they could continue their search for lifesaving therapies, the pharmaceutical companies instead presented the American public with medicine after medicine that was nothing more than a simple "copycat" drug, but with a truly breathtaking marketing strategy afforded by DTC advertising. No longer were pharmaceutical companies required by the FDA to show their new drug was significantly better than those available on the market. They only had to prove they were better than placebos, and many of the newer drugs were only slightly better than the sugar pills.

So despite the lack of new "blockbuster" drugs, the industry continued its meteoric financial success, with some companies posting profit margins as high as 25 percent. All the while, the American public continues to suffer. As more and more patients, especially the elderly and uninsured, get placed on more and more medications, the costs quickly become overwhelming and patients are forced to make difficult decisions. Does the eighty-three-year-old widow on a fixed income pay for this month's supply of her blood pressure medicine, her diabetes medicine, and her blood thinner? Or does she pay her heating bill, pay her telephone bill, or purchase enough groceries to last her through the month? Maybe she does what many poor are doing—skip doses or cut her pills in half in an effort to make them last a bit longer, without re-alizing the lower dose is ineffective, exacerbating the very problem for which she is being treated.

Does the unemployed single mom with newly diagnosed breast cancer pay for her Taxol therapy (a drug that was entirely discovered through the work of the National Cancer Institute and then licensed to Bristol-Myers Squibb who began selling it to cancer victims at about $10,000 to $20,000 per year), or does she pay the monthly rent on her apartment for herself and her two boys and just hope the cancer will stay in check?[34] Sure, there are a variety of programs sponsored by governmental agencies, philanthropic organizations, and even the pharmaceutical companies themselves, designed to assist those who are struggling to meet the costs of their medications. But these programs are woefully inadequate and people are dying because of it. In a recent survey published in *USA Today*, 41 percent of Americans reported that drug costs were a significant problem for them and 29 percent actually didn't fill the prescriptions they were given by their physician because they couldn't afford it.[35]

Don't get me wrong! I don't think pharmaceutical companies are mor-ally obligated to give free medicine to anyone who cannot afford it, just as doctors and hospitals aren't obligated to provide free care to those in need (although there are a plethora of governmental regulations that legislate the latter). But I do take issue with companies that realize profit margins far be-yond any other American industry. Companies that whine to Congress about how much they are forced to spend on R & D, but still seem to post record profits despite the fact that most of the products they produce are nothing more than "me too" drugs that offer no improved benefit to the population they pretend to serve, simply allowing a new cycle of patent protection to kick in. Companies like Bristol-Myers Squibb, who in 2001 paid their CEO, Charles Heimbold, Jr., almost $75 million in compensation, not including his $76 million in unexercised stock options. Or Wyeth, who compensated its CEO to the tune of approximately $40 million, also excluding his stock options of another $40 million.[36] I do take issue with those companies when thousands and thousands of Americans struggle just to pay for the medicines these companies provide.

But fighting back can be difficult. For neither that elderly widow nor that single mom are able to afford the lobbyists that prowl the halls of Congress to make certain our elected officials don't forget how they got there in the first place. Those unfortunate patients don't really have a voice in Washington to plead their case and help them get the medications they so desperately need. Big Pharma, on the other hand, is well represented. According to Public Citizen, Big Pharma spent $478 million between 1997 and 2002 on congressional lobbying. Marcia Angell was quick to point out that in 2002 the pharmaceutical industry employed 675 full-time lobbyists at a cost of $91 million.[37] But it has been money well spent.

When U.S. citizens realized that Canadians were buying the exact same drugs as they were at one-third or one-quarter of the price, they began organizing regularly scheduled bus trips and train excursions across the border merely for the sake of purchasing their medications. Well, PhRMA would have none of that and launched an aggressive lobbying campaign in Congress that resulted in legislation making the practice illegal. Even still, between one and two million Americans continue to obtain their medicines across the border. The pharmaceutical lobby contends that such practices are dangerous because many of these Canadian medications are fraudulent. Really? Then why isn't there an epidemic of drug-related deaths in Canada? Why aren't our neighbors to the north dying in record numbers from hypertension or diabetes that are being inadequately treated by these "fake" drugs? Oh, and one more thing. Why does Canada outperform the United States on practically every index on the WHO's comparison of health systems around the globe? Puzzling, isn't it?

The industry vehemently lobbied against a prescription drug benefit plan they thought Bill Clinton was going to add to the federal Medicare program. Yet several years later when Republican President George W. Bush did the same, the industry supported the passage. But that support was predicated upon the inclusion of a provision in the bill that banned Medicare from using their enormous purchasing power to force the pharmaceutical companies to reduce the costs of their medications for Medicare patients. Am I the only one who finds it interesting that Aetna, Health Net, Blue Cross, Blue Shield, and a multitude of other "privately run for-profit" insurance companies are allowed to do just that, resulting in a significant savings for their stockholders and lower prices for their patients? If those companies are allowed to bargain for price reductions in America's free enterprise system, why not Medicare? You want to know why? Just look at how much the pharmaceutical industry gave in campaign contributions to members of Congress during the 2008 election and look how much Medicare gave. The answer is clear. Whether the issue is Medicare's ability to bargain for price or some patent extension the result is always the same: money talks.

Just ask former New Jersey Senator Robert Torricelli. In 1999, Senator Torricelli was chairman of the Democratic Senatorial Campaign Committee. As such, he was charged with filling incumbent senators' reelection campaign war chests with money—lots of money. It just so happened that, at the time, the pharmaceutical company Schering-Plough was in trouble. You see, they were the manufacturers of the blockbuster drug Claritin, which was one of the most successful drugs in the company's history. But alas, the patent on Claritin was expiring and Schering-Plough was desperate to obtain an extension.

Company executives went into the office of Senator Torricelli and presented him with a generous check in the amount of $50,000 made out to the Democratic Senatorial Campaign Committee. Less than twenty-four hours later the New Jersey senator graciously stood on the floor of the Senate and introduced a bill to extend the patent on Claritin. Although the bill was ultimately defeated (some things are even too much for politicians to stomach!), it was really very kind of the senator to do so.[38] If you ask me, that's service! It's too bad our elderly widow or our single mom with cancer didn't have that kind of coin to throw around. Maybe they wouldn't have to choose between their medicines and their rent.

I don't know about you, but I think Torricelli should have been forced to give the money back to Schering-Plough so they could find something better to do with it . . . like investing it in R & D, perhaps?

The Politics of American Medicine

Show Me the Money and
I'll Show You the Problem

The Hospital Industry: $32,378,426.00
The Pharmaceutical Industry: $42,062,493.00
The Insurance Industry: $65,533,700.00
Health Professionals: $129,293,379.00
Lawyers: $298,577,620.00
America's Uninsured: *"WORTHLESS"*
For everything else, there's MasterCard.

After reading the previous chapters, it may surprise many of you to know that I am not as cynical as the average American when it comes to our politicians. I am convinced that the vast majority of those who enter politics do so motivated either by a sincere desire to serve their fellow citizens or by a specific cause that is near and dear to their hearts. It isn't until these same idealists reach Washington that they begin the metamorphosis into the money chasers we have all come to loathe and detest. Most first-time legislators arrive fresh from a heady victory and ready to change the world and to make a difference in the lives of those who entrusted them to the office. Yet once ensconced in that same office, the realities of what it took to get them there and, more importantly, what it takes to keep them there set in. Money, with a capital M, is the key to the kingdom, and soon even the most incorruptible begin their march in cadence to the new drummer. And with health care reform on the front burner throughout this last election cycle, the war chests of the special interests were opened widely.

The figures listed above were obtained from the website of OpenSecrets .org[1] and represent the total campaign contributions from individuals and political action committees to federal candidates and political parties reported to the Federal Election Commission from January 1, 2007, through April 25, 2010. As you can see, the special interests who had the most to gain or lose from health care reform were throwing lots of money at politicians to make certain that *their* interests remained *special* in the minds of the elected officials. And after witnessing the debacle of the health care debate unfold over the past three years, I have to conclude that the money was well spent.

When campaigning for the presidency, Barack Obama told us that in order for reform to be truly effective, we must hold the private insurance providers accountable for their egregious practices of denying coverage to those with preexisting conditions and rescinding the care of those who became ill with maladies that would require expensive treatments. He proposed, as did many others, a government-run "public option" that would place *patient* care back in the forefront rather than the *profit* care we have come to expect of the commercial carriers. This new entity was designed to provide affordable coverage to those who were priced out of the commercial market and would create a healthy competition for the private insurers who continued to raise premiums, spend greater and greater percentages of their resources on overhead, and offer their executives compensation packages that were becoming more and more obscene.

But $65,533,700 speaks volumes. In no time, the public option was being derided across the country by politicians and pundits who labeled it "socialized medicine" and a government takeover of health care. All of a sudden, a government-run public option for health insurance was a bad idea. But wait a second . . . I didn't quite hear the insurance industry complaining about a government option for the elderly, who are mostly on a fixed income and the high consumers of health care resources. No, Medicare is OK for them. And wait, maybe I'm wrong but I don't remember America's Health Insurance Plans (AHIP) complaining about a government option for the poor who won't be able to pay their high-cost premiums for insurance. No, Medicaid is OK for them. But what the insurance industry *did* complain about was a government option that might compete with them for younger, healthy, employed Americans who pay their premiums (or have their employer do it for them) and are relatively low utilizers of their insurance benefits. This is the group where all the profit is made and the insurance industry is convinced that a government option has no business there. And so faster than you can say $65,533,700, the public option disappeared.

Many Americans, especially the elderly, are also feeling the pinch of the high cost of prescription drugs. The industry has exploded in the past decade and a half, beginning when the ban on DTC advertising was lifted by Congress in 1997, thanks in large part to the efforts of PhRMA, the lobbying arm of the pharmaceutical companies. As mentioned in the preceding chapter, from 1997 to 2006, the average cost of a prescription drug rose from $30 to $68, and spending on pharmaceuticals skyrocketed from $72 billion in 1997 to $289 billion in 2006.[2] Increasingly, Medicare recipients were being forced to choose between their medicines and their groceries, between paying their pharmacists or paying their heating bills. But during the 2008 election cycle, there was hope on the horizon as candidate after candidate decried the high cost of medications and promised relief. Initiatives were introduced that would give Medicare the same right that every other insurance provider enjoyed: the right to negotiate prescription drug prices for their clients. Anthem Blue Cross, Kaiser Permanente, Health Net, Aetna, you name it; all could use the strength of their market share to negotiate lower prices for the medicines their patients needed. That is, all of them but Medicare, the insurance provider with the largest market share and thus the greatest bargaining power. Congress repeatedly rebuked any attempt to allow Medicare to flex its muscle and the elderly were left out in the cold. That's what Billy Tauzin and $42,062,493 will get you.

Billy Tauzin was the president and CEO of PhRMA, and one need only to look deeper into Mr. Tauzin's colorful background to appreciate just how money talks in the halls of Congress. Tauzin was a little-known attorney from Chackbay, Louisiana, who was first elected to the state legislature in 1972. Eight years later, he successfully ran as the Democratic candidate to fill the 3rd Congressional District seat, which had been vacated by the newly elected governor. Tauzin became an adroit wheeler and dealer who quickly worked his way up the ranks of the Democratic congressional establishment.[3] But when Bill and Hillary Clinton's ill-fated attempt at health care reform resulted in the Republican takeover of Congress in 1994, Tauzin abruptly denounced the Democratic Party and became a born-again Republican. The switch ingratiated him with the GOP power brokers, and Congressman Tauzin was soon rewarded with the chairmanship of the House Committee on Energy and Commerce.

Working closely (too closely, some would say) with the pharmaceutical industry, Congressman Tauzin was instrumental in designing the Medicare prescription drug bill championed by the Bush administration. Many in Congress, as well as in the public sector, were critical of the bill, seeing it as a windfall for the pharmaceutical industry. Included by Tauzin in the provisions of the bill was the prohibition of drug reimportation from Canada and other countries, as well as a specific ban on allowing Medicare to negotiate prices for the prescription drugs they were making available to their fifty million patients. PhRMA won big time, but so did Billy Tauzin, who, within months, announced his retirement from Congress to accept the job of CEO at PhRMA for a handsome $2 million per year.[4]

The relationship that Tauzin had established as an "opportunistic congressman" continued to serve him and PhRMA well as the new administration began to tackle health care reform. Although Candidate Obama derided Tauzin in his campaign ads, President Obama had little choice but to invite Tauzin to the table when the reform package was being crafted. PhRMA came to the party willing to provide $80 billion in discounted drugs over ten years ($8 billion/year) and offering to pay for television commercials in support of the reform plan. Of course, they reserved the right to set the prices of those drugs so that the discounts they offered might actually be offset somewhat by increasing the baseline prices. Genius! After back and forth negotiations with Max Baucus, the Democratic senator from Montana and the powerful chairman of the Senate Finance Committee, the backroom deal was struck and the emerging legislation perpetuated the prohibitions on drug reimportation and Medicare price negotiation.

Some estimate that giving Medicare the freedom to negotiate prescription drug prices would result in a savings of up to $100 billion per year![5] Let's see . . . PhRMA offers $8 billion per year in reductions to prices they are free to set and, in return, prevents Medicare from negotiating prices that would save up to $100 billion per year. It sure appears to me that Billy Tauzin earned every bit of his $2 million salary and Max Baucus every bit of the $781,113 in campaign contributions provided to him by the pharmaceutical industry since 2005.[6] And this was all occurring during the new administration of "transparency" promised by Barack Obama. It's transparent all right, but I'm not sure I like what I see.

Other "hot button" topics in the debate on reforming our health care system were the issues of medical malpractice, the wasteful cost of defensive medicine, and national tort reform. Throughout the debates, Republican candidates each emphasized the tremendous importance of malpractice reform to rein in the high costs associated with defensive medicine and allow physicians the freedom to practice without the fear of a frivolous lawsuit hanging over their heads. It should come as no surprise to anyone that the congressional Democrats were as silent as church mice on the issue of tort reform. Oh, sure, one or two would make a cursory remark in support of tort reform, but it was never more than just that. I was stunned to see John Edwards actually address the subject a bit more forcefully in several of the debates, especially since he earned much of the money to build his new 28,000-square-foot home by suing obstetricians in North Carolina when babies were born with cerebral palsy.[7]

But if you wonder, as do I, why such an important subject was for the most part glossed over or completely neglected, all you really need to do is look again at the chart that begins this chapter. Since January 1, 2007, America's lawyers and their minions have provided Congress with $298,577,620 in contributions.[8] If that kind of coin can't protect you, nothing will. And of course, it did. Also, if you find it unusual that Democrats would be so unenthusiastic about including meaningful malpractice reform in the new health care bill while the Republicans were so adamantly in support, you might be interested to know almost 80 percent of that $300 million went to the Democrats.[9] And guess what? Senator Max Baucus, who has been President Obama's appointed architect of health care reform, has accepted $768,954 in campaign contributions from attorneys since 2005.[10]

What is surprising to me is that America's health professionals, physicians and the like, were not more successful at including meaningful malpractice reform in the final bill. And why weren't they able to get the God-awful "Sustained Growth Rate" mechanism for Medicare reimbursement levels permanently eliminated? After all, they did shell out $129,293,379 in influence.[11] So why weren't they more influential? And why did the American Medical Association (AMA) support the legislation while the vast majority of medical and surgical specialty organizations and the overwhelming majority of American physicians were vociferously opposed to it? To answer that question, it is important to understand that most physicians are fiercely independent, exceptionally well educated, and accustomed to giving orders rather than taking them. In addition, although there are issues that are important to all physicians, the differences between primary care and specialty medicine are at times cavernous and their specific interests may be in conflict.

When the trial lawyers walk into Congress with almost $300 million in campaign contributions, they do so with one voice. When the AMA walks in, they don't have all $130 million focused on the same issue nor do they have control of all that "candy." Each specialty organization has its own agenda; thus, the influence of my own organization, the American Association of Neurological Surgeons, is going to be far less than that of the radiologists or internists, whose membership numbers dwarf ours. Tort reform is a huge issue to neurosurgeons or obstetricians, who can find themselves paying up to $200,000 per year or more in insurance premiums. The same issue may not be as important to a radiologist or a family doctor or a psychiatrist, who might spend one-tenth of that amount. Just as the insurance companies were able to force managed care contracts upon us by a process of "divide and conquer," the new reform bill was foisted upon *organized* medicine in much the same way.

The AMA, which has been around since the mid-nineteenth century, has seen a decline in membership over the past decade or so—only about 20 percent of physicians and medical students are members.[12] Yet the AMA purports to be the spokesperson for America's doctors despite the fact that

80 percent of America's doctors don't belong! This dichotomy and obvious incongruity reflect the divergent interests of its onetime members. A great example of this conflict that is clearly delineated in the current reform initiative involves the plan to provide insurance coverage for America's forty-seven million uninsured. The new bill plans to help achieve that goal, in large part, by lowering the eligibility requirements for Medicaid. Physicians went ballistic, noting that Medicaid already reimbursed at levels so low that in many areas of the country no physician would see a Medicaid patient. To placate the AMA, the crafters of the new bill offered to reimburse Medicaid patients at Medicare rates, but only for primary care physicians, not for specialists other than general surgeons who practiced in rural communities (and only for two years, by the way). "Yippee!" cried the AMA. As their majority primary care doctors celebrated the "victory," specialists were left out in the cold.

America's surgeons beseeched the AMA to demand meaningful tort reform in the new bill but were rebuked at the door. That explains why the American College of Surgeons, my own American Association of Neurological Surgeons, and every other surgical specialty organization lined up solidly against the bill while the AMA, "representing America's doctors," supported it. Divide and conquer worked again; physicians took it in the proverbial shorts and now go into this new program of health care reform kicking and screaming instead of partnering with the administration in attempting to improve the quality of care for the patients we serve. It should be remarkably instructive to the leadership of American medical organizations why PhRMA, the insurance industry, and the lawyers all came out winners in this exercise and why physicians, despite $129,293,379, got the shaft.

One of the more interesting special interests for me in this process has been the American Hospital Association (AHA). I am still at a loss to understand what they hoped to get out of the new bill and whether they were pleased or not with the final product. They dutifully lined up on stage with President Obama and pledged support for his plan alongside the AMA, PhRMA, and the AHIP, but have been relatively mute throughout the debate. It makes me wonder if they were expecting much worse cuts in Medicare reimbursement than what finally materialized or if there was some "backroom, not-so-transparent" deal that bought their silence, much like the pharmaceutical industry. I made multiple attempts to discuss the issue with AHA executives, calling their offices in Chicago and Washington and e-mailing them through their website, but was never able to get any individual to return my calls.

As I understand it, America's hospitals agreed to cuts in Medicare reimbursement in the neighborhood of $155 billion over ten years. The rationale for their acquiescence to these cuts is that with the eventual health insurance

coverage for an additional thirty-two million Americans, hospitals would realize an additional $171 billion in revenue over that same ten-year period—a
net gain of $16 billion.[13] I find it intriguing that the industry would spend
$32,378,426 in campaign contributions for a net gain of a paltry $1.6 billion
per year. The other consideration that makes such support puzzling is the
fact that as many as twenty million of those thirty-two million newly insured
Americans will be covered by lowering the threshold for Medicaid eligibility.
I find it hard to believe that a hospital would be pleased to know that more
than half of their newly insured patients were on Medicaid, a program with
the lowest reimbursement levels in the country.

One of the "conspiracy theories" that I have heard mumbled under the
breath of hospital administrators and political insiders is that the AHA has
become dominated by the larger, multi-institution hospital chains, both for-
profit and not-for-profit. Their vision for the future is that such models are
more cost efficient; they have greater market strength when negotiating reimbursement contracts, prices for hospital supplies, and even salaries for their
professional and nonprofessional employees. They are of the mind-set that
the local, independent community hospital is a thing of the past and would
like to see them vanish over time.

The Medicare cuts go into effect soon, yet it will be close to five years
or so before we start to see the large influx of Americans with their new, shiny
insurance cards. The larger hospital networks have a much greater financial
reserve than the struggling independent institutions and would be in a better
position to weather the five years of Medicare cuts while awaiting the influx
of newly insured clients. The conspiracy proponents suggest that the AHA
was quick to sign on to a plan with such modest advantages for the hospitals
in hopes that the smaller, independent institutions would find themselves in
financial trouble before the appearance of more universal coverage, making
them more susceptible to acquisition by the larger networks. Only time will tell.

My wife, who has been my social conscience in the writing of this book,
was appalled when I placed the term *"WORTHLESS"* next to "America's
Uninsured" in the opening of this chapter. I did not do it to insult the many
patients who are without coverage; I did it to make a point. The crafters of
this bill began their complex journey with every intention of helping the many
patients who have been shortchanged by the "best health care system in the
world." But as the money from the special interests poured in, the focus of
this effort began to change and the really important reforms that would have
resulted in sustained improvement in the delivery of health care to every
American citizen evaporated.

Gone is the "public option." After all, it's nothing more than socialized
medicine and the government intrusion into health care, right? Gone is the

ability of Medicare to negotiate prescription drug prices with the pharmaceutical industry. After all, don't you realize PhRMA has committed $80 billion over the next ten years already and allowing Medicare to negotiate would deprive the industry of that important "research and development" capital needed to cure cancer? Gone is any meaningful attempt at tort reform. After all, changing the current system, with its lottery mentality, would only reduce your access to a lawyer, right?

When all was said and done, the American public was told this was a great victory for patients denied care because of preexisting conditions, patients dropped by their carrier because their illness became too expensive, and patients whose employers did not offer coverage and were unable to afford it on their own. Do you really think now that you have a Medicaid card, things will change? Ask your friends and neighbors how it's working for them. With decreasing reimbursement (except for primary care doctors, for two years only), do you really think your physician will have more time to spend with you, to take an earnest interest in your health? And at the end of the day, ten years from now, when costs continue to soar, access continues to be a problem, and quality continues to decline, do you think there will be any politician willing to take up the mantle of health care reform after what we have been through these past few years? Maybe, but only if your column changes from *"WORTHLESS"* to something much more substantial, like $42,062,493 or $65,533,700 or $298,577,620. I wouldn't count on it.

It costs money, lots of money, to purchase your own senator, especially an influential one who sits on the Senate Finance Committee, which was charged with writing the new health care legislation. How much? Well, according to the Sunlight Foundation and OpenSecrets.org, the health care and insurance sectors have shelled out contributions to committee members (over the course of their tenures through 2008) in numbers outlined below:[14]

Max Baucus (D-MT): $3,967,694
John D. Rockefeller IV (D-WV): $2,068,303
Kent Conrad (D-ND): $2,152,550
Jeff Bingaman (D-NM): $1,022,626
John Kerry (D-MA): $9,542,508 (includes presidential campaign)
Blanche Lincoln (D-AR): $1,721,641
Ron Wyden (D-OR): $1,390,661
Charles E. Schumer (D-NY): $2,348,758
Debbie Stabenow (D-MI): $1,434,936
Maria Cantwell (D-WA): $653,926
Bill Nelson (D-FL): $1,683,226
Robert Menendez (D-NJ): $1,675,155

Thomas Carper (D-DE): $899,984
Chuck Grassley (R-IA): $2,734,703
Orrin Hatch (R-UT): $2,971,051
Olympia Snowe (R-ME): $1,153,130
Jon Kyl (R-AZ): $2,505,012
Jim Bunning (R-KY): $1,814,703
Mike Crapo (R-ID): $910,124
Pat Roberts (R-KS): $1,199,679
John Ensign (R-NV): $2,376,589
Mike Enzi (R-WY): $853,668
John Cornyn (R-TX): $2,562,606

How many unemployed Americans who lost their insurance with their jobs can afford such influence? How many patients who are denied timely access to quality care because they are on Medicaid can afford such influence? If the poor, the uninsured, and the underinsured want to really get representation, they had better start putting away their nickels, dimes, and quarters. Senators cost a lot and I expect, even in this struggling economy, the price is only going to go up. Now Senator Max Baucus will tell everyone that once he was charged with writing the new bill on health care reform he thought it was important to demonstrate his impartiality and fairness, so he refused to accept any campaign contributions from those special interests that had a dog in the fight. How disingenuous can you be? Senator Baucus did not have to accept new contributions, because as you can see above, those special interests were already on the layaway plan and had prepaid for their tickets to the dance.

OK . . . enough senator bashing. As I said in the beginning of this chapter, I firmly believe that most politicians enter the profession with good intentions. But sometimes those intentions lead to the creation of legislation that is so misguided and so poorly designed that it actually can exacerbate the problems it was created to address. I suspect, no, I'm convinced, that the overwhelming majority of these dysfunctional laws result from the fact that when crafted, legislators fail to enlist advice from the people who are best positioned to understand how such legislation will play out in the real world. Instead, they are captive to policy wonks, political strategists, or even the justifiably "outraged" constituents. Often they act, again with admirable intent, but without a full understanding of what effect such legislation will have in the real world, in the trenches. This is especially true when it comes to health care.

A good example is the Emergency Medical Treatment and Active Labor Act (EMTALA) passed in 1986.[15] This law makes a lot of sense from both a practical and a moral point of view. It was designed primarily to prevent patient "dumping," a practice where hospitals refuse care to uninsured or poorly insured patients who present to their emergency rooms, instead "directing" them to public facilities such as county hospitals or university medical centers, essentially "dumping" the undesirable patients into the public system. (No problem with a public option here, I guess!) Such practices put an undue financial burden on the receiving facilities but worse, many patients' conditions deteriorate in the time spent traveling to the second facility and some even die.

The public sector hospitals were rightfully indignant and urged Congress to put a halt to the egregious activity, which put patients and the survival of public sector hospitals at risk. Congress responded and enacted EMTALA, which mandates that all hospitals are required to evaluate and provide treatment to any patient presenting to their emergency rooms regardless of their insurance status or ability to pay. Each hospital is expected to maintain an on-call roster of medical and surgical specialists who are readily available and who are required to evaluate and treat the patients, again without regard to their insurance status. Additionally, if a given hospital does not have the specific specialty service required, they are directed to "stabilize" the patient and transfer them to the nearest facility where the appropriate care is available. Finally, if a facility with appropriate specialty care is contacted, they are obligated by law to accept the patient. Again, all of this makes perfect sense, on paper. How it has played out in the trenches is an entirely different issue.

To begin with, the law requires *every* patient to be evaluated and treated, not just those with real emergencies. As managed care models became entrenched across America, many primary care physicians were forced to increase the volume of patients they saw in order to maintain their incomes amid falling reimbursement. There was little room in their busy schedules for patients who called in with "a cold" or "a rash," and they were directed to simply go the nearest emergency room, using the ERs as uncompensated physician extenders. In addition, as more and more Americans joined the rolls of the "uninsured" or became Medicaid beneficiaries, they found it increasingly difficult to find a primary care physician who would accept them as patients. Without a physician they had little choice but to turn to the local ER for care more appropriately managed in the office of a family doctor or pediatrician.

It was not long before emergency rooms across America became overwhelmed with nonemergent patients, filling gurneys in the hallways and resulting in interminably long waits. As a result, when actual, life-threatening emergencies presented to the ER, we began to see emergency rooms temporarily closing their doors and "diverting" these patients to other facilities. These diversions resulted in delayed care, and once again, patients with real emergencies suffered and some died as a result of the precious moments lost in the transfer. Essentially, by demanding all patients be seen and treated rather than just those with emergencies, EMTALA succeeds in perpetuating and, at times, exacerbating the very problem it was enacted to prevent.

Since EMTALA does not have a requirement that community physicians bear the responsibility of evaluating *their own* patients, they are now free to "dump" their inconvenient patients into the system. Also, since EMTALA does not address the establishment of community clinics to provide nonemergent primary care to uninsured or Medicaid patients, it essentially guaranteed that our ERs would be overwhelmed. And they are. EMTALA also does not explain how local ERs are supposed to financially absorb this growing population of "underfunded" patients. There is no mechanism to reimburse the local hospitals for the uncompensated care they are expected to provide.

Specialists became affected as well. The law clearly states that if a specialist is "on-call," he or she is obligated to evaluate and provide treatment to any patient who presents to the emergency room and who requires their attention. Even more, they are required to accept patients from any outlying ER that does not have the necessary specialty services available. Thus, neurosurgeons, orthopedists, neurologists, gastroenterologists, and others find themselves providing increasing amounts of uncompensated care. EMTALA does not offer to pay for that care, and EMTALA does not offer protection from frivolous litigation as a result of that uncompensated care. Physicians were told they had to provide it, or face a $50,000 fine for every instance in which they refused.

Soon after EMTALA went into effect, medical and surgical specialists had enough and began to stop taking call at their hospitals. Why would they interrupt their busy elective schedules, filled with patients for whom they received reasonable compensation, to assess an uncompensated patient who might sue them in the event that things did not go as planned? EMTALA has no answer to that question. Thus, physicians have increasingly refused to be part of on-call panels and more emergency rooms are left without specialty coverage, *further* overburdening those ERs whose physicians continue to put patients first and provide ER care. Growing numbers of such community hospitals have found their specialists frustrated by having to provide uncompensated care for patients transferred from neighboring hospitals—hospitals with appropriate specialists on their staff who refused to participate in the call schedule, electing to spend the night in restful slumber and shifting the burden of their community's poorly insured to others.

EMTALA is a reasonable attempt to ensure necessary emergency care for those in need and to prevent hospitals from "cherry-picking" patients with good insurance and abandoning those without means to other facilities. It was enacted by well-meaning politicians who were earnestly concerned with the growing problem of patient "dumping." But the way the law was written and implemented has, in many physicians' view, only worsened the problem. If Congress had consulted with more physicians practicing medicine in community settings, we could have easily predicted the unanticipated and detrimental consequences of the legislation.

Another such initiative that was enacted on both the federal and state levels addresses the problem of communication between health care providers and patients with an inability to speak or comprehend English.[16] Certainly, an argument can made that when someone comes to the United States, the burden is upon him or her to learn our language. But the United States has a rich history of multiculturalism and has earned its moniker as a "melting pot." Indeed, in many communities across America, there is a predominance of Latino, Asian, and other cultural influence such that advertisements, street names, written driver's license tests, and other public resources are presented in various languages other than English.

Providing quality medical care requires an accurate history from the patient and a thorough understanding by the patient of proposed treatments, including dosing schedules and side effects of medication, risks and complications related to invasive procedures, as well as warning signs and symptoms that should prompt a return to the clinic or office. It can be difficult, if not impossible, for the physician who does not speak the primary language of the patient to be certain that the important information is exchanged. Recognizing this, lawmakers drafted legislation that mandated if a physician accepted Medicare or Medicaid patients, it was the responsibility of *the physician* to provide translators services if needed! Really? Let me understand this . . . if I happen to be one of the diminishing numbers of physicians who will see a Medicaid patient, I now have to pay for a translator if the patient doesn't understand English? Those of us who accept Medicaid are already losing money on those patients since their reimbursement does not even cover the costs of our overhead. Now we are told we have to pay out-of-pocket for a translator. How does that work?

Several years ago I saw a Medicaid patient in my office by the name of Geraldo Perez. In our practice, I tend to get the majority of Spanish-speaking patients since I am able to speak the language well enough to communicate in a reasonable manner with most of them. Now rest assured, I am not "fluent" and have never taken a Spanish class, but I grew up in East Los Angeles and went to an elementary school staffed by nuns who were Cuban refugees and less than adept at the English language. Many of my school friends had parents who spoke no English and thus by mere assimilation I was able to pick up enough Spanish to get by (although I must confess that some of the first words I added to my vocabulary were the more "salty and expressive" ones). I have traveled to Nicaragua on several occasions to teach physicians and perform surgery, so I am relatively comfortable with a Spanish-speaking patient.

Mr. Perez was a fifty-nine-year-old legalized U.S. citizen who spoke no English. He worked the fields for a company that did not offer health benefits, and his salary was such that he was eligible for the state Medi-Cal program. He was accompanied by his thirty-two-year-old daughter who was fluent in both languages and whose full-time job was "caregiver" to her father. She was paid by the State of California to cook, clean, and look after him. Mr. Perez had suffered a low back injury several years earlier and hadn't worked in twenty-six months. Eventually he progressed through the cumbersome and painfully slow Medi-Cal system and was referred to me for evaluation (*two and a half years* after his injury).

Over the next hour, I took a detailed history and performed a physical examination, directing him to perform certain tasks that would assist me in determining how we should proceed. As I mentioned above, my Spanish is adequate, not fluent, but we appeared to communicate fairly well. Several times during the evaluation I turned to his daughter and asked, "Como se dice?" or "How do you say?" a certain word. When we were done, I asked her to make sure Mr. Perez understood everything we had talked about and asked if he had any questions for me. We shook hands and I scheduled him for an MRI scan and a follow-up appointment to go over the results when it was completed. Three days later, I received a "bill" from his caregiver daughter for $45.00 for *translator services*.

This scenario really happened. I did not fabricate this story. I got on the phone with the daughter and instructed her to drop by the next afternoon to pick up her check as well as all of her father's records. I would not see him as a patient any longer. Once again, a law that seems to make perfect sense to a well-meaning legislator makes absolutely no sense in the real world of practice. Why wasn't there a physician at the table when this law was considered? We would have simply asked the question, "Why on earth would I consider seeing a non-English-speaking patient for the paltry fees provided by Medicaid if *I* also have to pay for a translator?"

Lastly, sometimes members of Congress try to pass laws that are just plain stupid and make absolutely no sense. Case in point: Tom Coburn is a Republican senator from the state of Oklahoma. Senator Coburn is not only a senator, Senator Coburn is an accountant. Not only that, Senator Coburn is a physician.[17] Senator Coburn is Superman! He understands politics, he understands finance, and he understands health care. I love this guy already. You da man!

A section of the new bill creates a program of "Comparative Effectiveness Research" designed to study various treatments in hopes of discovering more clearly what actually works in medicine and what doesn't. The bill earmarks $1.5 billion in the first year and an additional $500 million for each of the ensuing ten years to carry out such research.[18] Dr. Coburn was not pleased. As a doctor, he knew what worked and what didn't. He did not see the need to have government involved in such nonsense and viewed comparative effectiveness research as little more than the Obama administration's attempt to "ration" health care (I guess he prefers the way we ration it now, based on ability to pay).

So Doctor Senator Accountant Tom Coburn introduced an amendment strictly prohibiting any data that was the result of such research from being used to determine whether a treatment or procedure would be reimbursed.[19] Does anyone follow the logic of such thinking? We spend billions of dollars on well-grounded research and discover that a treatment is ineffective, and we are forced to continue to pay for this useless procedure, no doubt with the infinite health care resources that we obviously have at our disposal. Fortunately, Coburn's Kryptonite-laden colleagues defeated Superman's proposed amendment.

Truth be told, my initial disclosure that I don't share our nation's cynicism regarding politicians appears a bit hollow after rereading this chapter. I apologize. But I can only call it like I see it, so I had best end with the same disclosure that our politicians themselves love to use:

My name is Dr. Jeffrey M. Lobosky and I approve this message.

· 6 ·

America's Hospitals

Havens of Mercy or Dens of Thieves?

$\mathscr{D}$r. Chae Hyun Moon had no way of knowing that this particular June morning in 2002 he would be coming face to face with a patient who would forever change his life. He assumed that John Corapi was just another "ordinary" cardiac patient, similar to the thousands of others he had evaluated during the course of his long and distinguished career. But as Dr. Moon would soon learn, John Corapi was anything but "ordinary."[1]

The fifty-five-year-old Corapi was a Catholic priest who had recently relocated to the small town of Lake, California, just south of the city of Redding where Moon had been in practice since the late 1970s. Corapi's journey to the sacred priesthood couldn't really be considered "ordinary" either, as he took his vows much later in life than the usual seminarian. He had initially used his accounting degree to get a job as the assistant controller for the Tropicana Hotel in Las Vegas and later landed a position as an investigator with the Nevada Gaming Control Board.[2]

By the late 1970s, about the same time that Dr. Moon settled in Redding, Corapi moved to Los Angeles, obtained his real estate license, and was soon pulling down a six-figure salary and enjoying the trappings of "the good life": luxury homes, a yacht, fast cars, and fast women. But along with such successes came temptations, and soon Corapi found his life engulfed by drugs, sex, and other forms of debauchery. According to author Stephen Klaidman, in 1982, John Corapi went on a three-day drug binge that eventually landed him in the hospital and then a psychiatric unit for almost a year.[3] Once released, he returned to Las Vegas but soon relapsed and found himself homeless, broke, and at rock bottom. With encouragement from his mother, Corapi returned to the Catholic Church of his Italian heritage and, after experiencing an epiphany of sorts, entered the seminary and was ordained by

Pope John Paul II in 1991 at the age of forty-four. No, there was nothing "ordinary" about John Corapi.

And Corapi's ministry would prove to be just as unusual. He began his career as an itinerant preacher, spreading the word of the Lord from parish to parish across the United States and Canada and delivering his own conservative message of Catholicism. As his reputation grew, he began producing a series of DVDs filled with his sermons, and he started a company to distribute them. He was given his own show on the Eternal World Television Network (EWTN), and soon became a popular Catholic televangelist.

Despite his renown, Corapi was essentially a loner and chose Lake, California, because of its relative isolation, proximity to fishing, and quiet lifestyle, which appealed to him. Klaidman reports that he had few friends and mostly stayed to himself. He did develop close ties, however, with an Italian couple who lived next door, and it was they who encouraged Corapi to see a doctor when he began to complain of fatigue and shortness of breath. Although the family doctor who examined the reclusive priest did not find anything wrong, he did recommend he see a cardiologist because of his vague symptoms and family history of heart disease. An appointment was made with the area's most prestigious heart specialist, Dr. Chae Hyun Moon, and their date with destiny began.[4]

In his 2007 book, *Coronary: A True Story of Medicine Gone Awry*, Klaidman meticulously documents the ill-fated interaction between Dr. Moon and Father Corapi. After an initial series of tests, the Redding cardiologist told the priest he needed an urgent angiogram, a procedure where a small catheter is threaded from an artery in the groin up into the arteries that supply the heart, allowing visualization of the coronary blood supply. Corapi was understandably shaken by the news and worried about the fact that his father had developed heart disease at a relatively young age, so he agreed to the invasive procedure. The news was bad, life-threatening actually, as the chief of cardiology at Tenet Health Care's Redding Medical Center advised John Corapi to undergo an emergent cardiac bypass the next morning or face a real risk of death. According to Dr. Moon, Corapi's coronary arteries were dangerously narrowed, and in two arteries, the walls of the vessel were elevating from the side into the lumen, a critical condition known as "dissection."[5]

Father Corapi was stunned at the news and, after discussing the situation with friends, decided to fly to Las Vegas for a second opinion. He was able to get an appointment with a well-respected cardiologist in Las Vegas who reviewed the priest's studies, pronounced them "normal," and actually wondered out loud whether they had sent the wrong angiogram. They hadn't. A third opinion from a cardiac surgeon likewise agreed there was nothing on the studies to even remotely suggest the need for cardiac surgery.

Relieved beyond words, John Corapi returned home to northern California determined that Dr. Chae Hyun Moon would have to answer for his actions.[6]

With the help of his attorney, Father Corapi first tried to discuss the situation with the hospital's CEO, who simply suggested that he follow Dr. Moon's recommendations and have the surgery. Frustrated at Redding Medical Center's defense of Moon despite the evidence presented, Corapi eventually contacted the Federal Bureau of Investigation (FBI) and blew the whistle on Redding Medical Center's prestigious "Heart Institute" and the doctors who ran it. The ensuing investigation by the FBI uncovered an unprecedented number of surgeries and other procedures performed by Dr. Moon and his associate cardiac surgeon, Dr. Fidel Realyvasquez, on patients with relatively normal findings.[7]

When the dust finally cleared, 769 patients had filed malpractice suits against the physicians and the hospital. After several years of painstaking investigation, a settlement was eventually reached that would end the surgical careers of the principal defendant physicians and cost each in excess of $1 million in civil fines and their malpractice insurance carriers more than $21 million to compensate the injured patients. The Tenet Health Care System ended up paying hundreds of millions of dollars to the federal government in fines and restitution, and the health care giant was forced to divest itself of its premier heart surgery hospital, Redding Medical Center. In addition, the trust and civic pride that the greater Redding community held for the hospital and its renowned heart specialists were shattered.[8]

But this was not the first time that Tenet Health Care faced civil and criminal investigations for its business practices. As a matter of fact, they had a long and sullied history of fraudulent activities dating back to the for-profit hospital group's original owners, National Medical Enterprises (NME). In the 1990s, NME was convicted of unnecessarily hospitalizing a large number of patients in their psychiatric facilities and billing for unneeded tests and procedures until their insurance ran out.[9] As a result of that scandal, the large, for-profit company merged with American Medical International in 1995 and changed its name to Tenet Health Care—a different name, but apparently the same corporate culture and same corporate ethos.

Hospitals did not always behave like this . . .

In one of the preeminent books on the evolution of the hospital industry, *Mending Bodies, Saving Souls: A History of Hospitals*, Guenter Risse from the University of California, San Francisco, traces the development of the modern hospital from its ancestral roots. In ancient times, the Greeks would take their sick and dying to the various temples scattered across the empire, the most prominent being that dedicated to Asclepius, the god of healing. They would lay the infirm on the temple steps and offer prayers and sacrifices in hopes of returning health. As the popularity of Christianity began to expand, the rites associated with the pagan gods clashed with the tenets of the new religion. And in 391 CE, when Christianity was proclaimed the official religion of the Roman Empire, the many pagan temples were systematically destroyed, leaving Christian churches in their stead.[10]

As the Roman culture became more advanced, the leaders attempted to change the reputation of its army from a band of barbarians to soldier-heroes. In order to attract a higher caliber of warrior, they offered more money, prestige, and *care* for their forces. Eventually the Romans established a series of "valetudiuaria" to provide support for the sick and wounded Roman soldiers. The militia was indeed an important commodity, but so were the slaves who provided the labor force necessary to continue the expansion of the Holy Roman Empire. Consequently, care within the network of the valetudiuaria was soon extended to the slave population as well.[11]

As the principles of Christianity became woven into the fabric of the Roman culture, the concept of charity, especially toward the poor and the sick, became ingrained. Around the fifth century, the bishop of Edessa established a *nosokomeion* or "sick house" for the dying or ailing poor, and soon infirmaries began to spring up across ancient Europe, usually attached to Christian churches, to provide hospice care for lepers and other undesirables. In addition, many of these institutions provided shelter for travelers who were poor or ill. Still later, *xenodocheia* (hostels) were constructed in proximity to the growing number of monasteries. Rudimentary medical care was offered in these facilities to the resident monks, the poor, and the region's wealthy, each in separate buildings. This stratification of care would be a precursor to the private and public hospital systems that would later characterize treatment in Europe and the United States.[12]

With the fall of the Roman Empire, the monastic centers that emerged throughout the Western world became the dominant hubs for not only charitable care, but medical education as well. Medical science was still in its infancy, and soon the monastic healers waged an intellectual war against the "secular" healers who favored surgery and herbal medicines over prayer and the use of religious icons. Around the same time, Christians residing in the Islamic Empire helped establish the first "Muslim" hospital in Damascus in 707 CE and soon such institutions flourished throughout the Islamic nations. These *bimaristans* were usually erected under the guidance of secular rulers who wanted to assist the local population and ingratiate themselves with the tribesmen. Such early facilities were much less dominated by religious mores and more open to lay therapies than their European counterparts.[13]

In the 1100s, the Council of Clermont ended the tradition of monastic healing as the church leaders decided that the practice of medicine was interfering with the monks' spiritual development and piety. With the onset of the Hundred Years War in 1337 between France and England, Europe saw the systematic decline of the charitable "sick houses," which relied heavily on bequests for their continued existence. In those facilities that remained, greed and corruption became rampant as staff began extorting bribes from patients and their families.[14]

During the Middle Ages, hospitals became little more than specialized isolation wards for patients with everything from leprosy to the plague, but after the 1500s, they began to resurrect into centers for treatment, recovery, and rehabilitation. Around the eighteenth century, a new model began to emerge in Europe where communities established their own hospitals governed by boards made up of the local citizenry. In addition to providing care, medical teaching and research began to proliferate at these institutions, and with the rise of the British Empire, several prestigious hospitals became dominant centers, attracting students from across Europe and America for medical education.[15]

Across the pond as the American Revolution came to an end, the young nation had but two major general hospitals among its colonies: the Pennsylvania Hospital and the New York Hospital. In 1823, the seventy-three-bed Massachusetts General Hospital opened for business and would go on to become one of the world's leading institutions for medical care, teaching, and research. Soon other communities followed; religious, philanthropic, and educational entities established hospitals with the common goal of providing a "community asset" to care for their neighbors without regard to their ability to pay.[16]

Professor Risse notes that as America entered the twentieth century, it saw the most explosive growth of hospital construction in history. Slowed only temporarily by World War I, by 1930 American hospitals became entrenched in the fiber of American life as the development of general anesthesia, antibiotics, and surgical technology transformed the practice of American medicine from home-based care to institution-based treatments. As the sophistication of the U.S. medical community evolved, hospitals began to shift their focus from providing supportive care for poor individuals with chronic or terminal disease to offering innovative interventions and even cures. Much of this explosion actually resulted from the growth of small, proprietary hospitals established by physicians within a given community. More than one-third of hospitals in the 1920s were such institutions.[17]

At the time of the Great Depression, the hospital industry trailed only the steel industry in size and production. In the fifty years between 1880 and 1930, the U.S. population had doubled but the number of hospitals had increased by a whopping 2,500 percent. Hospitals proliferated across the

American landscape without much thought as to necessity or coordination. Having a hospital became an immense source of civic pride for a community, and soon the competition for patients became frenzied, similar to what we currently see throughout America. Hospitals began expanding, which required increasing infusions of capital to support. These institutions of care soon turned to business managers steeped in the traditions of American capitalism for leadership, bringing with them the drive for expansion and profit. At the same time, these community assets began paying attention to "payer mix" and developing marketing strategies to bring those patients with the ability to pay through their doors, so that they could continue to provide care for the community of patients of lesser means.[18]

For the most part, however, hospitals remained true to their mission of caring for the community in which they were established. This remained true even for those hospitals that were physician-established proprietary institutions. That isn't to say that good old-fashioned American marketing wasn't in play, but a generation or two ago, it was unheard of to have a hospital advertise its services on the radio, on television, or in purchased print ads. Reputations were built by word of mouth, by the strength and innovation of the medical staff, and by the occasional newspaper article or television news item trumpeting the acquisition of cutting-edge technology or the availability of new and exciting service lines.

During the 1940s and through the early '60s, hospital growth stabilized. In 1965, President Lyndon Johnson took up the mantle of health care reform that had been woven by his predecessor, John Kennedy. Johnson and his advisers realized that the new American model of health care, employer-based insurance, had within its design a fatal flaw. While employed, health coverage was not an issue, but when workers reached retirement age and left their jobs, most left their health insurance behind as well. For most Americans, it was during retirement that they actually began to experience acute and chronic illnesses and found the mounting medical bills prohibitively burdensome. As a result, in 1965 President Johnson and the Democratic Congress established both the Medicare and Medicaid programs, designed to assist the elderly and the poor across America.

Organized medicine was vehemently opposed to the new plan, labeling it "socialized medicine" and refusing to support the legislation. The Johnson administration was forced to make concessions to the AMA and other organized medical groups in order to secure their backing. First, he made it clear that both programs were to be completely "voluntary" and that no physician would be forced to treat a Medicare or Medicaid patient. Secondly, he reassured physicians that the program would allow reimbursement of their usual and customary fees. Lastly, as a carrot to both the physicians and hospitals,

Medicare would make available funding for the expansion of existing hospitals and the establishment of new ones, as well as for the capital equipment required to serve this population of patients.

Around this same time, America saw its first for-profit hospital "chain" appear when American Medical International purchased two existing hospitals. Within six years of the enactment of Medicare, there were thirty-eight such for-profit chains, which made their living buying up struggling hospitals, consolidating care, reducing staff, and making money. As David Vanderwater, former CEO of Columbia/HCA so aptly stated, for-profit hospitals "were not in the health *care* business. They were in the *sick* care business."[19]

We saw a second wave of hospital growth in the United States, and soon modest-sized communities found that they now had two or three independent hospitals competing for patients. Concomitantly, the for-profit sector surged, and by 1986 constituted almost 15 percent of the market.[20] Of course, such competition required that if Hospital A had a heart surgery program, Hospital B had to have one as well. If Hospital A provided neurosurgical services and a specialized ICU, Hospital B must do so in order to compete. The result was more and more community hospitals whose beds were half empty and whose expensive state-of-the-art equipment was left unused half of the time.

As long as Medicare was providing the funding, and as long as the commercial insurance companies were paying the going rates for reimbursement, the system worked. There was no incentive whatsoever to collaborate and centralize, for example, heart care at one facility and orthopedic care at another. However, in a relatively short period of time, the Medicare program was on the brink of insolvency with costs far greater than even its most vehement critics had predicted. And in the private sector, as "managed care" began to take hold, the resources to sustain such practices began to disappear, and many of these newly established or recently expanded institutions found themselves in financial peril.

The competition for patients to fill those empty beds was fierce, and for the first time community hospitals began public ad campaigns touting the merits of their various service lines. The new type of community hospital, the "for-profit" model, relied heavily on the principles of American capitalism and "market-based" practices. As we saw happen with the insurance industry, the focus of these new national networks of hospitals was, by definition, profit. Local community hospitals, which had long been created by and for the local citizenry, soon had a new master. Instead of being an asset for the "community they served," these for-profit institutions became an asset for the "community who invested." In a flash, National Medical Enterprises, Hospital Corporation of America, Paracelsus, Columbia Health Care, and Tenet became household names across many American communities. The Madison

Avenue marketing of hospitals became accepted practices and required both the for-profit and not-for-profit institutions to get into the game.

For the first time, we began to see the phenomenon of "medical bankruptcies" as families lost everything as a result of astronomical hospital bills when a spouse or child was afflicted with a costly illness and their insurance coverage was insufficient or nonexistent. In the past, hospitals and physicians simply "wrote off" such care, and could afford to do so, since reimbursement from Medicare and the commercial carriers was sufficient to allow the occasional "charity case." However, with reduced reimbursement from all sources and with the pressure on the for-profit hospitals to provide impressive revenue forecasts to Wall Street, the luxury of being "charitable" was just that—a luxury that could no longer be afforded.

Also, for the first time, we began to see, with an alarming frequency, news reports of scandalous practices involving hospitals as we saw in Redding. One month it was National Medical Enterprises, another it was Hospital Corporation of America, then Tenet, and then even the not-for-profits soon became sullied. Indeed, just recently, the *Baltimore Sun* carried a series of articles that questioned the insertion of unnecessary cardiac stents in patients with normal coronary angiograms at St. Joseph Hospital in Towson, Maryland.[21] In these challenging economic times, it becomes increasingly difficult for a hospital administration to question the practices of physicians within their institutions who are responsible for the hospital's continued financial sustainability. It becomes easy, and even necessary, to turn a blind eye to a Dr. Moon or Dr. Realyvasquez. And even the consumer "watchdogs" can often fail to protect the public from such professional and corporate greed. "Health Grades," one of the nation's leading authorities on hospital quality, actually gave Redding Medical Center's Heart Institute its highest award for quality at the time that Moon and Realyvasquez were fixing normal hearts.[22]

It is not surprising that the lion's share of for-profit hospitals are usually established in more upscale communities rather than inner cities. If the mission of an institution is profit, it would make little economic sense to build a hospital where there was a sizable population of poor, uninsured patients. No, it's only best business practice to situate such hospitals where a large proportion of your customers are affluent and well insured, thus guaranteeing that the number of money-losing Medicaid and uninsured patients is kept to a minimum. Indeed, the for-profit entities consistently provide less "charity care" than their not-for-profit counterparts, but they rebut such criticism by pointing out that there are just less charity patients in their designated market areas. They fail to tell us that such a phenomenon was by design.

We frequently hear that the answer to America's high-cost health care system is to encourage "market-based" medicine and allow unfettered competition to efficiently bring down prices while improving quality. Good luck with that, folks. How impressed are you with the market-based principles that guided Wall Street and the banking industry these past few years? How is that working for you? If the principles fail in the financial industry, either because they were wrong to begin with or because of unrepentant greed, investors stand to lose lots and lots of money. But when those principles fail in the health care industry, either because they were wrong to begin with or because of unrepentant greed, people suffer and some die. I have no problem with allowing the market to flourish or fail when it comes to selling cars or building homes or even investing our pensions, but there is no room for such risk in the management of our nation's health; there is simply too much at stake. The portals of access to care in this country are the insurers who provide the funding for that care and the hospitals who provide the infrastructure for it. Thus, both should answer only to their clients, the patients, and not to profit-driven investors. The conflict of interest should be obvious to all.

And this American "experiment" with market-based, profit-driven medicine has for the most part proven to be a colossal failure on many fronts. Several recent studies comparing costs, overhead, quality, and outcomes between for-profit and not-for-profit hospitals have consistently shown that the for-profits perform below the traditional community not-for-profits and public institutions across the United States. An August 1999 *New England Journal of Medicine* paper by Dr. Elaine Silverman et al. compared Medicare spending in the 208 communities where all hospitals were for-profit with the 2,860 communities where all the hospitals were not-for-profit during the years 1989, 1992, and 1995. In each year spending in the for-profit-dominated service areas was significantly higher than in the not-for-profit ones. The authors estimated that in 1995 alone, for-profits cost the Medicare system an additional $5.2 billion.[23]

In 2004, P. J. Devereaux and his associates published a provocative article in the *Canadian Medical Association Journal* comparing costs of care at for-profit and not-for-profit hospitals in the United States. At the time there was a growing movement in Canada to possibly experiment with the expanding American model of investor-owned health care facilities. The researchers painstakingly mined 788 articles from the pool of available medical literature and used the largest and best refereed studies to address the issue of cost between the two models. Devereaux and his colleagues found that charges at the for-profit hospitals in the United States were, on average, 19 percent higher than those at not-for-profit facilities, again dispelling the notion that for-profit hospitals were more cost efficient.[24]

Both of the aforementioned studies were accompanied by an editorial authored by Harvard Medical School Associate Professors Steffie Woolhandler and David Himmelstein.[25] The scathing editorials took the for-profit entities to task on everything from price to quality. They cited their own prior studies, and those of others, which demonstrated for-profit facilities consistently provided lower quality at higher costs. Administrative costs were 34 percent of budget at for-profit hospitals and 24.5 percent at not-for-profit institutions. They went on to point out that despite higher costs, they paid nursing and other clinical care providers 7 percent less than the not-for-profits. In addition, they claimed for-profit rehabilitation facilities cost Medicare more than if that care was delivered in not-for-profit rehab centers. Even the for-profit Medicare HMOs, Medicare Advantage Plus, cost the federal program in excess of $2 billion more than the traditional Medicare program. More recent figures demonstrate that overhead costs are 14 percent higher for the Medicare Advantage Plus plans.[26]

In terms of quality, Woolhandler and Himmelstein reported that for-profit dialysis centers had higher death rates than their counterparts, for-profit skilled nursing facilities received lower care quality scores than not-for-profit ones, and even hospice care for the terminally ill was of lower quality at those institutions that were investor owned and profit driven. They continued with a litany of the fraud and abuse charges levied against the major players in the for-profit health care facility arena, such as the $1.7 billion settlement paid by Columbia/HCA in 2003 for overbilling the federal Medicare program; the National Medical Enterprises psychiatric hospital scandal cited earlier in this chapter; as well as the 2004 admission by HealthSouth that it billed $3.4 billion in fraudulent claims arising from care in its network of rehabilitation facilities. They went on to point out that in each instance, the CEO who presided over the scandal eventually lost his job, but each severance package exceeded $100 million.[27]

Yet, before everyone reads this information and accepts it as dispassionate fact, it is important to point out that both Dr. Woolhandler and Dr. Himmelstein have been vocal critics of market-based medicine for over a decade. More important is the fact that each is a cofounder of "Physicians for a National Health Program," which for years has encouraged the adoption of a Canadian-like, single-payer health care system here in the United States.[28] Therefore, one must realize that although the data that they present may indeed be statistically accurate, their interpretation of that data most likely is influenced by their desire to promote a single-payer model in the United States.

Lest we all blindly (or otherwise) accept that all for-profit entities are bad and all not-for-profit ones are admirable defenders of the greater good, I would suggest you read an interesting article that appeared in 2006 on The Health Care Blog by Maggie Mahar, author of the 2006 book, *Money-Driven Medicine: The Real Reason Healthcare Costs So Much*.[29] Mahar wrote, "Do

Non-Profit Hospitals Deserve Their Tax Breaks?" in response to a *New York Times* piece reporting that the IRS was looking into the tax exempt status of several U.S. not-for-profit hospitals.[30] As she points out, not-for-profit hospitals were granted tax breaks because of the presumption that they provided care to the poor, enhanced their communities through neighborhood outreach programs, and supported teaching and research activities that the for-profit entities avoided.[31]

However, that same status is granted whether the not-for-profit facility is in the urban blighted neighborhoods of South Central Los Angeles or amid the upscale mansions of Beverly Hills. And ironically, the facility in Beverly Hills actually fares much better because the local property taxes are significantly higher, making their tax break much more lucrative. In addition, the demographics of Beverly Hills are remarkably different than South Central L.A., assuring that their patient population is much more affluent and has a much lower percentage of uninsured charity care and Medicaid. I imagine that philanthropic gifts to the two facilities sharply contrast as well.

Mahar correctly tells us that for-profit hospitals are free to do whatever they wish with their capital surpluses, usually directing them to programs or services that enhance profits or returning them to their satisfied investors. Not-for-profit entities do not enjoy such freedoms and by law are required to use their earnings to "promote the purposes for which the nonprofit was created."[32] Essentially they must reinvest their profits to support their mission—care for the poor, education, and research.

As the not-for-profit hospitals engage the for-profit ones in battle for patients, the distinction between the missions of the two have become increasingly blurred. We see nonprofit facilities now offering valet parking, touting their Botox services, and advertising their creature comforts as if they were a Ritz-Carlton hotel rather than the community hospital they once were. It is unclear how such activities really benefit the poor of a community other than increasing revenue by attracting more upscale patients. Indeed, the argument can be made that the nonprofit's surplus can be better spent developing outreach educational programs, immunizing children in lower socioeconomic regions of the community, establishing prenatal screening and monitoring clinics, and providing a whole host of other services that are more in line with their "mission."

With the emphasis on "capturing market share," we also see some community not-for-profit institutions trying to go head-to-head with the larger academic medical centers and developing service lines, such as organ transplants and other complex procedures they have no business performing, simply in hopes of increasing the "institutional prestige." It has been proven time and again that *practice makes perfect*; therefore, those institutions with higher volumes of such procedures consistently outperform those whose number are more meager. For this reason, such care should be regionalized for the sake of the patients, but there remains little or no incentive for hospitals (nonprofit or otherwise) to collaborate. The result is almost uniformly lower quality and higher costs.

And even our esteemed centers of academic excellence are not immune from the frenzied pursuit of the almighty dollar, sometimes exploiting the very patients they purport to serve. The University of California, San Francisco Medical Center (UCSF) is one of the world's leading teaching and research hospitals. Their reputation for innovation and quality is unquestioned. Yet a 2008 article by Elizabeth Fernandez in the *San Francisco Chronicle* revealed that UCSF and other bay areas hospitals were actually providing fund-raising vendors with lists of patients to be "mined."[33] In one such instance, the university provided the names, medical record numbers, and treating departments of 6,300 patients to a fund-raiser.[34] The information was inadvertently posted on the Internet, so that the world now knew that John Smith, MR#1187985, received treatment in the AIDS Clinic at UCSF. They learned that Mary Jones, MR#3345099, received radiation treatments through the Department of Radiation Oncology for her cancer. Such a breach of confidentiality is frightening and, although accidental, reflects the uneasy attitude that patients are sources of revenue, either through their insurance billings, their potential for philanthropy, or as in these cases, both.

As Americans, we rely on our hospitals to serve as "sick houses," as *nosokomeion*, as "havens" where we can turn for quality treatment should we become ill or injured. And our hospitals rely on us to provide the revenue stream necessary for the institution to fulfill its mission. It should go without saying that the hospital's mission should always be providing the best possible care for the community of patients that comes through its doors, rich or poor, insured or not. It seems that, in this market-based system of American medicine, our hospitals sometimes lose sight of that mission.

Profit is *not* the mission . . . compassionate care is.

· 7 ·

America's Physicians

Oops, Sorry, I Mean Health Care "Providers"

 $\mathcal{A}$ merica's doctors started vanishing sometime in the early 1990s. It began rather insidiously, and since the disappearance was subtle, the American public barely noticed. Actually, physicians themselves didn't realize it was happening before it was too late. U.S. doctors were not succumbing to an overwhelming bacterial infection or rapidly metastasizing malignancy. No, America's physicians were victimized by a more sinister malady that went by the rather benign-sounding term "managed care."

As market-based medicine began to evolve, the most essential components in our health care system, namely, the physicians who examine, diagnose, and treat patients, *devolved* into "health care providers." We were no longer doctors or physicians; we became providers and, as such, were awarded our provider numbers by Medicare, Medicaid, and the commercial insurance companies who held the purse strings. We were encouraged to enroll as "preferred" providers in the many insurance plans offered to the public. A preferred provider wasn't preferred because he or she was more skilled, had better outcomes, or was perceived as more caring and compassionate. Preferred provider simply meant you would provide your services at the reduced fee schedule offered by the insurance companies. The insurers really preferred that.

Oh, and by the way, our patients also began to vanish and were quickly replaced by health care "consumers." We became one big, happy family with liberty and justice for all. We became cogs, doctors and patients alike, in the machinery of managed care and market-based medicine. And we did it with nary a whimper. Here's to the free enterprise system.

It may surprise many of you to learn that I believe physicians must shoulder a significant share of the blame for the emergence of managed care in this country. I understand that this opinion is not going to get me elected president of the American Medical Association. I can live with that. But when I look at how and why market-based medicine came to dominate the American health care system, I can't help but hold organized medicine at least partly responsible for failing to recognize and address the multitude of problems that resulted in the development of our current system.

Traditionally, "fee for service" medicine was the model by which medical care was delivered in the United States. A doctor performed a "service" and he (usually he, since the influx of women didn't occur in significant numbers until the 1970s) charged a "fee" for those services. In the early years of American medicine, those services may have been bartered for livestock, grain, labor, or the like. As the United States became more industrialized and the population began migrating from rural regions to larger cities, Americans began relying on health insurance to pay for their physicians' fees. After World War II, the U.S. population expanded, people were living longer because of medical advancements, and an increasing number of Americans found their insurance premiums were being paid for by their employers as part of a benefit package usually negotiated by their trade or labor unions.

But unfortunately, America's prosperity did not encompass everyone, and as the population began to age, a significant number of elderly citizens found that they were actually outliving their resources. Since they were retired, their insurance premiums were no longer covered by their employers. In addition, with the population of the United States increasing, so too were the number of America's poor, without resources to pay for medical care. As I discussed in chapter 3, President Harry Truman recognized the approaching storm in the mid-1940s and began earnest discussions regarding governmental safety nets for these citizens, only to be rebuked by the Republican-dominated Congress and the American Medical Association, who wanted absolutely nothing to do with "socialized" medicine. To these groups, Truman's vision merely represented the Red Menace (i.e., Communism) infiltrating the fabric of American life. Consequently, his plan never got traction.[1]

In the mid-1960s, as part of President Lyndon Johnson's "War on Poverty," Medicare and Medicaid were finally enacted to provide medical coverage for the American elderly and poor. During the programs' early years, physicians did well and received reasonable reimbursement for their services. Medicare even paid for hospital expansions, capital improvements, and new technology. But the price tag for such generous programs soon skyrocketed as more and more physicians and hospitals took advantage of the largesse, and before long, Congress began to complain about the rapidly escalating cost of maintaining Medicare and Medicaid.[2]

At about the same time, the American business community began grousing about the high costs of health insurance for their employees. They saw premiums rise year after year and found that insuring their workers was adding significant costs to their products and cutting into their profits. They complained to Congress, they complained to the AMA, they complained to the unions, they complained to the media, they complained to anyone who would listen and even to those who would not. And what was organized medicine's response to these legitimate concerns? Not much of anything.

Physicians tend to be fiercely independent. We are accustomed to giving orders, not following them. Many of us practiced in an era when all we had to do was ask our hospitals for new equipment and we got it. Our wish was their command as hospitals competed for the patients we controlled. They were heady times and physician practices flourished. But because of our sense of power and control, we were less responsive to requests from hospitals and insurance carriers to participate in cost containment.

It was not uncommon for a community with five orthopedic surgeons to have four or five completely different sets of instruments to perform the exact same procedure even though each set could do the job just as well. If the hospital had purchased those instruments from a single vendor, the cost savings would have been significant. But the individual orthopedists wouldn't hear of it. They demanded their choice of instruments, sold by the company representative they liked the most (often the same company representative, by the way, who paid for their rounds of golf, expensive dinners, or trips to Hawaii to try out those instruments). Hospitals had no option but to accede to their demands.

Routinely, patients were admitted to the hospital the night before even minor surgery and remained in the hospital for days thereafter. The idea that, perhaps, it was just as safe to admit them the morning of surgery and release them that evening didn't get much support. Impossible! Dangerous! Malpractice! We had always done it this way and there was no motivation to change. Only years later, when the insurance carriers forced us to reassess these practices, did it become obvious that patients could survive with shorter hospital stays, had less risk of hospital-acquired infections, recovered more quickly because of earlier mobilization, and actually felt more comfortable recuperating in their own homes. Oh yeah . . . it also saved a boatload of money.

When I rotated through the internal medicine service as a student at the University of California, Irvine, one of my supervising residents made each student write down every test he or she ordered on a patient that week and then find out how much those tests actually cost. It was astounding to see how quickly simple blood tests and X-rays could add up. That experience has stayed with me my entire professional life and forces me to ask, "Is that test really necessary? Is the result of that test going to change what I will recommend for this patient?" If the answer is no, I don't order it. And I tell the patient I am not going to order it, and why.

Many physicians readily admit they routinely order tests they don't feel are warranted, for fear of being sued, so-called defensive medicine. This is certainly understandable, especially if you have been through a malpractice trial, but there is little evidence to suggest this immunizes the physician from a lawsuit. More problematic are physicians who order a $1,500 MRI at the drop of a hat because it's faster than taking the time to actually listen to and *examine* the patient, using all those years of education to figure out what's wrong. Additionally, doctors are pressured by their patients for the latest high-tech diagnostic study even if their complaints are minimal. Rather than expend the effort to explain why the test isn't needed, doctors decide it's easier to acquiesce. After all, it's the insurance company's money.

Organized medicine abdicated its leadership role in attempting to rein in the spiraling costs of health care. Because we failed to act, big business, who was footing the bill for their employees, and the insurance carriers (including Medicare and Medicaid), who were distributing big business's premiums, took control. Physicians responded by complaining rather than collaborating, and the insurers responded by infecting us with managed care. And doctors began to disappear, replaced by an entire generation of "providers." But physicians are by nature exceedingly bright and resourceful, so many of us found other jobs in the medical arena.

Some of us became "entrepreneurs." Instead of making our living taking care of patients, we made it by purchasing the infrastructure necessary for other providers to take care of our patients. We got together, pooled our resources, and began building MRI centers, freestanding outpatient surgery centers, renal dialysis facilities, and diagnostic laboratories. Our incomes began to recover as MRI machines became as common as Starbucks and we offered the public "whole body" scans without a physician referral so that we could catch those darn cancer cells early. And guess what? Studies began to show that utilization of services at facilities owned by physicians was significantly greater than hospital-based ones.[3] Well, isn't that a surprise? I order tests more often if I actually own the machine and get income from the test itself. Who would've thought?

Oh, sorry, I forgot to tell you one thing. My MRI scanner, my surgery center, my dialysis unit, and my chemotherapy infusion center are not for everyone; if you are uninsured or on Medicaid, you should go to the local community hospital instead. After all, I'm an entrepreneur and you folks will do nothing but cut into my profit.

When discussing physician-owned facilities, invariably the entrepreneurs will tell you the establishment of this freestanding center is truly a community benefit since it forces community hospitals to *compete* for patients by increasing productivity, efficiency, and consumer satisfaction. What a crock.

What it does do is increase the income of the entrepreneur at the expense of the community hospital. The practice of referring the healthiest and best-insured patients to your own facility while sending the sickest and the poorest to the community hospital is a phenomenon known as "cherry-picking" and it is widely practiced in these investor-owned entities. Additionally, in many communities where these facilities have emerged, the physician specialists have opted out of the on-call responsibilities in the community hospital emergency rooms, leaving the ERs and trauma centers without critical specialty coverage.[4]

How community hospitals are supposed to compete fairly under these circumstances and how this benefits the community at large are unclear, but I guess that's not the entrepreneur's problem. So it becomes ours, as hospitals struggle to survive when they are forced by federal and state law to accept any patient, regardless of their ability to pay, while their physician-owned competition is not.

Some physicians have returned to working the "assembly line." Ah, yes . . . yearning for the days of industrialized America. Maybe America's physicians should be represented by the United Auto Workers (UAW) or the Teamsters. One of the most common complaints I hear from patients is that their physicians have no time for them. We line 'em up and run 'em through. We make patients wait, sometimes for hours, and then if they are lucky enough to see a "physician provider" rather than a "physician's assistant provider" or a "nurse practitioner provider," we talk to them while standing with one hand on the doorknob ready to race to the next patient room as soon as a lull in the conversation gives us the opportunity. Get to your complaint quickly, madam, and don't complicate it with details. Tell me what hurts so I can order your scan and refer you to someone who might actually listen to you. Thanks for coming in. And by the way, we take Visa and MasterCard.

Part of a primary care doctor's responsibility is to evaluate their patients' myriad of complaints and determine if they really do need further testing and specialist referral. But today's factory working physician providers understand that time is money and volume is king. So increasingly they sit at their desks with pad in hand and simply refer the patient to a specialist who deals with the organ of complaint. It is puzzling to think one needs all that schooling to be able to figure out which organ gets sent to which specialist.

But specialists have joined the assembly line as well. The "entrepreneurial" assembly line workers among us have figured out that patient volume, and thus income, can be increased by having the physician assistant (P.A.) do the hand shaking, scheduling, and follow-up visits so that we only have to do the procedure and billing, thus not wasting our time with the lost art of compassion, caring, and communication.

Assembly line medicine is destroying the bond that a doctor and patient develop when thoughtful and courteous counseling occurs. Actual dialogue occurs when the physician thoroughly explains the nature of the problem in language the patient understands, subsequently crafting treatment options that take into account the wishes of the patient. Part of our job is to allay their fears and to *earn* their trust. It is hard to do either on the assembly line. But for some of us, that is the sad consequence of being infected with the managed care virus.

A growing number of physicians became "proceduralists," as we recognized that there was money to be made by *doing* things rather than by thinking about things. Surgeons had long realized that, but more recently, the primary care providers have seen the light. It is now quite commonplace for general practitioners, family physicians, and internists to perform in-office cortisone injections for your every ache and pain or ultrasound and traction for your throbbing back. They are even undertaking colonoscopies and other more invasive procedures usually performed by specialists with several years of additional training and experience. More and more, we see primary care offices becoming cosmetic boutiques, offering Botox injections, skin rejuvenation therapy, and the like. But try and get a patient in to see them for uncontrolled high blood pressure, diabetes, or another life-threatening condition and you're out of luck. There aren't many billable procedures for hypertension.

And speaking of Botox, a recent paper published in the prestigious *Journal of the American Academy of Dermatology* revealed a secret survey of dermatologists' offices across the country.[5] The authors posed as patients and called in asking for an appointment to have a suspicious mole evaluated to rule out melanoma. They then called the same offices and asked to schedule an appointment for a Botox injection. What the authors found was disturbing. When the patient had a possible life-threatening malignant melanoma, the average wait for an appointment was twenty-six days. If the patient wanted a Botox injection, it was eight days. As one Harvard dermatologist put it, "the study shows that the Botox needs of the United States are being met."[6] What has happened to our priorities when a cosmetic patient has better access to our system than one with potential cancer?

Ear, nose, and throat (ENT) specialists, ophthalmologists, and even oral surgeons are now doing face-lifts, chin implants, and other operations traditionally performed by plastic surgeons. Cross-specialty procedures are becoming commonplace as providers fight for shrinking pieces of the reimbursement pie. That may actually increase access but not necessarily quality. Within given specialties, the numbers of procedures are expanding, sometimes even in the absence of good scientific data proving efficacy. The number of spinal fusion surgeries in the United States, for example, has exploded to almost 300,000 per year from a little over 20,000 ten years ago.[7]

Much of the increase in spinal fusion surgery has been fueled by the medical device industry itself. Their representatives wine us and dine us. We are flown to exclusive conferences where we are treated like royalty. Believe me, it's great. The surgeons are ensconced in the best hotels and feted with lavish meals, a round or two of golf, and a night on the town. We get presented the "unbiased data" from the companies that make the instrumentation and then get to perfect our technique in their modern cadaver laboratories. The vast majority of these procedures occur without major complications but that's not really the point. The vast majority of these procedures are also being done without good evidence that they work better than less expensive and less invasive treatment options not sponsored by the medical device industry.

Entrepreneurial spine surgeons have actually now teamed up with the device manufactures and become "distributors" of those very same implants they recommend inserting in their patients. The obvious conflict of interest speaks volumes in opposition to these arrangements and the physician-owned distributorships (PODs) that are popping up across the medical landscape. A June 2011 article on WallStreetJournal.com reported that the Senate Finance Committee has directed the Inspector General of the Department of Health and Human Services to look into such entities. Usually the individual spine surgeon dictates to the hospital which company's devices he or she will choose to use on patients. If that same spine surgeon is actually the "distributor," then in addition to their surgical fees for the operation, they also receive the "commission" from the implant company for the sale of the hardware. Not surprisingly, many now feel this is a major driver of the veritable explosion of spinal fusion surgery over the past several years and may explain why many patients in a community are receiving multiple surgeries and why the costs of spinal fusion in the Medicare population have gone from $343 million in 1997 to $2.24 billion in 2008.[8]

Only recently has evidence emerged that the treatment of coronary artery disease with medications can be just as effective as invasive angioplasty or bypass surgery with much less risk and cost.[9] Bad news for the proceduralists. For years, patients with chest pain that resulted from narrowed coronary arteries were taken to surgery or had a balloon inserted into the affected artery and expanded to dilate it. That was the standard of care because *we* knew it worked; our angioplasty catheter manufacturer told us so. It wasn't until someone actually did a scientifically unbiased comparison of treatment options that the efficacy of medical therapy was revealed. Being convinced that something works is not the same as proving something works. So now, in order to make up for the lost revenue from coronary angioplasty, cardiology proceduralists are competing with interventional radiologists for the opportunity to perform procedures on the other arteries in the body. And the turf wars begin.

Some of us have become Madison Avenue marketing executives. A generation ago it was considered unethical and downright unseemly for a physician to advertise. Physician's reputations and their practices were built by word of mouth. If you were an exceptional diagnostician or skilled surgeon, the word got out and colleagues referred their patients to you. But once again, times have changed.

Currently, it's hard to pick up a newspaper or magazine and not find slick advertisements for an entire gamut of medical specialties. It amazes me to think that patients would choose to have their breasts augmented, carpal tunnel released, or hip replaced based on a layout in one of the in-flight magazines they browsed while traveling from Cleveland to Kansas City. Excuse me, miss, may I have some more peanuts and the phone number of that nationally renowned orthopedic surgeon whose ad is on page forty-seven?

A month doesn't go by for me without receipt of a letter saying that I have been named one of "America's Best Surgeons," or congratulating me on being recognized as one of "The U.S. Top Doctors." Along with the letter is usually an order form offering plaques, statues, and other trinkets trumpeting my distinguished honor, which can be prominently displayed in my office and the local hospital . . . at a significant cost of course. And if I really have money to burn, I could appear in the magazine ad as a centerfold model of "America's Top Best Greatest Number One Surgeon in the Whole Wide World," found in the seat pocket of my next flight.

I actually called one of these companies after being so honored and asked how they reached the conclusion that I was one of the living legends of American medicine. I asked if they had looked at my surgical results; they hadn't. I asked if they had interviewed my patients; they hadn't. I assumed they had interviewed my medical colleagues; they hadn't. I received this prestigious honor based on the number of years I had been in practice and the number of professional organizations of which I was a member. My ego was shattered. But I can send you a copy of the plaque depicting me in my surgical scrubs and looking much like my Little League All-Star picture when I was eleven years old. Just send me your name, address, and $25.99 for shipping and handling.

It used to be the ambulance-chasing lawyers who dominated local television programming with their unprofessional solicitations. Now they are forced to compete for airtime with the "Madison Avenue Medics" who boast of their exceptional skills, provided at a significant discount if you act now. Cut out the coupon in your local newspaper and you are entitled to a free vasectomy with your next procedure. Such practices, although widespread, involve very few physicians but still reflect poorly on the entire profession. I don't know about you, but I still would rather choose my surgeon based on the recommendation of my family doctor or the nurse who lives down the street.

But some of us defected to the other side. We realized the battle was lost and succumbed to the offers to become part of this vast network of the managed care complex. We stopped complaining about the heartless system that looked over doctors' shoulders and insinuated itself between physicians and their patients and decided we would be better off being paid to do the looking and the insinuating. We became medical directors and physician reviewers, accepting bonuses for the number of surgeries we refused to approve and promotions on the basis of the money we saved by denying care. We *then* became the ones that doctors complained about, but it didn't really matter, since we were no longer treating patients and those doctors were no longer our colleagues. The money we could no longer make providing patient care was returned in spades when we concentrated on rejecting it.

Finally, and sadly, many of us have become professional whiners and we have perfected the art. As physicians grow increasingly frustrated by the realities thrust upon us by the managed care virus, we also feel impotent in our battle to defend ourselves against it. We have come to the realization that the insurance carriers are the bosses and the days of physician control are long gone. So for many of us, the response is to whine . . . to whine in the doctor's lounge, to whine in the operating room, to whine at our national conferences, to whine to our families, to whine to our friends, and even to whine to our patients.

The problem is that, although we may be good at whining, it does very little to address the problems we face in the current health care arena. Once again, we are abdicating our role in addressing the health care crisis as we did a generation ago. I cannot imagine that the outcome will be any different. The time is now for the emergence of a new generation of physician leaders who will slap us across the face like Vito Corleone did to Johnny Fontane in *The Godfather Part I* and tell us to quit crying and act like a man (or a woman). We need to aggressively engage in battle with this managed care virus and unite with our hospitals and our patients to wrest back control of health care. It is imperative that organized medicine identify strong and capable physician leaders to champion the cause.

And by the way, whiners need not apply.

· *8* ·

Physician Reimbursement

You Can't Always Get What You Want, but if You Try Sometimes You Might Find You Don't Even Get What You Need

I'm a baseball addict. I readily and shamelessly admit it. As a matter of fact, I am such a fanatic of the game that I often confess that my priorities in life are the Los Angeles Dodgers, my family, and my job . . . in that order. My wife oftentimes fails to see the humor in that admission, but then again, wives don't always appreciate their husbands' clever wit.

Now any true fan of the game will have to concede that Alex Rodriguez of the New York Yankees is currently the premier player in the game and may actually turn out to be the best who ever played. He hits for power but still has a lifetime average over .300, steals bases with his remarkable speed, and is an exceptional infielder to boot. A-Rod really has all the tools. He grew up in Miami and was an outstanding football and baseball player in high school. Rodriguez received numerous offers of college scholarships to play both sports but decided to forgo school when he was drafted in the first round by the Seattle Mariners in 1993. At the ripe old age of eighteen, Alex Rodriguez played in his first major league game and his career was well on its way.[1]

He became an instant superstar in Seattle and caught the attention of the entire nation in the process. In 2000, A-Rod became a free agent, meaning he was no longer bound by contract to the team that drafted him, allowing him to market his exceptional talents to the highest bidder. Interest in the future hall of famer was rabid, and when the dust finally settled, Alex Rodriguez signed the largest contract in the history of professional sports with the Texas Rangers—an unheard-of $252 million (that's right, over a quarter of a *billion* dollars) ten-year deal. Across the nation, jaws dropped and Rangers owner Tom Hicks was ridiculed in the media and demonized by his fellow owners. With one swift stroke of the pen, the salary bar was elevated, although "launched" might be a more appropriate word.[2]

Many of you may be wondering why a book on health care would devote print space to a discussion of Alex Rodriguez. That's a legitimate question. First, as I told you earlier, I love baseball and it is never far from my thoughts. But more importantly, I include this information as a way of initiating a discussion of just how we Americans prioritize the many aspects of our lives. So let me begin that discussion by sharing with you some information regarding America's doctors rather than America's baseball players.

Let me introduce you to Dr. John Doe. Dr. Doe is an internist practicing somewhere in Middle America. A specialist in internal medicine starts by spending four years in college and must finish close to the top of his or her class in order to secure one of the highly coveted slots in an American medical school. Dr. Doe then spends another four years in medical school experiencing some of the most demanding and competitive challenges in our educational system. But wait, he's not done yet. Dr. Doe then must complete four years of an internal medicine residency working at least one hundred plus hours per week while trying to master the nuances of being a competent physician. Finally, mercifully, at the ripe old age of thirty (rather than eighteen like A-Rod), Dr. Doe embarks upon his career with great intentions and a six-figure debt from college and medical schools loans.

An internist is one of the many "primary care" doctors who treat a wide array of diseases and provide preventative care for their patients. It is truly a noble calling. And they are well compensated for their efforts. A 2001 report that collected and compared data from ten different sources, including the American Medical Association, found that the average internist in the United States made $127,366 per year.[3] Not bad, really. But for what the Texas Rangers were paying Alex Rodriguez to play baseball in 2001, namely $25.2 million they could have supported *199* internists! *One hundred ninety-nine!* One hundred ninety-nine men and women who spent a minimum of twelve years in school, graduating with significant loan debt, and who on average work seventy to eighty hours a week saving people's lives and restoring health. The magnitude of that number boggles my mind and I hope yours, as well.

Believe me, this is in no way an indictment of Alex Rodriguez (although subsequent disclosures that he used performance-enhancing drugs have sullied his reputation), of the Texas Rangers, of baseball (never), or of professional sports in general. More power to them. Last time I looked, this is still America, home of the free enterprise system. Professional athletes, as well as other "entertainers," should be entitled to what the market will bear. In the spirit of full disclosure, I must confess that my own son-in-law was also a major league pitcher (and yes, A-Rod did take him yard once, but he still beat the Yankees that night), and I am pleased he has been able to make a comfortable living and support my daughter and granddaughters playing the game he loves.

Instead, this is an indictment of American society, myself included, who think nothing of paying $100 or more to see the Lakers play the Knicks, the Colts play the Cowboys, or the Yankees play the Red Sox. Throw in a Dodger dog and a couple of Bud Lights and now we're talking real coin. But heaven forbid we be asked to fork over a $15 co-payment for spending twenty or thirty minutes with our internist who is struggling to adjust our blood pressure and diabetes medicines. After all, your insurance company has already given him $31 for the visit. Shouldn't that be sufficient? At $127,366 per year, the internist still makes more than 95 percent of the U.S. population. So why are physicians griping?

We're griping because we don't feel appreciated. It's unfortunate, but in society today, we measure value or worth in dollars and cents, and increasingly, my colleagues are finding themselves working longer hours, seeing a greater number of patients, and performing many more procedures only to see their incomes decline. A national survey by the Center for Studying Health System Change found that between 1995 and 2003, physicians' net income, adjusted for inflation, actually declined 7 percent. This resulted from the fact that Medicare payments for physicians were 8 percent lower than inflation during the same time frame. Additionally, commercial insurers also reduced their physician fees from an average of 1.43 times the Medicare rate to 1.23 in 2003.[4]

Whenever someone tells you, "It isn't about the money," you can bet it usually is, but money is only part of the puzzle. Traditionally, doctors have been some of the most financially successful members of a community, not filthy rich, but very comfortable and able to afford the neighborhood's nicer homes, to finance their children's education, and to put sufficient funds aside for their retirement. This was society's reward for protracted schooling, long hours (day and night) away from family, and the intense and frequently lifesaving nature of their work. But as every American knows, times have changed. Housing costs have soared and college tuition has skyrocketed, but physician incomes have not kept pace. More and more of my colleagues are commenting on how their incomes are now below those of their own accountants, lawyers, realtors, and stockbrokers. Indeed, in the same time span that doctors have seen their incomes fall by 7 percent or more, all other private sector professionals have found theirs increase.[5]

The diminished reimbursement that accompanies managed care medicine, when coupled with the escalating costs of office overhead and malpractice insurance premiums, has had a profound effect on doctors' net incomes.

There was little physicians could do in response to this crisis. Reimbursement rates are fixed by Medicare, Medicaid, and the commercial insurers. For physicians in practice there are only two choices—take it or leave it—and if they choose to leave it, there is a long line of other practitioners willing to take it. As far as overhead costs are concerned, you can only cut staffing so much. The only viable option for most of us is to increase the volume of patients and number of procedures, which then, of course, requires more staffing and even higher overhead. As I mentioned in chapter 1, this leaves little time for face to face interaction between physicians and their patients and further erodes the traditional doctor-patient relationship.

I read with interest a fascinating article in the *Wall Street Journal* entitled "Why $70 Million Wasn't Enough."[6] The article discusses the departure of financial superstar Mark McGoldrick, affectionately known as Goldfinger, from the venerable Goldman Sachs investment firm. McGoldrick was the genius behind the company's hugely successful mergers and acquisitions division. Now understand, Mr. McGoldrick didn't start his own business, he didn't create a revolutionary product that entertained or benefited the public, he didn't utilize his extraordinary talents to find a cure for cancer or even author the great American novel. Nope. Mr. McGoldrick did none of these things. What he did do was buy companies that other individuals created through their own hard work and sell them to other individuals or companies who sought to acquire or merge. He was the ultimate middle man. And by all accounts, he was remarkably successful at what he did. And remarkably well compensated at $70 million per year (about $200,000 per day give or take a few bucks). At the grand old age of forty-eight, Mark McGoldrick was actually earning significantly more than his boss, Goldman Sachs's CEO Lloyd Blankfein, who only pulled down a mere $53 million.[7]

But McGoldrick was reportedly unhappy. He was doing an incredible job for his company and generating enormous profits, and how did Goldman Sachs show their appreciation? They did it by paying him a "paltry" $70 million (although he did also get a key to the executive washroom and preferred seating in the company cafeteria). If you think *he* was feeling underappreciated, how do you think Dr. John Doe felt when he read the article and learned that McGoldrick made more money in one day than Dr. Doe did in a year? What's worse, the article did not even hint at the excess of such figures, but instead talked about how hard McGoldrick worked, sometimes twenty-one hours a day to the detriment of his own health. I am sure that evoked great sympathy in Dr. Doe.

One needs only read the daily newspaper to see the excesses of American business. Think of Kenneth Lay and the Enron scandal. Think of Dennis Kozlowski, the former CEO of Tyco. And don't forget the Rigas brothers,

John and Tim, whose corruption ran Adelphia into bankruptcy. And these are just the guys in the orange jumpsuits. The business section of any newspaper is replete with astounding figures on executive compensation, and even compensation that is lavished on CEOs whose companies perform poorly and whose stockholders suffer as a result. Screw up . . . you're fired. But thanks a lot for playing and here are some nice parting gifts to the tune of tens to hundreds of millions of dollars. It's insane. And Dr. Doe and his associates are paying attention.

According to the New York State Comptroller's Office, the average Wall Street bonus in 2006 was $137,580.[8] That's the average and that's just the bonus, not the salary. And by the way, this figure represented a 15.2 percent increase from the $119,390 average bonus for the same group in 2005. According to figures published in *USA Today*, the average salary of the top twenty fund managers in 2006 was $657,000,000![9] The same article reported that the average salary for a CEO of a major U.S. corporation was $10.2 million. And please don't forget that for some of these CEOs, this figure represented compensation despite their companies' poor performances, dwindling profits, and reduced returns for their stockholders. You may not have read this stuff, but I assure you, Dr. Doe and his associates have and they are paying attention.

I don't expect you to feel bad for American doctors. Obviously, all of the issues that confront physicians, such as housing costs and college tuition, significantly affect every American—teachers, plumbers, and auto workers alike. And it is hard to evoke sympathy for a group that earns, on average, among the top incomes in the nation. But what I am trying to do is have you, the American public, at least understand our frustration when we see how others in society are rewarded for work that is much less essential. American society bestows enormous wealth on our entrepreneurial business tycoons, gifted athletes, and talented actors, even when their character is questionable. Physicians are taken for granted by politicians, insurance companies, and even our patients. Several years ago, an economist who was an invited speaker at one of our conferences reported a majority of patients would switch physicians if their co-payments were reduced by $10 or more. How about that for loyalty?

And it is physicians who bear the brunt of diminished reimbursement. Income levels for all other allied health professionals have increased over the years. Your physical therapist, your X-ray technician, your speech pathologist, your lab technician, your dietician, your scrub tech, your nurse practitioner, your physician's assistant, and even your hospital administrator all make more money now than they did before managed care. The gap between doctors and support staff is shrinking and shrinking fast, and doctors have to pay the bills for the practice, including hefty insurance premiums.

I was at a conference in San Francisco in May of 2007. At the conference, a prominent local hospital official shared with us some interesting statistics. The average primary care physician in San Francisco County made a little over $130,000 per year. The average nonsurgical specialist made a little over $200,000 per year. And a registered nurse, working in a critical care setting, made between $90,000 and $120,000 per year.[10] In March of 2008, Robert Merwin, the CEO of Mills-Peninsula Health Services, took out a full-page newspaper ad proclaiming that the average wage for a nurse at their hospital was up to $116,000. This is in addition to a fully funded retirement plan, as well as a free health care benefit package. The new contract on the table with the nurses' union would, over the next four years, raise the average salary to $140,000.[11] I am pleased to see nurses financially rewarded at a level commensurate with their training and job complexity. But I am appalled at the income levels for physicians relative to other Bay Area professionals.

What many Americans fail to recognize is that the bill they receive from their doctors (or hospitals) has very little relationship to what they are actually getting paid. I'll offer an example from my own neurosurgery practice. One of the most important operations I perform, in terms of lifesaving surgery, is the removal of acute subdural hematomas. A subdural hematoma is essentially a large blood clot that results from trauma and compresses the underlying brain. If not removed immediately, the patient will oftentimes die or be left significantly disabled. By removing the clot emergently, the compression is relieved and recovery is more likely.

But removal of the blood clot is just part of the care involved in recovery. Invariably these patients are very ill for extended periods of time and require careful monitoring in an intensive care unit, sometimes for weeks on end. After their release from the ICU they are followed for three months or more in a rehab facility or as an outpatient in the office. A surgeon's fee is "global," which means that it includes not just the operation, but the ICU care and three-month follow-up as well.

My standard fee for such an operation is $3,808. However, I never come remotely close to receiving that amount. Each commercial insurer negotiates a reduced fee for these services, and if I don't accept those reductions, I'm out of business. The vast majority of trauma patients we see through the emergency room are either uninsured (I can charge them full price, but good luck collecting anything) or on Medicaid. In California, where I practice, Medicaid pays me $1,180 for that service. When you calculate the overhead (cost of malpractice insurance and office expenses to see the patients), I net $755 for a three-hour, middle-of-the-night lifesaving surgery, three to six weeks of ICU care, and three months of follow-up. Now think about what you paid your mechanic, your plumber, or your house painter for their services recently . . .

Let me relate to you a true story that more clearly reflects the disregard that many physicians are experiencing. Sometime in the late '90s, after the collapse of Hillary Clinton's health care reform effort, our hospital invited a prominent member of her task force (who shall remain nameless) to speak in front of our hospital board and the entire medical staff. We were extremely fortunate to attract someone of her stature to our community and the house was packed. She began her talk with a discussion of her beloved Chicago Cubs (now I was really getting interested). At the time of her presentation, major league baseball was just beginning to recover from a devastating players' strike that resulted in cancellation of the World Series. One of the leading keys to that recovery was the battle raging between St. Louis Cardinals slugger Mark McGuire and the Chicago Cubs' own Sammy Sosa to surpass Roger Maris's single-season record of sixty-one home runs. The intensity of the race captivated the American baseball fan as much as the personalities of the two players themselves. Unfortunately, just like Alex Rodriguez, both McGuire and Sosa were later found to be users of performance-enhancing drugs.

Our speaker spent the first five minutes of her talk in unbridled enthusiasm as she described the excitement generated by this race for baseball immortality, and it became clear that Sammy Sosa was her guy. It was Sammy Sosa this and Sammy Sosa that. I was waiting for Pope John Paul II to appear on stage and canonize the Cubs' star right on the spot. Oh, and by the way, the one thing she failed to mention was that Sammy Sosa's salary that year was $8,325,000.[12]

After this warm and entertaining introduction, the speaker went on to tell us what was wrong with America's health care system. Of course, at the top of the list were the avaricious insurance companies, putting shareholder profits over patient care (standing ovation). In second place were the pharmaceutical companies and their felonious practice of price gouging for their lifesaving medicines (standing ovation). Next were the uncaring and profit-driven hospitals that charged patients $12 for a single Tylenol tablet (standing ovation from the medical staff while the hospital board chose to discreetly remain seated). And last, but certainly not least, were the overpaid, arrogant doctors (the only applause coming from our head nurse in the neurosurgery operating room).

As an example of the latter, she proceeded to relate to us a conversation she had several months earlier with an orthopedic surgeon who had attended one of her lectures. He came up to her after the presentation and explained how, since the advent of managed care, his workload had dramatically increased, his paperwork had became overwhelming, and yet his income had dropped from $350,000 to $190,000 (as best I can recollect). Our speaker, health care policy expert, Sammy Sosa fan club president, turned to us and essentially said, "Can you believe this guy? He's complaining about only making $190,000 a year. Well, boo hoo, pass me the handkerchief."

Sammy Sosa, with no college education, working six months a year, playing a *game*, was making $8,325,000 per year and was admired by this woman more than you can imagine. This orthopedic surgeon, who spent four years in college, four years in medical school, and five years in residency, who works ninety or more hours a week, who gets up in the middle of the night to take care of any patient that presents to his hospital regardless of their ability to pay, who exposes himself to hepatitis C, AIDS, and a variety of other infectious agents in the course of his caring for patients, is somehow greedy and arrogant. Maybe the next time our speaker comes into an emergency room with a broken hip, that greedy and arrogant orthopedic surgeon might be the one on-call and his response might be, "Well boo hoo, pass her a handkerchief."

Or maybe she could call Sammy Sosa.

· 9 ·

Pretty in Pink

The Influence of Women on America's Medical "Man"power

$\mathscr{I}$ have to confess at the outset that the title of this chapter is somewhat disingenuous. The real subject of the pages that follow is the physician shortage that plagues many communities across America. But I figure that most people are like me and that before they buy a book, they peruse the table of contents to see if the chapter titles pique their curiosity. I cleverly determined that the above title would surely compel both feminists and misogynists alike to want to take a closer look.

I really do think that any discussion of medical manpower should begin by examining the remarkable influence women have had on the recent evolution of medicine in the United States. Indeed, currently almost one half of students entering medical school are women, and in some specialties they have already become the majority, an astonishing accomplishment considering that only a generation or so ago, men dominated the profession.[1]

I should begin by telling you about my academic experiences with intelligent and accomplished women. The short answer is there aren't many experiences to relay. The long answer starts during my teenage years. I attended a Catholic high school in southern California that was technically coed, but classes were segregated into boys' and girls' sections. It wasn't until my senior year that I first had classes with girls—the high-end math and science curricula that had such few students of either sex that they were combined. I found the women to be just as bright as my male classmates, but they did seem a bit reserved and were less inclined to speak in class. Years later, it was interesting to talk with a female classmate at our reunion and learn that she had gone to one of our science teachers (a nun) and voiced her desire to go to medical school and become a doctor. She was encouraged to consider a career in nursing instead.

Following high school, I had the good fortune to major in premed at the University of Notre Dame, a truly outstanding academic institution that is actually better known to many for its storied football program. I had the distinction of being in the last all-male Notre Dame freshman class, so consequently, for most of my college years as well, I had little interaction with smart women in a classroom setting. Although many alumni and students were dismayed at the decision to go coed, I have no doubt that it made Notre Dame a better university and made her male students better men.

By allowing women to attend Notre Dame, the university doubled the pool of outstanding applicants and raised the bar for admission. Notre Dame was always one of the country's elite academic schools, requiring high GPAs and exceptional SAT scores to secure admission. But with the inclusion of women, the competition was even keener and the quality of the student body soared. I'm not so certain those of us in the "pre"-coeducational era could currently gain admission. Fears that the admission of women would result in a loss of traditions and change the intangibles that made Notre Dame special to so many of its students were never realized.

But the university did indeed change, and for the better. Having women on campus had a profound effect upon the behavior of the male students. How we spoke, how we ate, how we dressed, how we acted, and how we perceived women all began to undergo a metamorphosis. In an all-male environment, it was only natural to view women as objects of desire and to assume a sense of academic superiority since there was little opportunity to experience meaningful intellectual interaction with them. However, sitting next to a woman in the classroom or having one as a lab partner changed all of that. But unfortunately, I once again missed the boat and spent the vast majority of my college experience in class with the guys.

Medical school was better but still far from balanced. When I attended the University of California, Irvine's School of Medicine in the mid-'70s, it was one of the more progressive campuses, and we had a significant number of women and traditional minorities in our class of approximately seventy students. Still, the vast majority were white and male. However, it was here that I really appreciated the women as equals. We studied together, we dissected our cadavers in anatomy class together, we took the same tests, we worked the same hours. We examined the same patients, we assisted at the same surgeries, we were equally exulted and abased during rounds, we got dead tired, and we survived . . . as equals.

Nevertheless, in the 1960s and 1970s, women had to fight not only the rigors of medical school but the subtle and oftentimes not so subtle discrimination inherent in the male-dominated profession. I was surprised to find that some female surgical residents acted tougher, told cruder off-colored jokes, boasted of working longer hours, and berated their underlings more mercilessly than many of their male counterparts. In order to succeed, they had to show that they were not only as good as the men but actually better, smarter, tougher, and more determined.

But as more and more women entered the profession, and as a greater number of these women began to assume leadership positions in medical schools and specialty associations, the entire culture of medicine began to change. When I was in residency, we worked 100 to 120 hours per week, and we rarely saw our families, but we were proud of the fact that we were bent but not broken. At least *we* didn't consider ourselves broken; I suspect our wives and children may have had a different perspective. The pervading philosophy was that a medical career was demanding, unforgiving, and unrelenting and one had to become tempered in the furnace of residency to survive on the outside. Indeed, there is much truth in that philosophy. When I get called in at 2 a.m. to perform an emergency operation, fatigue must be eliminated from the equation and my skill and judgment must not be diminished because of the hour. The grueling years of residency training prepared me for just these types of challenges and have served me and my patients well over my twenty-seven years in practice.

Typically, when young doctors completed their residencies, they moved to a community where they could "hang up their shingle" and establish a successful practice. But it took hard work and long hours to launch a new practice. New doctors had to see any patient sent to them, often the less desirable or less well insured, in order to break into the established referral patterns of the primary care doctors in town. You took extra ER call in hopes of building a patient base to get your name recognized throughout the community. New physicians gave talks to various civic groups on a variety of disease entities or new treatment options they were bringing to town.

All of this took time away from family—missed baseball games and school plays, dinners without Dad, lost opportunities that could never be recovered and a shifting of the burdens on to spouses. These were the same spouses who had endured the rigors of residency in hopes of a better life at the end. The same spouses who now felt like widows, just as lonely as they had been before. And our children always had to understand why Dad couldn't make the soccer game or coach the team: "He's a doctor and his patients need him!"—instilling a guilt for their resentment of his absence. It should be of little surprise that divorce, depression, alcoholism, drug abuse, and infidelity are not uncommon issues in a medical marriage.

As women gained a considerable foothold in the medical profession, they began to do something their male counterparts never did. They dictated how they would play the game and they changed the rules that had dominated medicine for so many generations. Once they were represented in sufficient numbers that they no longer had to be concerned with repercussions from their all-male superiors, women started questioning the very tenets that traditionally defined both medical training and medical practice.

I saw the changes subtly, while still a neurosurgery resident at the University of Iowa. In my sixth year of training, the Department of Pediatrics, which had a large contingent of female residents and staff, spearheaded a movement that encouraged program directors to grant "paternity" leave to male residents upon the birth of their children. Studies showed that early bonding was critical in child-parent relationships, and the long hours of work often precluded such interaction. Many departments embraced the movement (especially those with a significant number of women), but others complied only grudgingly. One surgical program director informed his male residents that all were entitled to paternity leave if their wives had a baby, but added that they might just as well apply for a residency in dermatology or pediatrics if they availed themselves of the new policy. But the fact of the matter remained—the floodgate was inched open and no matter how much resistance followed, it would never again be closed.

Women medical students and residents confessed that they were not as skilled after being up twenty-four or thirty-six hours straight. They openly admitted that the severe fatigue affected their judgment and the care they were providing. Male residents, myself included, would rather have died (better us than our patients) than surrender such an admission. As a surgical resident the old mantra was that the only problem with being on call every other night was that you missed half of the good cases. We were tough, we were macho, and we knew that any breach in that rugged exterior would be viewed by our peers, as well as our superiors, as a sign of weakness. With the competition for a residency slot in specialties like neurosurgery or cardiovascular surgery so intense, we all played along to get along.

In 2001 and 2002, the potential liability of physician fatigue was recognized, and several bills were introduced in Congress that limited the number of hours per week a resident could work.[2] In July of 2003, the Accreditation Council for Graduate Medical Education mandated an eighty-hour work week for residents, and training programs were forced to initiate compliance measures that assured the rules would be obeyed.[3] It seemed only logical that long working hours could adversely affect patient outcomes. Much to the chagrin of many residency directors, the new regulations were quickly adopted and incorporated into teaching hospitals across the country. Yet quite surprisingly, a comprehensive study of the issue published in *The Journal of the American Medical Association* (JAMA) in 2007 revealed no difference in patient mortality rates at teaching hospitals in the years preceding and after the change.[4] But the rule remains, and there is talk of reducing the hours even further.

As a result, even at major university teaching hospitals, intern and resident physicians are being supplemented by nurse practitioners and physician assistants to fill the gaps created by the restricted work week legislation. Previously when you were admitted at an academic medical center, you were bombarded with an army of medical students, interns, residents, and professors. Currently, even some of those doctors *"won't see you now"* as the physician extenders have taken their place to preclude them from working over eighty hours.

Indeed, there is much debate still being waged throughout academic medical centers regarding the work restrictions. As expected, directors of surgical specialty programs, as well as their residents, feel the new guidelines significantly impact resident learning. For example, most neurosurgical residencies are seven years long and if one reduces the work hours from 120 or 100 hours per week down to 80, it doesn't take an advanced math degree to calculate the diminished educational experience that results. In an attempt to adjust for these changes, some programs are now considering adding an eighth year of training to the residency.

This new "culture" characterized by a more humane and supportive training experience is a welcome transformation from traditional medical education. Intuitively, we must all recognize that young physicians learn better when they are well rested and perform better when their personal lives are in order. We give up much to become doctors, everything from our financial resources to our youth. We should not have to also sacrifice our spouses and children on the altar of medicine. But changing the work demands doesn't address the loss of educational experience and simply adding additional years to already interminable residencies is not a reasonable solution.

Of course, there were a variety of factors that forged the initiation of this new medical culture, and it would be simplistic to attribute these changes solely to the emergence of women as a force in organized medicine. But it is equally simplistic to observe the timing of these policies, to acknowledge the growing influence of women in the medical arena, and to assume the two phenomena are merely coincidental. Just as the women students made Notre Dame a better university, the influx of women physicians has enhanced the study as well as the practice of medicine.

So what does any of this have to do with medical manpower and the physician shortage? Actually, the impact is considerable. As I touched on previously, the physicians of my era (baby boomers) were used to arduous work hours and expected to continue the pace once we entered practice. America's new physicians, both men and women, bring to their chosen communities the work ethic and practice culture unique to their generation. And their work ethic rejects one-hundred-hour weeks and their culture places a premium on family time and shared family responsibilities. Therefore, one doctor from Generation X does not completely replace one of the boomers who came before her or him.

Several studies have noted that on average, women physicians in practice work significantly fewer hours than their male colleagues.[5] They devote more of their time to child rearing and domestic responsibilities, and they actually enjoy the balance that they seem to achieve in their personal and professional lives. In addition, women are avoiding those specialties that demand greater personal sacrifice, such as surgery, and migrate toward dermatology, pathology, and certain primary care careers that offer more flexible lifestyles. Their male counterparts are beginning to appreciate the advantages of such choices and increasingly are using similar criteria when considering practice opportunities. This will undoubtedly have a profound effect upon the practice of medicine for generations to come.

Look, I think it's great that doctors of today are just as good at being fathers, mothers, husbands, and wives as they are at being neurosurgeons and cardiologists. But ponder this for a moment . . . there was only one new medical school built in the United States between 1980 and 2000 and the number of medical students in America has remained constant since the mid-'80s.[6] Yet the population of the United States has expanded in the same time frame and the number of elderly (who require the majority of medical attention) has grown out of proportion to any other sector of society. It is projected that the U.S. population will increase to more than 439 million people between 2010 and 2050 and that Americans over the age of 65 will increase from 35 to 88 million at the same time.[7]

So my question is simply this: if we continue to produce the same number of physicians and they now work significantly fewer hours than their predecessors, how do we propose to provide care to our ever-expanding citizenry, many of whom are elderly and will require more and more attention? And where exactly will our new wave of surgeons, cardiologists, and intensivists come from as an increasing number of our young medical students decide that the demands of some of our most critical specialties are more than they wish to endure?

Believe me when I tell you that the physician shortage is upon us and it is real. This is especially true in fields such as neurosurgery, orthopedics, general surgery, gastroenterology, and cardiology. These specialists are in high demand and, as such, are able to dictate where they go, how hard they will work, and what they will be paid. It is increasingly difficult to find young physicians to join established practices, especially outside of large urban regions. If a community is fortunate enough to attract a young specialist, he or she comes to town fully expecting a ready-made practice with a preordained schedule of well-insured patients and a guaranteed income that is equal to or exceeds that of the practitioners who have been there for twenty-five years.

Most are not interested in the "business" aspects of medicine and are looking to work as employees of the hospitals or existing group practices. They are disinclined to promote themselves through community presentations or by manning satellite clinics in outlying regions. They have come to expect their senior associates and hospital administration to be responsible for such activities. And they soon find that caring for uninsured patients at inconvenient hours in the emergency room significantly impacts their lifestyles with little impact on their incomes. Therefore, they began to opt out of on-call responsibilities while shifting their now established practices to physician-owned surgery centers and freestanding specialty facilities.

And not uncommonly, once they have fulfilled the contractual obligations necessary to secure their income guarantees, some simply move on to greener pastures in even more desperate communities that offer more generous financial incentives. They become medical "free agents," leaving behind a void in the community they departed, a community that feels betrayed and used—a community that now needs to replace a physician they worked so hard to attract. They also leave behind a population of patients who relied on them for care, only to be told the doctor "*won't see you now.*"

I am sure that all young doctors and many readers consider my previous comments unduly harsh. I guess I can kiss the 2012 "Mentor of the Year Award" good-bye. That truly was not my intent. Although my words are certain to be interpreted as an indictment of the new generation of physicians, my objective was to make everyone aware of the profound challenges faced by established practitioners and most community hospitals in trying to meet the demand for medical manpower now and in the foreseeable future.

To many who entered practice twenty years ago, this new generation of practitioners appear to be concerned more with their incomes than with the communities they serve. Just eavesdrop on the conversation of any group of docs in their fifties or sixties and you will hear a litany of complaints about their junior colleagues—they want it all and they want it now. But remember, my generation did not come out of residency with an average debt of more than $150,000.[8] When my generation started practice, insurance carriers were still reimbursing us at a rate that made charity care much easier to absorb. The words "managed care" were not part of medicine's vocabulary. We did not have to rush patients through in high volumes just to make ends meet, so we had deeper and more rewarding personal relationships with those for whom we cared. It is hard for a physician to develop a sense of loyalty to a community or for a community to develop a sense of loyalty to a physician in today's model of assembly line medicine.

Young physicians of today are exceptionally bright and intellectually inquisitive and must master far more knowledge and surgical expertise than their colleagues of even a generation ago. The era of powerful new wonder drugs, breathtaking technological advances in surgical treatments, and exciting new and innovative therapies has been ushered in by these very same doctors. Their ability to eradicate disease and to relieve human suffering knows no bounds. And yet a growing number of Americans are finding they have no access to the healers of tomorrow simply because their numbers have not kept pace with America's expanding population.

The answer to how this shortage occurred is somewhat convoluted. In the 1920s and 1930s, the American Medical Association established rigorous guidelines for the education of U.S. physicians and closed the institutions that failed to meet those guidelines. This resulted in a reduction in the number of doctors practicing in America, but markedly improved the quality of care. It is frequently suggested by the critics of organized medicine that the AMA and the accreditation committees that govern medical education have a vested interest in keeping the supply of practitioners artificially low, thus increasing demand and, as a result, maintaining fees. Truthfully, their primary concern is not maintaining fees but maintaining quality. Also, it is Washington, not the AMA, that gives these organizations their marching orders in regard to expanding the number of medical schools across America.

In the 1970s, the Nixon administration, in an effort to rein in the skyrocketing costs associated with the federal Medicare program, became convinced that the future of medical care was the Health Maintenance Organization (HMO) model and began encouraging the population to embrace such health plans.[9] The general feeling was that with more stringent oversight by the "gatekeeper" primary care physicians, there would be fewer referrals to expensive specialists, resulting in a net reduction in the cost of care. The managed care paradigm continued to be promoted throughout the '70s and '80s, and decisions regarding physician supply were predicated upon the success of just such a system.

The policy makers deduced that what we really needed were less specialists and more primary care physicians. They also surmised that as the number of physicians increased, costs went up because of greater utilization. Hence, the absolute number of entering medical students and residents remained static for almost a quarter century. There was an emphasis upon the training of internists and family doctors and a de-emphasis on producing those damn expensive specialists. There was only one little problem: Americans demanded access to specialists and refused to embrace managed care. The gatekeeper system, as originally designed, failed miserably. But now we were left with an overabundance of primary care givers and a relative shortage of specialty physicians. This imbalance continues, as fewer students opt for longer specialty training and those that do work fewer hours than their predecessors.

Another phenomenon that is having a profound effect on physician supply is the fact that colleagues of my generation are retiring from medicine earlier than those before us. It was not uncommon for doctors trained in the 1940s and 1950s to work until they were well into their seventies and beyond. This clearly demonstrated both the "workaholic" nature of these practitioners as well as their enduring love for their job. But today, most doctors in their fifties are thinking of ways they can retire and put an end to the travails that have characterized the practice of medicine over the past twenty years.

Others are leaving the *practice* of medicine, obtaining their MBAs, and assuming roles in the *business* of medicine as hospital and insurance executives, medical directors, reviewers of health plans, pharmaceutical or medical device manufacturer consultants, and a variety of other industry-related occupations. Although they are considered American physicians, they have no impact on providing direct patient care and are contributing to the physician shortage. Still others are leaving the field of medicine altogether to find employment in other sectors that have nothing to do with their prior careers.

Why the early exodus? For the most part, it is a reflection of the growing dissatisfaction that boomer generation doctors are experiencing as a result of the changes initiated by managed care. They are frustrated by what they perceive as losses of autonomy, respect, and income. They are working harder to make less money with a much greater hassle factor. So those that are able to get out do just that, one way or another. It is disturbing to note that the rate of suicide among physicians has steadily climbed over the past twenty years and is currently well above that of the general population.[10]

Additionally, as discussed earlier, there is a disconnect between the boomer generation physicians and those now entering the field of medicine. They view their younger colleagues as having an entirely foreign work ethic and find it difficult to adjust to the new mind-set, so they leave rather than mentor.

If we do nothing to address the current trend, it has been estimated that in the next ten to fifteen years we will reach negative growth in terms of physician supply, and that by 2020, the United States will realize a shortage of 200,000 physicians.[11] This bodes poorly for a nation that is aging rapidly, developing chronic diseases (such as diabetes and hypertension) at an alarming rate, and anticipating the need for medical professionals at a level that will be clearly unsustainable.

Another worrisome trend in terms of physician manpower is the apparent diminished interest in a career in medicine among our most talented young men and women. When I applied to medical school in the early '70s, the competition was daunting, with over 50,000 students seeking one of the coveted 10,000 slots in American schools. Despite the increasing population over the past twenty-five years, the trend has been downward. In 1996, for example, the number of medical school applicants was about 47,000. Just six years later, that figure declined to 33,500. Although the number has recovered slightly since then, it is still far short of what we would traditionally expect based upon our population.[12]

Our best and brightest look at the profession of medicine and see a generation of unhappy physicians who are not shy in letting them know how dissatisfying their careers have become. Indeed, a recent study by the physician recruitment group Merritt-Hawkins found that 52 percent of surveyed physicians would not choose a career in medicine if they had it to do over.[13] In addition, 64 percent (*two-thirds* of America's doctors) would not encourage their children or their children's friends to pursue a career in medicine. This attitude is pervasive among my own close colleagues as well, which may be the single most important factor contributing to the decline in the number and quality of individuals who will serve as our doctors of tomorrow.

Young people look to role models when choosing careers, just as I did so many years ago during my emergency room visit. Where will the doctors of tomorrow find their role models when so many doctors currently practicing present such a bleak view of a medical career? Beyond physician unhappiness, our best and brightest are asking themselves why they would enter a profession that requires between twelve and sixteen years of advanced education, resulting in a six-figure debt, and then work eighty plus hours per week to make less money than their stockbroker, real estate agent, prison guard (in many cases), or the salesman who sells them the medical devices they utilize to save patients' lives. Young people are young, not stupid.

So just how are we, as a country that boasts of providing the best medical care in the world, supposed to meet the needs of our growing population while faced with the challenges I outlined above? Hey, I've got an idea. If we can no longer attract the best and the brightest in our country, why don't we try and attract the best and the brightest from other countries? Well, we've been doing that for years. European physicians began trickling into America in the 1920s. It wasn't until the mid-1950s that a formal governing body was devoted to the influx of foreign medical graduates (FMGs), or international medical graduates (IMGs), as they are now known. The Educational Commission for Foreign Medical Graduates (ECFMG) was established by the

AMA to oversee the credentialing and testing of physicians who were trained outside of our borders.[14]

Most enter practice in the United States by matriculating into American residency programs after completing medical school in their home countries. For years, there has always been a surplus of five to seven thousand residency positions in American teaching hospitals that are left unfilled by graduates of U.S. medical schools.[15] Those positions are the ones usually occupied by the IMG pool. The competition for these slots is ferocious, and it is usually the top graduates of foreign schools that gain admission.

The use of IMGs to address the physician shortage has always been cloaked in controversy. Critics contend that medical education in many foreign countries is substandard, that language and cultural barriers interfere with the delivery of high-quality care, and that the population of IMGs competes with our own graduates for jobs. They correctly point out that residency programs are supported by the federal Medicare program and U.S. tax dollars, which they suggest should not be spent to educate noncitizens.

Proponents argue that IMGs must pass a written test that is at least as difficult, if not more so, than the one administered to U.S. graduates. In general, those who secure a position in a U.S. residency program represent the crème de la crème of their country. They question the validity of the oft-repeated assertion that IMGs provide a lower quality of care to American patients, pointing out the lack of any scientific basis for such a charge. Most importantly, they point out that instead of competing with U.S. medical graduates for jobs, they tend to practice in medically undermanned areas that American-born and American-educated doctors are reluctant to serve.

For the past two or three decades, IMGs have accounted for between 20 and 25 percent of practicing physicians in the United States.[16] We count on them to bridge the gap between what we need and what we produce in terms of medical professionals. However, now even that safety net may be in jeopardy. Two significant factors have led to a 20 percent decline in IMG applicants since the dawn of the new millennium. The first occurred in 2000, when a new oral exam called the Clinical Skill Assessment Test (using paid actors as mock patients) was initiated to evaluate the medical knowledge and the language skills deemed essential for proper patient evaluation. The IMG must pay a fee of $1,200 to sit for the exam, a cost that is prohibitive for a large number of individuals from the poorer developing countries.[17]

The second factor occurred on September 11, 2001. As a result of the terrorist threat, there has been a substantial restriction on the admission of foreign nationals to American institutions of higher learning. The attempted bombing of the Glasgow airport by two foreign-born physicians in 2006 attests to the pervasive nature of terrorism, both in the United States and abroad, as well as the absolute necessity to maintain vigilance. It also demonstrates that no single group (i.e., well-educated physicians) can be considered above suspicion. Consequently, fewer of the federal agencies that have traditionally supported the visa applications of IMGs are willing to continue doing so.[18]

Beyond addressing the needs of our own country lurk the ethical issues involved in recruiting the best and brightest from developing nations. Most IMGs will remain in the United States after completing their training rather than returning to their native countries where the needs are so much greater than our own and where the resources are so much less. Approximately 75 percent of IMGs eventually practice full time in the United States, much to the detriment of the population in their home countries. The effect can be devastating. For example, 40 percent of all physicians who have graduated from Lebanese medical schools in the past twenty-five years now practice in America. Between 1995 and 2005, Peru produced approximately 5,000 physicians, yet in that same decade realized only a net increase of 1,200 doctors to serve their people.[19]

As mentioned earlier, current projections predict a shortage of up to 200,000 physicians in the United States by 2020. In June 2006, the Association of American Medical Colleges sounded the alarm and called for a 30 percent increase in enrollment in American medical schools.[20] So far, little progress has been made. You must understand that even if there was the political will to address the problem, it will take years to implement. In the meantime, the U.S. population gets larger (in both number and weight) and older, the newer doctors work less hours, and IMGs will find increasing barriers to entering the American medical establishment.

So if you're frustrated that the doctor won't see you now . . . just wait.

• 10 •

The Medical Malpractice Crisis

How Many Lawyers Does It Take to Chase an Ambulance?

How easy is it going to be to write this chapter?

Few professions are more maligned than the practice of law. America's attorneys are collectively demonized in the media and abased by almost every sector of society. Most Americans look upon the bar as greedy and unscrupulous, insinuating themselves unwelcomed into every aspect of American life. We blame them for everything from the ridiculous warnings on hot cups of coffee to the unfathomable celebrity verdicts of O. J. Simpson and others. As the old joke goes . . . How do you tell the difference between a dead lawyer on the freeway and a dead snake? There are skid marks in front of the snake! I could probably end this chapter here and now and my point would be made without the need for further discussion. You could just move on to the next chapter and we could discuss the crisis in America's emergency rooms.

If it were only that simple.

Lawyer bashing is a popular pastime and I admit that I enjoy it as much as the next guy. It would be nice if we could blame the lawyers, as some of my medical brethren would like, for all that is wrong in medicine. Why stop there? Let's blame them for all that is wrong in America and the entire world. But unfortunately, it is just a bit more complex than that and I would be doing a disservice to the subject by succumbing to such a temptation. Therefore, I promise to try and practice some restraint. After all, two of my roommates and several of my close college friends became attorneys. One of my attorney friends is godfather to my middle daughter and several have been instrumental in helping me to gather information for this book. Fortunately, none are personal injury or malpractice specialists; they have chosen fields that take them into the boardrooms of corporate America and the halls of Congress. (OK, maybe not that different.)

I want to be clear from the outset that despite my close relationship with these talented individuals, I am no apologist for much of the legal profession. I become disgusted almost to the point of nausea when I see the ads on TV beckoning people to call the number on the screen if they were in a car accident, exposed to asbestos, or had their doctor prescribe Vioxx or fen-phen. I was appalled on a recent trip to spring training in Florida when I saw a billboard every quarter mile with the name, picture, and phone number of a different personal injury attorney. It's no wonder Florida has one of the most unfavorable malpractice climates in the United States, where specialists such as neurosurgeons and obstetricians can pay over $250,000 annually just for insurance.[1]

Of course, this army of righteous litigators will repeat the mantra that they are only striving to protect the unfortunate victims of careless drivers, uncaring corporations, or incompetent physicians. Personal injury lawyers actually care so much for these poor suffering souls that the attorneys work hard to find *them* just to explain how badly they have been injured, even if the individuals weren't aware they were hurt. Many care so much for their potential clients that they will even send them to a doctor or chiropractor whom they know is very good at discovering these hidden injuries. And the attorney will be there to make sure the injured parties receive justice, real American justice, hopefully in the form of a six-figure settlement or more. And by the way, although they are doing this out of the goodness of their hearts and a true concern for the injured, they do have to eat too, you know. So if you don't mind (or even if you do) they'll keep 35 to 40 percent of that settlement as a token of the victim's gratitude.

The majority of Americans, including most attorneys, abhor the ambulance-chasing tactics that characterize the prominent cadre of lawyers whose faces are plastered across billboards, whose voices inundate the radio waves and television screens, and whose expensive print ads fill our newspapers. But in truth, people *are* injured because of reckless or drunken drivers; people *are* harmed by poorly designed products made by companies who place profit over safety; and some patients *do* suffer at the hands of incompetent or negligent doctors. Without a lawyer, many of these victims would have little or no opportunity to be compensated for their injuries.

As I see it, the problem with personal injury litigation is that the system is poorly designed to accomplish the goals for which it was established. In addition, there is ineffective oversight to rein in the charlatans who have become the most visible of practitioners. But these practitioners are not limited to attorneys alone. As I mentioned earlier, a number of physicians, chiropractors, physical therapists, and the like are complicit in the deterioration of the system; the common bond among them is greed. Such greed is only matched by their complete lack of ethics.

Now don't get me wrong. A personal injury practice can be a very lucrative proposition that efficiently profits a number of people at the same time. In my office, it is not uncommon for me to see the following scenario: An individual gets rear-ended at a low rate of speed with little damage to either vehicle. The party involved eventually does "call the number on their screen" and makes contact with an attorney. I am always suspicious of a patient who claims a significant injury but has an attorney, rather than a doctor, as their first contact. Lo and behold, the attorney astutely determines their potential new client has indeed been injured. (Thank you, Dr. Perry Mason.)

Next, the patient is usually referred by the new attorney to a chiropractor, who recommends treatments three to five times per week for several months, and to a medical doctor, who prescribes muscle relaxants, narcotic analgesics, and sleeping pills to help with the pain, which, not surprisingly, has become "excruciating." Despite all these efforts, and money, the victim doesn't improve and actually worsens as the trial date nears. Imagine that! In an attempt to add legitimacy to the claim, the patient usually obtains an MRI scan and is referred to our offices for an evaluation. In the vast majority of these situations, the MRI scan is normal or very underwhelming and the patient's complaints far exceed what would be expected. When I say as much in my report, along with my recommendation that the chiropractic adjustments be discontinued since they have been of no benefit for four months, the patient is simply sent to another neurosurgeon or orthopedist until they find the desired opinion.

The case eventually goes to trial and I, of course, do not get called as a witness, but the "victim" receives justice in the form of an agreed-upon settlement by the insurance company or a jury-rendered verdict. The victim wins, the attorneys on both sides win, the chiropractor wins, the drug-prescribing medical doctor wins, the consultant who finally gave the sought-after opinion wins—even *I* win since I was paid for my consultation. But everyone else in America loses as insurance premiums rise.

The above example illustrates the sordid side of personal injury litigation, but I am not implying that it is representative of all, or even the majority of, cases involving individuals who have been harmed in some way. When a person does suffer because of the negligence of another, accountability is important, and without a system to address such issues or attorneys to represent the victim, justice cannot be served. But the current system is abundant with fraud and greed and there is no way to efficiently curtail frivolous suits. With the lottery mentality of many lawyers and their clients, even overtly ridiculous cases get their day in court. Do you remember the burglar who filed suit against a school district because he fell through an unmarked skylight on the roof of a gymnasium as he was attempting to steal the oversized lights to illuminate his own backyard? This happened very near to where I practice, and believe it or not, the plaintiff won! The school district should certainly have posted a sign reading, "Burglars, Beware! Skylight Ahead."[2]

Medical malpractice is a uniquely complex form of personal injury litigation. An "adverse event" occurs in medicine when a patient suffers a complication or an injury as a result of an act of commission (something done to them, like a surgery) or an act of omission (something that wasn't done, like getting a timely MRI scan). However, not all adverse events are the result of malpractice; indeed, most are not. Malpractice implies negligence or incompetence on the part of the physician when compared to community standards.

For example, if a patient comes into the emergency room with a headache, the list of probable causes can be extensive. If, after taking a history and examining the patient, I conclude it is likely that the headache is suggestive of migraine, I may treat the patient appropriately and forgo more definitive tests. If the patient returns later with more significant symptoms and is found to actually have a brain tumor, although I was incorrect in my initial diagnosis, that was not malpractice. I diligently extracted a history, performed a physical examination, and prescribed treatment based upon the data that I had. Now, if that same patient kept returning to the emergency room week after week with their symptoms worsening and I failed to explore the cause further with an MRI scan, *then* one could hold me negligent.

My specialty, neurosurgery, is one of the most vulnerable in terms of malpractice litigation exposure. Note that I said malpractice "litigation," not malpractice. We are sued more often than most specialties, but this reflects the dangerous nature of our work. Navigating through someone's brain or spinal cord, within millimeters of vital structures, carries a unique risk not shared by other medical or surgical specialties. Despite our years of training, the remarkable technological advances that we have at our disposal, and the impeccable attention to detail that characterizes the vast majority of neurosurgeons, adverse events do occur. And when those adverse events occur in one of our patients, the results can be devastating. Death might be considered the ultimate adverse event, but in many cases it may be preferable to the disabilities that result from our attempts to save lives by removing tumors from highly dangerous regions of the brain, by placing a small titanium clip across the neck of a complex aneurysm, or by meticulously dissecting a tumor from deep within the substance of the spinal cord.

When the patient dies or is left with a devastating disability, it is only natural to feel a profound sympathy for that patient and their family. Further, when that condition results from a medical intervention, such as surgery, it is equally natural to lay blame at the hands of the surgeon. Distraught over the loss of their loved one or facing a lifetime of disability and lost income, some families or patients then turn to the courts to find relief in the form of a medical malpractice suit. If the case goes to trial, the jury selected represents a broad spectrum of individuals with varied occupational and educational backgrounds. This group of people is supposed to represent a jury of peers for a neurosurgeon with fifteen years of higher education and a scope of knowledge regarding the central nervous system that is shared by maybe three thousand to four thousand individuals throughout the country.

When you have a sympathetic plaintiff, it is difficult for a jury to deny them help. It is equally difficult, if not impossible, for that same jury to understand the intricacies of neurosurgery. Try explaining to a cashier at Wal-Mart, or to an autobody mechanic, or to a high school P.E. teacher, or to a stay-at-home mother the neurophysiology of neuronal cell loss and the surrounding ischemic penumbra. This is not meant to demean these occupations or to question their intelligence. It took the neurosurgeon four years of college, four years of medical school, and seven years of residency to understand the anatomy of the corticospinal tract. How can we expect this "jury of peers" to understand it in a matter of days? Furthermore, most juries realize that doctors have insurance and that insurance companies are rich. They have what is referred to by lawyers as "deep pockets."

The risk that every neurosurgeon faces when he or she undertakes a dangerous operation is that if the case does not go well, he or she will be sued. If so, the plaintiff will have significant disabilities that will certainly evoke sympathy from a jury, and the jury will not truly be able to comprehend and objectively review all of the complex medical issues involved in the case. Also, the jury will know the wealthy insurance company is probably responsible for any payment to the poor patient. What they don't realize is that most malpractice policies cover only $1 million per claim and that the physician is responsible for judgments above that amount. Consequently, even though the physician provided the best care for the patient, this sympathetic jury could return a verdict in favor of the plaintiff that far exceeds the limits of the doctor's policy, which could potentially lead to his or her own personal financial ruin. So we stop doing difficult cases.

More and more neurosurgeons are eliminating cranial operations from their practices and instead limiting their caseload to the less risky spinal procedures, which, ironically, are better compensated. Very few general neurosurgeons continue to treat pediatric patients, for there is not a more sympathetic plaintiff than a disabled child who now must be supported for the remainder of his or her life. Trauma patients oftentimes present in critical condition with a poor prognosis despite the surgeon's best effort. Most are uninsured or underinsured, and thus a growing number of neurosurgeons, orthopedists, and general surgeons refuse to provide emergency room coverage for fear of being sued.

The result is the loss of access to specialty care for many communities. Patients now must travel to distant academic medical centers for treatment that a decade ago was available in their own towns. It is one thing to endure the hardship of receiving care for your brain tumor in an unfamiliar environment, miles from family and community support. It is quite another when you need an emergency operation to save your life and no one is available to provide your care. The hours required to transfer you to that distant facility can literally mean the difference between life and death.

Consider, if you will, the case of John Lucas, who was critically injured in an auto accident in Mississippi. As a result of the medical liability crisis in Mississippi at the time, every local neurosurgeon had either relocated to another state or stopped seeing trauma patients altogether. His father, who ironically was a physician, fought frantically until he could arrange a transfer to a facility able to provide the care his son needed. But John died before the treatment could be initiated.[3]

Nevada had a horrific reputation for medical liability suits and their legislature did little to address their crisis. Jim Lawson was unfortunate enough to be injured in an auto accident in Las Vegas, but the local trauma center had closed because of a lack of specialty coverage. He was transferred to another hospital, but it did not have the resources needed to treat him. Eventually, Jim Lawson also died while awaiting helicopter transfer from Las Vegas to Salt Lake City. You read that correctly, Salt Lake City, *Utah.*[4]

And it's not just the trauma patients or those with high-risk problems that suffer. One in seven obstetricians-gynecologists (OB-GYNs) in the United States have stopped delivering babies, and over 25 percent of those who still do have significantly reduced the high-risk obstetrical care they are willing to provide![5] Sixty percent of all malpractice payouts among obstetricians is related to the charge of neglect when a child is born with cerebral palsy.[6] The true cause of cerebral palsy is unknown and research continues, but plaintiffs' attorneys seem to know that the cause is an incompetent physician who didn't deliver the baby quick enough or should have performed a cesarean section or shouldn't have used forceps for extraction. Amazing, isn't it, how a mere three years of law school can bestow such insight into medical conundrums that have eluded researchers for years. We have one of the highest rates of cesarean section births in the world, many of which are done "defensively" for fear that a lawsuit may result if the birth were allowed to proceed naturally and the baby were to have problems.[7] Yet our infant mortality rate and maternal death rates are abominably higher than almost all other developed countries similar to our own.[8]

But let me tell you, an infant with cerebral palsy can cost an obstetrician millions of dollars despite a lack of scientific evidence to support a claim of malpractice. The baby turned out bad, you were the doctor, therefore, you must have done something wrong. As a result, in some parts of the country OB-GYNs pay more than $250,000 per year for malpractice coverage. They can either pass that cost on to their patients (good luck with the insurance companies) or they can choose to do what one in seven has already done. They can refuse "*to see you now.*" It does not bode well that as recently as 2004, one-third of all OB-GYN residency positions were vacant.[9] Young medical students are avoiding high-liability specialties like the plague.[10]

The history of silicone breast implants represents a perfect example of how astronomically absurd judgments can be rendered by juries in the absence of any scientific evidence to support a plaintiff's claim. The use of silicone gel for cosmetic breast augmentation became widespread in the 1970s. Toward the end of that decade, the occasional nuisance suit began to appear, alleging various injuries as a result of the implants. The suits usually involved rupture of the implant, and much of the early litigation was directed toward the "potential" risk of breast cancer associated with the silicone exposure. However, the scientific community did not substantiate such claims, and in the early '90s, two large epidemiological studies actually showed that silicone implants were associated with a *decreased* rate of breast cancer.[11] The trial lawyers were forced to uncover other potential injury-causing agents that could punch their ticket to the litigation lottery.

In December 1991, that opportunity arrived when a jury awarded a woman a $7.5 million judgment after her attorneys successfully argued she suffered from nonspecific illnesses as a result of the damage the silicone implants caused to her "immune" system.[12] The trial made national headlines and subsequently the Food and Drug Administration (FDA) banned implants for cosmetic surgeries. The ban did not result from evidence that the implants were associated with immune disease, but by the lack of any evidence that they *didn't* cause immune disease.[13]

The floodgates were blown open and ads began to appear across America inviting women with silicone implants to join a class action lawsuit against the manufacturer, describing the wide variety of nonspecific symptoms that proved their immune systems had been compromised. Seeing the $7.5 million award for just one plaintiff, Merrell Dow Pharmaceuticals eventually settled with the four hundred thousand plaintiffs for $4.25 *billion*.[14] There were many ways the defendant could have better utilized $4.25 billion, such as new product development, but that was not to be.

By the way, in June 1994, one of the first major studies that investigated the association between silicone implants and autoimmune/

connective tissue disorders was published in the prestigious *New England Journal of Medicine*—it found absolutely no correlation between the two.[15] Several subsequent studies have also been published with similar findings.[16] A jury awards $7.5 million to a woman without a stitch of scientific evidence. The terrified manufacturer was forced to settle a class action suit for $4.25 billion, initiated by personal injury attorneys. Yet when the science is eventually available, it shows that silicone implants do not cause immune or connective tissue disorders. The four hundred thousand plaintiffs got to keep their money anyway, as did their attorneys. How about that for American justice?

According to the group Doctors for Medical Liability Reform (DMLR), a neurosurgeon practicing in America can expect to be sued at least once every two years. In addition, one out of every three trauma surgeons, orthopedic surgeons, and emergency room physicians will get sued in any given year.[17] These individuals form the backbone of America's trauma system. These individuals are there waiting when you or your spouse or your child are injured in an auto accident and fight to save your life and the lives of your loved ones. But increasingly, they're refusing to answer the call for fear that their efforts will be rewarded with a malpractice suit. In a seven-year period alone, between 1995 and 2002, the state of Pennsylvania lost 36 percent of their general surgeons and almost 15 percent of their neurosurgeons because of the rising costs of malpractice insurance.[18]

Juries are also growing more generous. Over 50 percent of all malpractice judgments now exceed $1 million and the *average* award is now up to $4.7 million.[19] Of course, those figures include a number of high-profile cases with judgments in the $50 to 100 million range, but the fear for these specialists is that they could be next. Furthermore, the lion's share of the money is awarded for "noneconomic damages" (pain and suffering), greatly surpassing the compensation for medical bills or lost wages. No one should argue that pain and suffering is not a legitimate claim in a malpractice action, but they are intangibles and impossible to measure. It is one thing to justly compensate injured patients for the medical costs they incur and the economic losses they will realize in the future as a result of their injuries. It is quite another to award them millions more for their perceived suffering. But that's exactly what the attorneys count on.

Since 1975, the costs of medical liability in the United States have skyrocketed over 2,000 percent. In 2003 alone, the average cost of malpractice insurance increased 18 percent, and it continues to climb.[20] Between the years 2000 and 2004 the average premium for neurosurgeons jumped 84 percent.[21] Even when the physician prevails in a malpractice action, the costs are colossal. DMLR reports that in a jury trial where the physician is exonerated, the average cost of defending the case is almost \$88,000.[22] Understand that for a physician, the cost of a malpractice trial cannot be measured in dollars and cents alone. The doctor's reputation is at stake, and the psychological toll that results from being sued is oftentimes overwhelming.

I have been exceedingly fortunate in my thirty-eight years as a medical student, resident, and practicing physician. I have actually been sued only once. On four or five different occasions, I was named as a defendant in a malpractice suit only to be dropped from the case as more information became available to the plaintiff's attorney. But that single instance where I actually had to defend myself in front of a jury was one of the most agonizing experiences of my life.

A young college student was at a fraternity party drinking beer with his girlfriend when he exchanged angry words with another attendee. As they moved the argument outside, a fight broke out and the student was knocked to the ground, striking the back of his head on a car bumper as he fell. He immediately became unconscious, the paramedics were summoned, and he was transported by ambulance to our emergency room. Since I was the "on-call" neurosurgeon, I evaluated the patient and found him to be deeply comatose. His CT scan revealed a large cerebral contusion (brain bruise) to his frontal lobe with evidence of swelling of the surrounding brain.

I phoned his family, who lived about five hundred miles south, explained the situation to his parents, and told them I needed to insert a small catheter into the brain so that we could measure the pressure inside his skull and drain off some cerebrospinal fluid. The danger was that the contusion might expand and the pressure rise to the point that it could put the remainder of the brain in great jeopardy. The parents were obviously distraught, but the father agreed over the phone (with a nurse on another line serving as a witness) to allow me to proceed. The surgery went smoothly and he remained stable overnight. His parents arrived the next morning. Initially, the patient's mother was hostile and suggested the procedure was unnecessary despite my efforts to convince her otherwise.

The following morning, the pressure measurement inside the skull was rising rapidly. The patient remained comatose and a follow-up CT scan indicated that the bruise was indeed enlarging. I met with the family once again and explained to them that their son's life was now at risk and that I needed to operate on him as soon as possible to remove the bruised portion of the brain so that the remaining uninjured brain could survive. In my estimation, if we did not intervene, he would likely die. The mother was adamant that she would not give permission. Despite the fact that I showed her the CT scan and beseeched her to allow me to save him, she continued to refuse and reiterated that she felt that surgery was unnecessary.

The boy's father called a physician friend who suggested that they contact one of the university medical centers near our town. Time was becoming critical as the pressures were now dangerously high. The father contacted the closest university hospital, University of California, Davis Medical Center. He was told that we were highly regarded neurosurgeons and was urged to let us proceed. Still, they declined, despite my pleadings for four to five hours. They next contacted the University of California, San Francisco, and were essentially told the same thing. Still they did not waver. I then took the father aside and told him that I understood his wife was distraught, but that he must allow me to operate immediately if there was any hope to save his son. He agreed and signed the consent.

We operated immediately and the surgery went well. We removed the damaged brain and created room for his swollen but still functional brain to expand. The pressures normalized and within a few days he emerged from his coma. The patient was eventually transferred to a rehab facility and regained his speech, his ability to walk, and his ability to care for himself. Because of his initial injury, there remained some cognitive deficits, but his recovery was truly gratifying . . . at least to me.

About ten months later, I received notice that the patient and his mother (but not the father) were suing me for medical malpractice. In the complaint, the mother suggested that I should have ignored both her and her husband's refusal to give consent and taken him to surgery anyway. Further, they alleged that his cognitive deficits were the result of the delay and could have been prevented if I had operated earlier. This was the basis of the suit. Now what you must understand is that in the state of California, if a physician operates on a patient without consent, that physician can be charged with battery. Furthermore, if the patient dies, then the surgeon can be charged with murder. Malpractice insurance covers neither of those situations.

Initially, the mother filed the lawsuit herself because she was unable to find an attorney to accept the case. In a letter to the court asking for an extension, she revealed that she had contacted somewhere between forty and sixty attorneys, who all refused to represent them. Fortunately, she finally found one, from the Stockton area south of Sacramento. In order for a malpractice case to proceed, the plaintiff must produce at least one physician who concurs that the defendant was practicing below the standard of care. That was a problem for the plaintiff's attorney. He was unable to find even a single neurosurgeon who would agree to testify to that admission. So he did the next best thing. He enlisted the assistance of an acquaintance of his who was an emergency room physician in the Stockton area and who would testify that I should have ignored the family and operated anyway. The case was allowed to move forward.

From the outset, my attorney tried to reassure me that we had little to worry about. The case was very straightforward, we had a parade of distinguished physicians willing to testify on my behalf, and the plaintiffs were unable to get any additional "medical experts" beyond their attorney's friend to testify against me. Despite all the reassurance, I found myself unable to sleep in the months leading up to the trial. I lost weight, became distracted at work, and constantly went over in my mind what could happen to my reputation and practice if I lost. I missed time in my office for attendance at meetings and depositions. Thank God for my wife, who gently saved my sanity and soothed me even though I had become irritable and aloof at home.

When the case finally went to trial, it unfolded mostly as we had expected, and after a week of testimony, the jury took just two hours to return a verdict exonerating me from any wrongdoing. But the verdict was not unanimous. Ironically, the one juror whom *we* had selected when the plaintiff's attorney had run out of challenges was the one who voted against us. After the trial, we were allowed to speak to the jury and ask them questions regarding their deliberations. It was revealed that they immediately voted 11–1 in my favor, and they took the remaining two hours to try and convince "our" juror to make it unanimous. She was adamant and would not change her mind (much like the patient's mother). When asked why she voted against me, she told the other jurors, "All doctors are liars and I don't believe what any of them said."

I prevailed in my only malpractice suit. But this case is a glaring example of all that is wrong with the system. You have an irrational plaintiff, an unscrupulous attorney, a juror who refuses to act on the evidence, and sizable cost in terms of the money and time required to defend it. But none of those costs can compare to the emotional toll this took on me as a physician. I begged the patient's mother to let me save her son; I used all my skill and training to eventually do just that. And what was my reward? It was a malpractice suit. How eager do you think I was to see the next patient that came into the emergency room?

As I mentioned, I have been fortunate in terms of medical malpractice claims. Having been sued only once in thirty-eight years while practicing high-risk medicine is nothing to complain about. I'd love to tell you the reason is because I'm the best brain surgeon in America, but it's possible I might be exaggerating just a bit. The truth is that I communicate well with my patients and I take the time to explain to them in detail their conditions and their treatment options. We talk about realistic expectations and the possible risks of those treatment options. More importantly, I listen to them, encourage their questions, and try to answer them in language *they* understand.

The emergence of managed care has forced physicians to vastly increase their patient volume and rely on "physician extenders," like P.A.s and nurse practitioners, to deliver care. By necessity, they spend less time with their patients, who then feel alienated and neglected. When the patients get sick enough that they need to be hospitalized, they are told to go to the emergency room and they are cared for by hospitalists who know nothing about them as a patient or as a person. I can't help but feel that a significant amount of blame for the current malpractice crisis in America must lie at the feet of the managed care system.

Talk to any malpractice insurance claims expert and he or she will tell you that most people sued their doctors not because they were injured but because they were angry. Physician arrogance, lack of compassion for the patient, rushed patient care, failure to return phone calls or address concerns, all conspire to create an adversarial relationship between the patient and the doctor. Thus, when a complication does occur or an outcome is less than perfect, even if the physician did everything correctly, he or she is at risk for being sued. It is enigmatic that some of the most skilled and brilliant physicians can find themselves as defendants in malpractice lawsuits more frequently than some of their grossly incompetent colleagues.

Additionally, where one chooses to practice plays a major role in determining how often one will be sued. I live in Northern California in a college town surrounded by farms and orchards. Many of my patients (and many of the potential jurors in a possible malpractice trial) are hardworking, straight-talking, salt of the earth people. They respect physicians and appreciate the care they are given. Most plaintiffs' attorneys understand this and their threshold for filing a malpractice claim in our region is rather high. (Remember, in my own case, the plaintiff was forced to find an attorney out of the area to represent her after contacting dozens of lawyers.)

California has one of the nation's most favorable malpractice climates after going through their own crisis in the 1970s. To address the same problems that plague places like Nevada and Mississippi, our state legislature passed the Medical Injury Compensation Reform Act (MICRA), which capped the awards on noneconomic losses (i.e., the intangibles of pain and suffering) at $250,000.[23] This immediately stabilized malpractice insurance premiums, but still allowed patients to recover fully all of their economic losses that resulted from a physician's malpractice. MICRA now serves as the gold standard in the national debate on malpractice reform.

Lastly, being a member of the clinical faculty of the University of California, San Francisco (UCSF) confers an additional legitimacy to my practice. UCSF enjoys the reputation of being one of the world's most prestigious teaching hospitals, and my reputation benefits (deserved or not) from merely being on the faculty—guilt (or innocence) by association. But this also forces me to remain current in my chosen field and allows me to interact and consult with some of the most gifted neurosurgeons in the world.

As you can see, the frequency with which one may be sued and the success of such suits are a crapshoot, a crapshoot that may have less to do with clinical competence than with the time you spend with patients, the state or county in which you practice, or whether or not you are associated with a highly regarded university program. On the other hand, patients who have truly been injured are at the mercy of similar forces. They may have a very legitimate claim against a physician, but their attorney may find himself or herself up against the "wall of silence" when trying to find a respected physician who will testify against another doctor regardless of the defendant's obvious incompetence. They are then forced to use one of the many "hired guns" who will testify anywhere, against anybody . . . for a price. This weakens the plaintiff's case and makes it more difficult for them to obtain equitable justice.

I confess, I have never agreed to testify against a colleague in a medical malpractice case. I have, on occasion, *refused* to testify in defense of a colleague who I felt committed malpractice and, in that situation, encouraged the insurance company to settle the case. For the system to work, fairness is paramount. My hesitancy to publicly acknowledge another physician's mistakes and my willingness to continue to maintain the wall of silence undermine that fairness. So I am as complicit as the trial lawyer in the failures of the current system.

Just how well do our courts address medical malpractice when it does occur? How well do we ensure that patients are justly compensated in the presence of a medical error? Unfortunately, I must admit, not very well at all. For every "frivolous" case that I can cite, plaintiffs' attorneys can counter with equally egregious examples. In 2007, Rhode Island Hospital in Providence had their neurosurgeons operate on the wrong side of the brain not once, not twice, but *three* times in one year![24] In March of 2008, surgeons in Minneapolis took a patient to the operating room to remove a kidney that had become cancerous. The surgery went well except for one detail—they removed the patient's normal kidney by mistake.[25] In June of 2006, a forty-seven-year-old Air Force veteran checked into a V.A. hospital in Los Angeles to have his cancerous testicle removed and . . . you guessed it![26]

Simply trading horror stories like the aforementioned does little to address the failure of our system to adequately compensate injured patients or adequately protect America's physicians from frivolous lawsuits. David Studdert and Michelle Mello have published a wealth of information on the subject and their findings are illuminating. In one study, they looked at almost 1,500 malpractice suits to determine whether the claims were justified. In

37 percent of the cases, there was no evidence that a medical error had even occurred, yet the suits were allowed to proceed to trial. And in those cases where a medical error had occurred, 54 percent of all compensation went to administrative expenses such as attorney's fees, expert witness fees, and court costs. Less than half of the settlement in justifiable claims went to the injured party.[27]

Another disturbing study by Brennan et al. in 1996 found that jury awards to plaintiffs were more directly related to the extent of disability of the patient than to physician culpability. And it worked both ways: juries were more likely to award compensation when patients had significant disabilities even when the physician was deemed to have done nothing wrong, and in cases where gross malpractice was obvious, they were much less likely to find for the plaintiff when the injuries were modest.[28] These and other studies reinforce the idea that our system is in dire need of significant reform, both for the patient and for the physician. But as long as our politicians continue to finance their campaigns through the contributions of special interests like the American Bar Association or the American Medical Association, there is little hope of genuine progress.

I'll end this chapter with an interesting story I came across while paging through my morning paper. In March of 2008 Eliot Spitzer, then governor of New York and a former federal prosecutor, was forced to resign from office amid revelations that he had been a repeat "customer" of a high-end call girl escort service. In the media frenzy that accompanied the story, Kathleen Pender, a reporter for the *San Francisco Chronicle*, wrote a story on the price of call girl services across the country.[29] In the article, she interviewed a former prostitute who had worked as a call girl and asked how they determined what to charge. She responded that prices varied in different parts of the country and different settings (urban, suburban, or rural). In general, however, she indicated that a good rule of thumb was to see what lawyers in the region charged for an hourly fee—that pretty much paralleled what the call girls in the region would charge. How interesting. Whores and lawyers are both getting paid the same. I suppose that falls under the equal pay for equal work statutes.

I know, I know, I said I would restrain myself and not succumb to the temptation to lawyer bash. Well, I lied.

So sue me.

· 11 ·

Crisis in America's Emergency Rooms

Take Two Aspirin and Call 911 in the Morning

$\mathcal{N}$owhere is the collapse of our current medical system more blatantly apparent than in America's emergency rooms. What's worse, when the system fails in the ER, it doesn't simply result in frustrated patients who are unhappy with the lack of attention from their primary care doctors, or interminable arguments with insurance company bureaucrats over the authorization of an MRI scan, or many of the other multitude of complaints that we have come to associate with American medicine. No, when the system fails in the emergency room, people die. Real people—husbands and wives, mothers and fathers, sons and daughters—die. They die because we failed them, all of us. It doesn't have to be that way.

Imagine a warm summer day. You're mowing your lawn and your two children are playing catch in the yard. The ball gets away and rolls into the street and as you turn, your young son is dashing after it. You scream a warning, as you have so many times before, but this time it is unheeded and too late. The neighbor driving home didn't see him running behind your parked car and in an instant your life and your son's are changed forever. The injuries are severe, but your son is clinging to life. The prayers begin.

But you and your son are fortunate because your local community hospital is a trauma center, well prepared to deal with the most life-threatening of injuries and staffed by superb surgeons and nurses ready to fight for your child's life. Your spouse dials 911 and frantically accesses the emergency medical system (EMS). Within minutes the rescue team arrives from the hospital or local firehouse and begins resuscitation and stabilization right there on your front lawn. They load your son into the ambulance and begin the mad dash to the hospital, sirens blaring, lights flashing. They radio ahead to the emergency room to mobilize the trauma team, ready an operating room, and make sure all components of the system are in place to receive your son and continue the battle to save his life.

But there's a problem. The emergency room is currently filled beyond capacity, all operating suites are occupied, there's no room at the inn for your son. The ambulance is "diverted" to the next closest trauma center, forty-five miles to the south. As they reroute to their new destination, they are told that this weekend no neurosurgeon is available to take trauma call and that the rescue crew will have to find yet another facility. Time is running out and the closest hospital with available resources is the university medical center ninety-five miles to the north.

Again they reroute, battling valiantly to keep your son alive as they desperately race to the university hospital. As we learned nearly fifty years ago, with traumatic injuries, time is of the essence, and it was that lesson that led to the establishment of trauma centers. But time has run out for your son, and despite a system that was designed to save his life, that system fails him as he dies en route to the third trauma center accessed to provide his lifesaving care.

Does this sound far-fetched or melodramatic? The scenario would be great stuff for a fictional Hollywood movie, don't you think? Well, think again. Scenarios like this are happening across America with a disturbingly increasing frequency. They are happening in America, where we have had a regionalized trauma care system in place since the late 1960s. They are happening in America, where we now spend over $8,000 per person annually for medical care[1] and consume in excess of 17 percent of the gross domestic product to provide that care.[2] They are happening in America, where despite these expenditures, we can do no better than fifty-seventh in the world in surviving traumatic injuries.[3] They are happening in America, home to the best health care system in the world . . . who are you kidding?

I practice in a pleasant college town of about one hundred thousand people and we have been a designated trauma center since the late 1980s. In all of those years, my partners and I have never missed a single night on call, but I can't say the same for some other trauma centers or other specialties in the region. Somewhere around the mid-'90s, we started experiencing the fallout of the current ER crisis. Trauma centers to our north and south found it impossible to get their neurosurgeons to provide continuous coverage and were sometimes forced to divert anyone with a serious neurosurgical condition to our institution. This was especially prevalent during the Christmas and Thanksgiving holidays; despite the fact that some of these communities had more neurosurgeons than ours did.

We started getting calls from hospitals several hundred miles away, desperately looking for a neurosurgeon to accept critical patients from their emergency rooms. Their helicopters or ground ambulances bypass San

Francisco and Sacramento on their way to us because there are no available beds to provide that care in these large metropolitan areas. We then accept the onus of treating these patients, many uninsured or underinsured, and shift the responsibility for that care from those communities on to our own, further crowding our ER and further depleting our already strained resources. But even more important is the fact that by the time some of these patients finally do reach us, the window of opportunity to help them has closed. Patients do die because of these delays in care and even those who survive may pay the price for those delays for the rest of their lives.

Devon Kramer was one of those victims. At forty-six years old, this unemployed, divorced father of two spent the lion's share of each day drinking up to a fifth of cheap vodka and occasionally supplementing it with marijuana when he could get it. On this particular evening Devon had the misfortune, in his intoxicated state, to trip on the curb and fall to the ground, striking the right side of his head against the pavement and opening a four-inch gash in his scalp. As he tried to rise and right himself, he fell again and several passers-by stopped to help. Someone with a cell phone summoned 911 while another Samaritan applied pressure to his wound.

When the paramedics arrived several minutes later, Devon was still conscious, had stable vital signs despite the bleeding, and was whisked to the local trauma center where the emergency room crew quickly assessed his condition. In his short time in the ER Devon became less responsive and more difficult to arouse. The capable ER doctor ordered an emergency CT scan, which can quickly provide a picture of the brain and disclose any underlying injuries. Indeed, Mr. Kramer was developing an expanding hematoma (blood clot) in his brain and would need emergent surgery to relieve the pressure and stop the bleeding. The local neurosurgeon was called.

However, this neurosurgeon realized from the description of the patient that Devon Kramer was nothing more than your typical uninsured drunk. So without coming in to examine him or even review his CT scan, the surgeon decided Devon's case was "too complex" and should be transferred to a university hospital. After all, the neurosurgeon had a full schedule of elective surgeries on well-insured patients the next morning and devoting the next several hours to save Mr. Kramer, who wouldn't be able to pay, was not very cost effective.

The ER physician tried valiantly to arrange a transfer to UC Davis, UC San Francisco, and Stanford, but there were no beds available in any of these hospitals to provide the ICU care his condition would require. In a panic, he called our ER and was put through to me, the neurosurgeon on call. Devon Kramer had now lapsed into a coma and the desperate doctor begged me to help. I immediately told him to send us the patient by helicopter and asked him to intubate (insert a plastic tube into the windpipe) Devon and give him a large dose of Mannitol, a drug that temporarily reduces pressure in the brain.

I called our operating room to have them ready a surgical suite, threw on my clothes, and drove to the hospital to await the patient's arrival. About seven minutes out, the flight nurse reported that Devon Kramer had lost his pulse and they were initiating CPR. While rhythmically applying compressions to his chest in the cramped confines of the helicopter, the crew administered various drugs to restart his heart. An electric current was applied in hopes of shocking him back to life. But it failed. At 2:11 a.m., Devon Kramer died from an epidural hematoma. I reviewed his accompanying CT scan. There was nothing complex about Devon Kramer's clot. He didn't succumb to an untreatable injury; he died because the system failed him.

How did this happen? A multitude of reasons are responsible for the collapse of emergency care in the United States. The current crisis in American emergency rooms is a mere microcosm of the greater collapse of American health care in general, and a review of how our emergency care system devolved can be instructive.

Fifty years ago, emergency care in the United States was a mere afterthought for most hospitals. The ER was usually a low priority in most institutions, housed in some out-of-the-way place and staffed by a mishmash of physicians with no specific training in the care of emergency patients. Some physicians were new graduates, with little experience, using the ER to build their practices. Some physicians were the dregs of their community, unable to sustain a successful practice and relegated to emergency room duty to make a living. Others were still in residency training, working as "moonlighters" to supplement their incomes.

A coordinated emergency medical system was nonexistent. There were no paramedics, no emergency flight helicopters, and no 911 system to summon help. Over 50 percent of the "ambulance" services across the country were supplied by local funeral directors using their hearses as ambulances. First responders to the scene of an accident were more than likely the local sheriff or one of his deputies. If the patient did make it to the ER, there was no guarantee that hospital had the necessary equipment to care for the patient's injuries. Specialty care was sparse and usually limited to large urban hospitals or university medical centers. Surviving a life-threatening illness or injury was the exception rather than the rule.

All of that changed in 1966 when the National Academy of Science published a scathing report on the appalling state of emergency and trauma care across the nation. Entitled "Accidental Death and Disability: The Neglected Disease of Modern Society,"[4] the report brought to light the virtual epidemic of traumatic injury and death in the United States and the woefully inadequate system we had in place to combat it. Release of this document resulted in public outrage and quickly got the attention of Congress and the American Medical Association.

As a result of this landmark report, emergency care in the United States was vastly improved. The specialty of "emergency medicine" was developed in U.S. medical schools, producing a new generation of physicians who received focused training in the evaluation and management of life-threatening emergencies.[5] Emergency rooms were soon staffed with these new ER specialists, first in the larger cities and then in smaller towns as well, greatly enhancing the quality of care in those fortunate communities.

Protocols were developed for everything from the acute care of a myocardial infarction (heart attack) to severe head injury. Standardized treatments that resulted in higher rates of survival for a variety of entities soon became commonplace in emergency rooms across America. CPR training, Advanced Cardiac Life Support, and Advanced Trauma Life Support programs emerged, saving countless American lives.[6]

We recognized that severely injured patients were best managed by trauma "teams" that had the training and resources available to intervene quickly and efficiently. These teams were composed of surgical specialists who were either in house 24/7 or immediately available to the ER in a moment's notice. Precious time was wasted when one of these patients was taken to a facility without those capabilities so regional trauma centers were established. Patients who met the given criteria were automatically routed there for treatment.

We also realized that we could do better by initiating treatment at the point of injury rather than waiting until the patient arrived at the hospital. A sophisticated network of first responders known as the Emergency Medical System (EMS) evolved with the advanced training of nurses, paramedics, and firefighters to provide that lifesaving care as soon as they arrived on scene.[7] Supported by ambulances (now essentially mobile emergency rooms rather than hearses) and helicopters to aid in the rapid transport of patients to these regionalized centers, the benefits of this newly developed system soon spread from large urban areas to remote rural landscapes. The result was improved outcomes and survival for the large majority of American patients. And this wonderful new system was available to everyone by simply dialing three little numbers—911.[8]

So how is it possible that a scenario such as the one I depicted in the beginning of this chapter can occur in America? Why did the system fail your son? Why did the system fail Devon Kramer? The answer is complex but it is an answer that is relevant to many of the problems we now face in American health care.

As with many issues confronting America today, be it education or transportation or government or even health care, the root cause is often the "M" word: *money*. And our emergency rooms are no exception. Just like so many grand ideas born from public outcry and enacted by indignant politicians in response to that outcry, initial funding is provided to launch these initiatives and essentially appease the public. However, once the economic realities of these programs become apparent, the resources to support them disappear, the responsibility to maintain them is thrust upon state or local officials, and we are left once again with another unfunded mandate.

The federal government responded to the National Academy's report by enacting legislation that resulted in the desperately needed revamping of the emergency care system. They continued to support the expansion of trauma centers across America until the early 1980s when Washington ceded their oversight to the individual states and gave them the discretion to use available federal funding for the programs as they deemed best. This helped to create a fragmented system of variable quality as states began to divert (ironic, the same thing we now do to patients) funds into other programs and services in dire need of resources.[9]

Despite the cutback in federal and state funding, hospitals still recognized the essential benefit of trauma centers and continued to expand and support them. Several hospitals within a given geographic region would compete for the trauma center designation, realizing the prestige it brought to their institution in addition to the improved care and, in many instances, positive cash flow. The number of uninsured patients in the United States was modest in the late '70s, and commercial insurers were still reimbursing hospitals and physicians at a level that allowed them to cost shift revenue from insured patients to help offset the losses associated with charity care. But to paraphrase Bob Dylan, "the times they were a-changin'."

With the emergence of managed care and the commercial carriers' insistence on indexing their reimbursement rates to Medicare standards, hospitals and physicians alike began to see their incomes declining. They found themselves having greater difficulty absorbing the financial burden of uncompensated or undercompensated care. This forced many physicians to severely limit the number of Medicaid or uninsured patients they could see in their offices, and these patients began to use the local ER as their primary care clinics. In addition to the critically ill or severely injured patients, our ERs began seeing a steady rise of patients who had minor aches and pains, colds and runny noses, earaches and tummy aches. And their beds began to fill.

As the 1990s progressed, America's uninsured grew and grew and grew. Also, more and more physicians began to feel the economic pinch of managed care, and more and more patients found the local ERs as their only source of access to medical care. The beds continued to fill until there were no beds available to care for your injured son. But it was not only the poor who inhabited your son's bed; it was also the insured whose own physicians no longer had the time to "squeeze them in" for an unscheduled visit. Reduced reimbursement forced their primary care doctors to greatly increase the volume of patients they saw to make up for the loss of income. Interrupting that flow of patients with an unexpected and possibly time-consuming problem could not be tolerated; therefore, even the insured patient was simply told to go to the emergency room. Local physicians began to use the ER as an extension of their office and the ER staff as noncompensated physician extenders. The beds continued to fill, so your injured son was "diverted" to the next closest trauma center.

But they had a different problem. They had a bed for your son; they just didn't have a doctor. With alarming frequency, physicians across America are choosing to opt out of emergency room call responsibilities, leaving their institutions without the necessary specialty expertise to care for the life-threatening problems that pass through their doors. The reasons for this physician reluctance are varied yet universal.

Most of us who practice medicine are truly dedicated to our calling. And most of us agree that caring for a patient in need, especially when his or her life is at stake, is an ethical responsibility that we have to our communities. But forces beyond our control or yours have conspired to create significant barriers to providing that care, leaving many of our hospitals and their patients in dire straits. Of course, the "M" word is a prominent issue, but not the only one.

As I have illustrated throughout this book, many of the changes in the delivery of medical care were the result of the emerging managed care paradigm and the resultant diminished reimbursement to the very doctors who provide that care. As the population of underinsured patients began to swell in emergency rooms, specialists began to find themselves providing an expanding volume of uncompensated care. Simultaneously they were witnessing a dramatic decline in their own incomes as revenues from the commercial carriers began to contract. Unable to absorb this burden for long, medical and surgical specialists looked for innovative ways to make up the difference.

They turned to their hospitals, which housed the emergency rooms, and demanded that they find ways to supplement specialists' lost income that resulted from ER care responsibilities. Some hospitals offered to assure Medicare rates for all uninsured and underinsured patients. Some offered their physicians a stipend for each day they took ER call or for each patient they cared for while on call. This plan succeeded for a short time, but soon physicians began to ask for more. Stipends increased and hospitals found that the revenue they were forced to devote to such plans was beginning to limit their ability to purchase new equipment, expand their facilities, or develop new programs.

Once the physicians were in the driver's seat with the hospitals (in a way they never were able to realize with the insurance carriers), greed began to erode this model as some doctors demanded exorbitant stipends because they knew they could—they essentially held their institutions and their communities hostage to those demands. In addition, the inevitable jealousy among different specialists with regard to the variation in stipend levels further exacerbated the crisis. When hospital administrators failed to meet the demands of their specialists, the docs simply walked away, leaving the ER uncovered.

But money alone was not the only factor leading to the exodus of physicians from America's emergency rooms. For some, the inequity of the system became more than they could bear. As discussed earlier, in 1986, Congress passed the Emergency Medical Treatment and Active Labor Act (EM-TALA), which mandated that all patients who presented to an emergency room be evaluated and stabilized regardless of ability to pay.[10] This law was enacted to prevent hospitals from refusing to see patients in need of emergency care because of lack of insurance, in turn "dumping" those patients on public facilities, such as county hospitals. This was certainly a virtuous idea, but with many unanticipated results.

One of the provisions of EMTALA mandates that if an emergency room patient is in need of care not available at the presenting hospital, they must transfer the patient to a facility that does have the capability to provide that care. In addition, if a hospital is contacted by the referring institution, it is illegal for them to refuse to accept the patient if they have the resources (i.e., specialists) to provide that care. As I explained in chapter 5, all of this sounds great in principle but can be quite problematic in practice. EMTALA never explains how either facility is supposed to pay for that care they provide if the patient is uninsured. What often ensues is the shifting of responsibility for uncompensated care from smaller, local hospitals to the larger regional centers and the "cherry-picking" by specialists in these smaller centers to the detriment of those in the larger ones.

The magic catchphrase in this rerouting of undesirable patients is simply "we don't feel comfortable." This implies that the hospital ER docs, or the appropriate specialists, feel the patient's problem is beyond their expertise and thus they "don't feel comfortable" providing the needed care at their institutions. Consequently, they want to transfer that patient to our hospital where we "do feel comfortable." Many times the situation truly is what they represent it to be, and indeed, it is appropriate to have the patient transferred. But it is not uncommon for larger regional centers to receive patients who could have easily been cared for in the referring hospital. What the patients did was fail the "wallet biopsy," and suddenly the problem became "too complex" to be handled locally. Remember Devon Kramer?

The typical patient involved is usually a drunk or drug abuser who is injured in an auto accident. He may have had a brief loss of consciousness at the scene but on arrival at the local hospital he is alert, abusive, and most importantly, uninsured. The patient undergoes X-rays revealing a broken leg, but because of the questionable loss of consciousness, the ER doc has a CT scan of the head performed, which turns out to be quite normal. The orthopedist on call at the local hospital is aroused at home around 3 a.m., but instead of getting out of bed to evaluate the patient, he determines that because there was a possible loss of consciousness he "doesn't feel comfortable" managing the patient since there are no neurosurgeons on staff at his hospital. He then tells the ER doctor to transfer the patient.

Because of EMTALA regulations, our facility is then obligated to accept the patient, our orthopedist is obligated to operate on him, and our neurosurgeons aren't even asked to be involved since there was no significant head injury. So the orthopedist from the referring hospital gets to sleep and be bright and awake for his schedule of elective, insured patients the next morning. Our orthopedist, on the other hand, is up all night repairing the broken leg, must cancel his elective schedule the next day, and doesn't get reimbursed. Pretty fair system, wouldn't you say?

Well, that gets old real fast and eventually the orthopedists or neurosurgeons or general surgeons or cardiologists get fed up. It frustrates them to see outlying communities supporting their own specialists with the more lucrative referrals, while determining that these same specialists are not sufficient if patients present in the middle of the night, on weekends, or on holidays or have no resources to pay for their care. So even the dedicated docs—the good guys if you will, who have always been there to take call—"just don't feel comfortable" and drop off the call schedule altogether. It exacerbates the specialist shortage in the ERs and is another reason there was no doctor available to care for your son.

Another huge issue that affects the willingness of specialists to provide emergency room care is the risk of medical malpractice lawsuits. In many regions of the country, the malpractice crisis has spun out of control. Ridiculously exorbitant judgments have led to neurosurgeons, orthopedists, and anesthesiologists paying as much as $200,000 or more per year for malpractice insurance.[11] Some communities have seen *all* the practitioners of a given specialty relocate to other states because of the cost associated with malpractice insurance, leaving large geographical areas without needed specialty coverage.[12] In the recent Institute of Medicine report on hospital-based emergency care, the authors cite a survey that reveals that 36 percent of neurosurgeons were sued by patients they saw in the ER.[13]

By its very nature, emergency medicine is a high-risk endeavor. The patients are often in critical condition, many have mitigating factors such as drug or alcohol intoxication, life and death decisions have to be made in an instant, and the prognoses are not nearly as favorable as in other settings. Americans have been ingrained with the idea that if an outcome is less than perfect, someone must be to blame. Thus, if your loved one dies despite the heroic efforts of each and every member of the trauma team, they must have failed him or her. And there are plenty of personal injury attorneys around to try and help you prove it. My own personal encounter with a malpractice suit (detailed in the previous chapter) was the result of a patient I treated through the emergency room.

As a result, more and more specialists are wondering aloud why they would put themselves in jeopardy caring for emergency room patients. Why should they interrupt their elective practices, expose themselves to HIV and hepatitis C infections, work long into the night, all for little or no compensation? And then be at risk for being sued by that same patient or their family if things don't turn out just right? EMTALA doesn't answer that question. So the specialists just stop responding to ER consults and also drop off the call panels. Now, they too are unavailable to care for your son.

Finally, specialists throughout the country are abandoning the emergency room simply because they can. As physicians search for more efficient ways to maintain their incomes, one innovation has been the development of specialized, doctor-owned hospitals and surgery centers. This phenomenon has been remarkably rewarding for physicians by allowing them to select the least risky, best-insured patients for treatment in *their* facilities while diverting (there's that word again) the less desirable patients to their community hospitals. As I discussed in chapter 8, this practice gives specialists a venue in which to practice without the demands that may be imposed upon them as members of a community hospital staff. If the administration requires that specialists take ER call to maintain hospital privileges, those specialists can simply tell the hospital to stick that demand where the sun don't shine and take the work to their own facility.

An example of this was documented in a May 2007 article in *Modern Healthcare* entitled "Docs on the Do Not Call List."[14] The article tells of the situation in Rapid City, South Dakota, where the 26-bed Black Hills Surgery Center has five neurosurgeons on staff, but the area's major medical facility, the 369-bed Rapid City Regional Hospital, had only *one* to take ER call. Although they recently hired a second neurosurgeon, they also had to hire "locum tenens" brain surgeons to care for the people in their community who present to the ER with neurosurgical emergencies. So, you may ask, what about the other five neurosurgeons across town? Well, once again, these docs are no longer available to care for your son.

But what about that third and final trauma center, the venerated university hospital? Well, once again . . . good luck, amigo. You see, more often than not, the university centers are inundated with not only their own patients but fallout from the patients who couldn't get into the regional trauma centers because they were already inundated with fallout from the local hospitals who couldn't get their specialists to care for the patients because—all together now—"they didn't feel comfortable." So, all the university beds are filled, waiting lists stretch into days, and there is nowhere to care for your son. As a doctor in this country, I apologize.

Where does all of this leave us? It leaves us with an emergency room crisis that gets worse by the day. Between 1993 and 2003, the number of visits to U.S. emergency rooms increased by 26 percent from 90 million to almost 114 million, more than one visit for every three Americans![15] Many of these patients did not need emergency room care but had no other access to a physician, so the crowds began to swell. Yet during that same time span, our country actually saw the closure of 425 hospital emergency rooms, further exacerbating the overcrowding problem.[16]

In 2003, 501,000 ambulances were diverted to other facilities, almost one every minute of every day.[17] Imagine the precious seconds lost; imagine the lives that slipped away as they struggled frantically to find care . . . in America. Those numbers are only worsening. A 2007 study on the availability of specialty coverage in emergency rooms reported by the Washington-based Center for Studying Health System Change found that 73 percent of U.S. emergency rooms experienced inadequate coverage by medical and surgical specialists. In addition, they reported that 21 percent of patient deaths or permanent injuries from delayed treatment were the direct result of lack of specialist availability.[18]

On and on it goes. And people die. Like Devon Kramer . . . and your son.

· *12* ·

The Great American Patient

You Didn't Really Think I Would
Let You Off That Easily, Did You?

*S*everal years ago, I attended an interesting conference discussing health care reform in the United States. I was captivated by the bevy of speakers who were more than happy to indict the multitude of villains at the root of our health care crisis and was not too surprised by the list of the usual suspects paraded in front of us like perps in a police lineup. We heard how insurance companies rescinded care, how pharmaceutical firms gouged us for our much-needed drugs, and how hospital CEOs got rich by exploiting the unfortunate patients who entered their institutions. The list was endless . . . well, almost endless.

I was intrigued by all of the information and I was filled with righteous indignation by what I had heard. But I was also just a bit perplexed by the conspicuous lack of any mention of the individual patient's responsibility for the failure of the American health care system. When the final speaker had finished and the floor was opened for discussion, I ambled up to the microphone and asked the panel what I thought was a relatively innocuous question. Specifically, I wanted to know what role the panel thought the American public played in creating the health care crisis since we are, in general, a population of obese patients who smoke too much, drink too much, use illicit drugs, drive without seat belts or motorcycle helmets, and demand that our doctors order a $1,500 MRI scan within twenty-four hours of straining our low back muscles after moving our cooler of Budweiser from one corner of the patio to the other.

You would have thought that I had asked the question in a white hooded robe while holding a burning cross in my left hand. I was told, in no uncertain terms, that such a question smacked of racism and social elitism. I was not so courteously informed that poor behavior like smoking, drinking, and drug abuse occurred more commonly in minority and lower socioeconomic populations and that middle- and upper-class white America always tended to use the downtrodden as scapegoats for the country's problems. To the panel, my question was more of the same; I was blaming the victim. Duly chastised, I sheepishly retreated from the microphone, slipped quietly out the back door, and immediately went over to St. John's Catholic Church to confess my egregious sin to Father McCarthy.

And that, folks, is where the problem begins.

In the volumes of books and articles I have read on the American health care system, there is very little mention of the American patient as a "co-defendant" in the creation of our current crisis. As in the above exchange, most books, including this one, contain stories that portray patients as victims of unscrupulous insurance companies, avaricious pharmaceutical giants, incompetent physicians, and uncaring hospitals. But there is another side to those stories that must be told if we are going to honestly explore the issue of health care in America. And it is a side that at times exposes that the American patient is as culpable as Health Net or Pfizer for our current predicament.

It is probably appropriate to begin by examining America's lifestyle *choices*. I emphasize the word choices because I am truly convinced that's what they are. The apologists who chastised me for my insensitive question viewed obesity as an inevitable result of poverty, relating how it was less expensive for poor families to satiate themselves with empty calories from fast food meals than prepare healthy options with fresh vegetables and lean meats. They bemoaned the fact that many of these "victims" were single parents who worked long hours at a low-paying job, leaving them too little time and too little money to prepare nutritious home-cooked meals. It was quicker and cheaper to order a pizza or a Whopper with cheese and French fries. Now, I understand how difficult life can be for America's poor, I really do. But if that is the case, why not drive through McDonald's and order the salad and a Diet Coke rather than requesting the Big Mac Meal? Do you want that supersized? You bet!

Obesity in the United States is epidemic and it reaches across all socioeconomic boundaries; it is not merely a disease of the poor. According to the Centers for Disease Control and Prevention, two-thirds of all American adults are overweight and half of those are actually obese (defined as having a Body Mass Index of thirty or greater).[1] Not overweight, mind you, but obese. That figure places the United States as one of the most overweight, unhealthy countries in the world and is truly at the root of many of the health problems that plague our population. We have been aware for years that obesity is the direct result of poor dietary practices coupled with a lack of regular exercise—not so much of "big bones" or "glandular" problems.

In 1970, Crosby, Stills, Nash and Young released a hit song entitled "Teach Your Children." Unfortunately, it appears that we have. In 1980, 5 percent of children under the age of nineteen were considered to be obese. In 2006, that figure literally "ballooned" up to 17.6 percent and fully one-third of all American kids are now overweight.[2] It should come as no surprise since our young people now spend an average of three hours per day watching television, playing video games, or sitting in front of their computers doing who knows what. Physical education programs in schools have been disappearing at an alarming rate, so that currently only 25 percent of U.S. school children participate in any organized exercise program.[3]

This bodes poorly for America's future on many fronts. Obviously I wouldn't be betting on Team USA to win Olympic Gold in the 100-meter dash in the years to come, but more important is the effect on the general health and well-being of the American population as a whole. Obesity itself is bad enough, but the associated co-morbidities, such as heart disease, hypertension, and diabetes, are going to exact an overwhelming toll on our health care system. And that toll will be coming sooner rather than later, as 90 percent of overweight children already have at least one "avoidable" risk factor for heart disease.[4]

When my financial adviser and I discuss investment opportunities, I usually tell him to liquidate everything and put it all into kidney dialysis centers. Take it from me, that's where the smart money should go. Diabetes is spreading throughout our country like wildfire and currently afflicts almost twenty-five million Americans. The future is dismal for this dreaded disease, as another fifty-seven million of us are "borderline" or "pre-diabetics."[5] Diabetes has moved into seventh place among the leading causes of death across the United States, but the mortality figures are just the tip of the iceberg. In 2006, more than seventy thousand people died as a direct result of diabetes and it significantly contributed to the death of almost a quarter of a million others.[6] These deaths are indeed tragic, but once these patients die, they cease to utilize our finite health care resources. On the other hand, we now have a growing population of Americans living *with* diabetes who suffer the multiple complications associated with the disease and cost the nation $175 billion a year in care.[7]

Diabetes has become the leading cause of chronic kidney failure, and in 2005 almost 175,000 diabetics were placed on chronic renal dialysis (thus my investment tip). Blindness, neuropathy, and heart disease resulting from poorly controlled diabetes promise to emerge in the not so distant future as major causes of disability and are certain to voraciously devour health care resources in the years to come.[8] But let's not forget these are "victims," so show some compassion! Don't expect them to watch their diet or to initiate a program of regular exercise; after all that Subway "Foot Long" sandwich is only $5.00 and it's almost as "finger lickin' good" as a bucket of KFC. And did you say exercise? Dude, really, I'd love to but *South Park* is coming on in ten minutes. No, it's the fast food industry that's at fault for creating all those high-calorie, nonnutritious meals. We should leave these "victims" alone and really be going after Ronald McDonald and his band of merry "Hamburglars" for pinning these poor individuals down, prying open their pie holes, and stuffing them full of cheeseburgers. Oh, by the way, pass me my milkshake, please.

I understand that in the 1950s smoking cigarettes was "Kool." All of our cultural icons—movie stars, sports heroes, television personalities, and politicians—they all smoked. The tobacco industry and their Madison Avenue marketing firms were quite adept at convincing the American public that smoking was sophisticated, relaxing, even sexy and safe. In 1946, the R. J. Reynolds Tobacco Company actually began a six-year ad campaign featuring physicians with the tagline "More doctors prefer Camels than any other cigarette."[9] So it is difficult for me to take issue with the millions of Americans who adopted the habit before the long-concealed health studies linked smoking with heart disease, emphysema, and lung cancer. In 1964, the U.S. surgeon general, Luther Terry, finally shared with the American public the tremendous health risks associated with smoking and began waging an endless uphill battle to eliminate tobacco from the fabric of American lives.[10] Smokers in that era really were "victims." They were victims of an addictive drug and they were victims of an influential industry that suppressed the information exposing the risks associated with the use of their product. And now, almost fifty years later, most of those victims are dead and gone.

I have more of a problem characterizing today's smokers as "victims." The overwhelming majority of Americans who currently smoke were born after the surgeon general's proclamation and grew up in a society that hammered home the antismoking message long and hard. But somehow it's still not their fault. The most current estimates reveal that twenty-five million men and twenty-one million women over the age of eighteen in the United States smoke cigarettes. Those numbers represent about 23 and 18 percent of the population, respectively.[11] And indeed most of these smokers grew up in an era where the risks associated with smoking were clearly delineated and where a tobacco company's ability to advertise was significantly curtailed. These Americans also came from an era where they were inundated with antismoking campaigns in schools and in the media.

Yet . . . they *choose* to smoke.

According to the CDC, smoking costs Americans almost $100 billion per year in direct health care costs and almost as much in indirect costs due to missed work and loss of productivity.[12] At first glance, these annual costs should infuriate the rest of us who are bearing the burden of the smoker's poor choice. And we are indeed bearing that burden; for just as the panelists I mentioned at the opening of this chapter told me, smoking is a vice associated with lower educational and lower socioeconomic status. It is safe then to assume that smokers are well represented among those who are uninsured or on Medicaid. That has certainly been my experience in practice.

Much of what we do as neurosurgeons involves stabilizing the spine. Oftentimes this requires a "fusion" to restore alignment or prevent the vertebrae from slipping out of their normal position. There are multiple studies that clearly demonstrate a marked reduction in successful fusion rates in smokers. Nicotine exerts a deleterious effect upon the ability of bone cells to mature and solidify; therefore, many of us will refuse to perform an elective fusion on a patient who smokes. If we do, the outcomes are more often disappointing, so we tell patients they must quit smoking prior to and for at least six months after their surgery. I explain to these patients in great detail the consequences of a "failed" fusion.

In response, the vast majority of these patients spend the remainder of the consultation reciting a litany of reasons why they cannot quit and become angry with me for refusing to perform their surgery and depriving them of the treatment to which they feel they are entitled. They're victims! Even worse are those who promise to quit then show up just before or just after surgery with a positive nicotine level in their urine. And of course when they go on to a "nonunion" and have continued pain six months after the surgery, it becomes my fault.

But from a purely economic viewpoint of health care costs, in the long run smokers actually save the system money. Certainly in the short term, the direct costs associated with their care for lung cancer, heart disease, and emphysema are much higher, but on average, smokers die thirteen to fourteen years earlier than nonsmokers.[13] Studies have shown that over time, the resources saved by not having to support them for those additional years outweigh the costs incurred as a result of their care.[14] So maybe the politicians whose view of health care reform is primarily "cost containment" should introduce a bill to repeal all smoking bans.

Nicotine is just one of our country's "legal" drugs. However, its popularity among Americans is dwarfed by the other one: alcohol. Once again, I could devote pages to the recitation of statistics regarding the use of alcohol among Americans and the deleterious impact on the health of our citizens. According to the National Institute on Alcohol Abuse and Alcoholism (NIAAA), in 2001 alcohol consumption was costing America $185 billion each year.[15] Sixty-five percent of our population drinks alcohol to the tune of $90 billion per year. High school and college students actually spend more money on alcohol each year than they do on soda, milk, coffee, juice, or textbooks *combined!* Alcohol is involved in 50 percent of all motor vehicle fatalities, in 40 percent of all industrial work-related fatalities, and in almost half of all work-related injuries. At any given time, somewhere between 25 and 40 percent of all hospitalized patients are confined for alcohol-related accidents or illnesses.[16]

How much more should we spend on these "victims" at the expense of immunizations for America's children or effective cancer therapy for the uninsured or necessary medicines for our seniors? No one seems willing or able to answer that question. Why doesn't someone tell me what we should do with George Sutterfield? George is a thirty-two-year-old carpenter who for the past five years has been "between" jobs. He is married with two small children, but his wife kicked him out nine months before I met him because of his excessive drinking. He lives for the most part on the streets or in homeless shelters, and since he is unable to find work, he cannot afford to support his wife or the two children he fathered. He also cannot afford health insurance, although he somehow finds the resources to buy two six packs of beer and a pint of Wild Turkey each day.

Over a three-month period, George presented to our emergency room six times either for injuries sustained while drunk or as a result of seizures induced by his use of alcohol. In that three-month span, he received five CT scans of the brain, was hospitalized twice (and signed out of the hospital against medical advice on both occasions), and refused on each visit his physician's recommendation to enter a county-sponsored alcohol rehab program. On ER visit number seven, George suffered another seizure, fell to the ground, struck his head, and developed a large blood clot over the surface of the brain, rendering him comatose. I was summoned to the hospital, took him to surgery, evacuated the clot, and then nursed him in the ICU for nine days. Fortunately (or not), George recovered and once again refused a rehab program. His wife and his parents both refused to allow him to recuperate at home and George became *my* problem. He signed out of the hospital despite my strong objections, but he promised me he would stop drinking, take his medicine to prevent seizures, and keep his follow-up appointment with me in the office in a week.

Much to my surprise, George did keep his appointment (although he was an hour late) and told me he had quit drinking despite the fact that I could smell the strong odor of Wild Turkey on his breath. I was actually concerned he would spontaneously combust when he walked past the pilot light of our furnace. Also, he stopped taking his seizure medicine because didn't think he needed it since he hadn't had a seizure since his last hospital visit. George did have one question for me, however. He wondered if I could prescribe OxyContin for his headaches rather than his Vicodin because he heard it worked much better. And just for good measure, you should know that neither the hospital nor I were paid a penny for saving Mr. Sutterfield's life. So what do we do with George?

George Sutterfield is not an isolated case. Those of us who practice in a busy trauma center see a parade of George Sutterfields who drive drunk, crash, and expect us to put Humpty Dumpty together again, all at our expense. And what about those individuals who fill 25 to 40 percent of U.S. hospital beds with alcohol-related illnesses that prevent them from working, leaving them uninsured? Who is to bear that burden? Is it you? Is it the alcohol industry? Is it Congress? I'd really like to know where to send my bill.

Of course, obesity, tobacco, and alcohol abuse are all legal vices; the impact by the illegal ones overwhelms the system even further. Again, according to the National Institute on Drug Abuse, illegal drugs such as cocaine, marijuana, methamphetamine, and heroin add $161 billion to our economic burden annually.[17] It can be argued that the *choice* to use drugs should be left to the individual as many libertarians would maintain. Additionally, there is validity to the viewpoint that recreational drugs such as cocaine and marijuana are no different than alcohol. Since I often have a glass of wine with dinner, I consider it a harmless "enhancement" to my meal, but since I don't smoke a joint when I get home from a busy day, marijuana becomes a "vice."

I have always maintained that individuals should be free to live their lives and make their choices as long as those choices do not infringe upon the freedom of others and as long as they are willing to accept full responsibility for the consequences of such choices. But that isn't always how it works. Millions of Americans are mired in the downward spiral of drug abuse that prevents them from gainful employment, squandering the limited resources they do have and oftentimes wreaking a wave of destruction on their health and well-being. As a responsible society, we are left holding the bag. Once again these "victims" access our health care system much more frequently than the rest of us with what is essentially a self-inflicted condition and they expect us to foot the bill.

The devastation to the individual who abuses drugs is bad enough, but with increasing frequency, we find the consequences of their actions thrust upon their offspring in terms of neglect, abuse, and even health status. As many as forty-five thousand babies are born each year with prenatal exposure to cocaine or other drugs, resulting in low birth weights and possible lifelong developmental and neurological impairments.[18] Their cocaine-addicted mothers can't afford to take care of them, and even if they could, their own behavioral patterns probably exclude them from being effective parents. As a result, we now have an entire population of infants and children that truly should be considered "victims." The responsibility for their health care, as well as their daily existence, falls on our shoulders.

While we're on the subject of drugs, it seems like an opportune moment to segue into my "rant" on the subject of medical marijuana. I live and practice on the "Left Coast" in beautiful California, where for years the debate about the medicinal use of marijuana dominated health care forums. On one side of the issue are those who supported the drug's use and argued that it would effectively control pain in the terminally ill who, for various reasons, developed a tolerance to increasing doses of opiates (such as morphine) or could not tolerate their side effects. In addition, with the AIDS epidemic raging through San Francisco and Los Angeles, proponents pointed to the appetite-stimulating effect of cannabis in hopes of offsetting the emaciation so often associated with the disease. They looked back on their college years and recalled fondly how smoking a joint induced "the munchies" and led them to devour an entire box of Cap'n Crunch in one sitting. On the other side, of course, were those who saw no rational basis to "legalize" another drug and facilitate the acceptance of marijuana use for any reason.

Well, of course, this is California, so the compassionate arguments trumped any objective scientific discussion of marijuana's benefits, and the voter-sponsored initiative Proposition 215 was passed in 1996.[19] I have been seeing patients continuously for the ensuing sixteen years since the law was enacted, and in all that time I have not *once* encountered a patient using legally prescribed medical marijuana for terminal cancer or AIDS-related emaciation. Sixteen years! Every single patient in my practice who is using medical marijuana does so for chronic low back pain, although I did come across a young patient recently who was prescribed marijuana for what I assume was his "terminal" carpal tunnel syndrome. Invariably, these patients are also on high-dose oral narcotics (I thought the pot was supposed to replace that?), are usually unemployed, and are either uninsured or on the state Medicaid program. Now you can argue that the reason they are uninsured and unemployed is that pain precludes them from working. However, in my experience most of these patients have normal or very underwhelming MRI findings and present with a multitude of contradictory complaints that do not conform to their objective physical or radiological exams.

So California now has a plethora of medical marijuana clinics (or cannabis clubs, as they are called) manned by an army of Dr. Feelgoods who open the candy store to anyone with the money to make the buy. For the life of me, I cannot understand why we can't treat marijuana like any other pharmaceutical and have the FDA simply require Class I randomized, double-blinded, and controlled studies assessing the drug's efficacy and side effects while comparing it to the medications currently available on the market. I guess that would be depriving needed treatment to all those "victims" of cancer, AIDS, and, of course, chronic back pain and carpal tunnel syndrome.

American patients have become a population of "whiners" (similar to the doctors who care for them as I discussed in chapter 7) who demand an operation, a pill, and now even a marijuana joint for whatever ails them. They recoil at any suggestion that they participate in their health care by exercising moderation when they belly up to the bar or the dinner table. They swear to their physicians that they "hardly eat anything," really do exercise regularly, and are at a loss to explain the five- to ten-pound weight gain at each annual checkup. It then becomes the responsibility of the system to deal with their illnesses. Obese? How about a gastric bypass or maybe one of those motorized wheelchairs that will get you to and from Hometown Buffet for the all-you-can-eat lunch? Diabetic? Here's some insulin and an appointment with the dialysis center. Emphysema? I know it's too hard to quit smoking so let me get you a portable oxygen tank but please be careful when you light up around it. As an added bonus, all you "victims" will be put on permanent disability just to make sure you don't have to contribute a dime for your care. Let your children and grandchildren do that for you. After all, isn't that what families are for?

We hear American patients whine about the expectations that physicians have for their role in maintaining their well-being. It's just too hard. But they also whine about the high cost of the health care system to which they have abdicated their responsibility for treatment. And they do far too little themselves to help control those costs. The American public is appalled at the cost of their insurance premiums. They are outraged at the price of their medications and downright incredulous when they have to plop down a $10 co-payment when they see their physician. They don't seem to be quite as agitated when they are asked to fork over $175 for an "awesome" ticket to the latest Eagles concert or $65 for a bleacher seat in New York to see the Yankees play Boston or even that same $10 co-payment to see Avatar in 3D. For some reason a $7 hot dog, a $10 beer (or two or three or four), and a $5 bag of peanuts is perceived as greater value than the thirty minutes their primary care doctor spent with them the day before trying to get a better handle on their diabetes and hypertension.

As to insurance, it always amazes me when I see patients who elect to enroll in the least expensive insurance plan go ballistic when they finally have to access that plan and come face to face with the limitations. They never complain while they are healthy and saving hundreds of dollars a month in a restrictive HMO Plan that limits which specialists they can see and what medications they can be prescribed. They aren't really concerned about a

$10,000 deductible plan since they're never sick and don't go to the doctor much anyway. Every month their sad sack of a neighbor is paying higher premiums when those dollars could be put to better use at the Indian Casino or buying the winning lottery ticket. But if they are unfortunate enough to develop a brain tumor or suffer a heart attack, then to hell with the HMO provider panel, they want to see the best surgeon in town even though he is not contracted with the HMO. Even though they have been saving thousands every year in premiums, it is now the insurance company who is greedy and who wants to force them to see the neurosurgeon or cardiologist contracted in their network. It's unfair! They're victims! Well, guess what? You can't have it both ways so just jump in the freaking "*Waa*mbulance" and quit whining.

But Americans won't quit whining. They'll whine about how government interferes in their lives and how socialism is right around the corner. I wonder how many of those who screamed and yelled bloody murder at the Tea Party rallies or town hall meetings denouncing health care reform are covered by Medicare, a government program. I also wonder how many receive social security benefits, another government program. How many are on disability, receive veterans' benefits, or access their state's Medicaid program? No, they'll rant against government-sponsored programs, but are quite comfortable, thank you, taking advantage of those "government programs" that benefit them.

Heaven forbid that intrusive government forces them to behave responsibly. How dare those bureaucrats pass a law mandating they wear a seat belt while driving? This is America, buddy! I don't need some stupid law telling me what I can and can't do in my own car! And where does Big Brother get off telling me that I have to wear a helmet when I ride my Harley or force my kids to put one on when they get on their bikes? It's my life and they're my kids! This is America, damn it . . . land of the free and home of the brave!

Well, America is becoming less the land of the free and more the land of the freeloader. In my own state of California, when a motorcycle helmet law was being debated in the state legislature in the 1990s, as expected there was strong opposition to it by motorcyclists, as well as civil libertarians, who felt government had no right to micromanage the lives of its citizens.[20] There were cries that helmets significantly diminished the pleasure cyclists experienced while driving along the gorgeous California highways with the wind blowing through their flowing hair. They even argued that helmets caused more accidents as a result of diminished hearing and vision, despite evidence to the contrary.

However, these opponents had a more difficult time addressing the data that showed that helmet use significantly reduced death and disability rates in those who wore them.[21] More compelling was the revelation that half of all motorcyclists treated in emergency rooms are either uninsured or eventually covered by the state and federal Medicaid programs.[22] Once again, we must return to the argument that people should indeed have the right to make choices, including the choice to wear a motorcycle helmet or not, as long as they bear the full responsibility of the consequences for those choices. Since at least half of California's bikers are not covered by private insurance, the rest of us become financially responsible for their care when they are injured. If we're paying the bill, then we do indeed have the right to expect those individuals to take measures, such as the use of a helmet, to reduce our potential liability. Otherwise, we become the "victims."

When the HIV epidemic was in full bloom, many health care providers, including doctors, nurses, and first responders, such as firemen and paramedics, were duly concerned about the transmission of the disease in uncontrolled emergency situations where blood and other body fluids flow freely. Those of us in trauma centers across the country simply adapted by assuming every patient was HIV positive, and we took the necessary precautions to protect ourselves and our loved ones from inadvertent transmission. Gowns, masks, gloves, and goggles became the uniform de jour in ERs across America. Yet, despite all these precautions, there were the rare instances of health care workers being infected by the patients for whom they provided care.

Some physicians and nurses responded by refusing to treat patients who were known to be infected with the virus or who were members of the demographic population of high-risk individuals. Understandably such actions infuriated the gay community, who classified such behavior as discriminatory. In addition, refusing to care for a patient with AIDS was contrary to all principles of the Hippocratic Oath and contrary to the traditions of American physicians. Thus, heated debate ensued and eventually laws were enacted that prohibited health care providers from selectively refusing to treat patients.[23]

HIV-positive patients did receive treatments and those of us who provided the care did take precautions, but still there were occasions when blood or other body fluid contamination occurred. When that occurred and the HIV status of the patient was unknown, we would simply order an HIV test of the patient so that we could put the provider's mind at ease. But lo and behold, the patient once again became a "victim." By ordering an HIV test we were seen to be *invading the patient's privacy*. Consequently, it became illegal for health care workers, exposed to blood or body fluids of a patient while providing care, to order an HIV test on the patient without the patient's permission or that of his or her family.[24] So now, if I come into the emergency room to treat a head-injured, uninsured heroin addict who was driving drunk and I get splattered by his blood in my attempts to resuscitate him, I have to ask his permission to run an HIV titer on him. If he refuses my request, I have to assume I am infected and take serial blood samples until I can prove otherwise, all the while taking precautions to protect my wife, my children, and even my patients. How about that? Finally, I'm a victim.

Lastly, all of us who make up the intricate quilt we call the American public deserve just what we are getting for sitting back idly and allowing our elected leaders to lead us like sheep to the slaughter at the altar of special interests. We let televangelist-like political commentators spoon-feed us the information we want to hear and ignore reasoned debate on the other side, all the while regurgitating the hogwash on both ends of the political spectrum. We are too lazy to research information ourselves and prefer to let others do the work and tell us how to think. Whether we subscribe to MoveOn.org or Rush Limbaugh, it's much easier to simply accept blindly the "facts" they want us to believe and wave our banners and scream our liberal or conservative slogans in front of the rolling cameras of CNN or Fox News. We continue to tolerate a political system where elected officials receive obscene amounts of campaign contributions from a wide range of special interests, then believe those officials when they look into the cameras with all the sincerity they can muster and tell us such gifts had no influence on their votes. Shame on them, but more importantly, shame on us.

As the debate over health care reform moves forward and as we scrutinize the roster of players responsible for the debacle, let's not overlook the culpability of the American patient in the discussion. Certainly, at times they really are victims who fall prey to insurance companies they are impotent to confront, to pharmaceutical manufacturers who have convinced them they are sick and in need of the magic pill they have to offer, to physicians who are too busy to listen to their complaints, to hospitals whose care sometimes comes at a cost too great to bear, and to their elected representatives who serve their campaign donors and well-heeled lobbyists rather than those who put them in their position of influence. But sometimes these victims deserve their share of the blame for the demise of quality health care whether it's politically correct to do so or not.

Yo, Father McCarthy! Keep that confessional door open, will you? I'll be right back in.

• 13 •

Solutions to the American
Health Care Crisis

My Wife Has Always Accused
Me of Being a "Know-It-All,"
So Here's My Chance to Prove It

$\mathcal{O}$nce again, as Americans, we find ourselves in the throes of a national debate on health care reform that never seems to end. Even the passage of the Patient Protection and Affordable Care Act, signed into law by President Obama on March 23, 2010, has not quieted the critics on either side of the issue. To many of us the raging controversy is not a new one. From Theodore Roosevelt to Harry Truman to Lyndon Johnson to Richard Nixon to Bill Clinton and now to Barack Obama, America's leaders have long realized that our health care system is broken. We are beginning to understand that a sizable population of our fellow citizens have little or no access to the advanced technology that defines American medicine. Many of us are embarrassed, or certainly should be, when the family of a young leukemia patient is forced to have their neighbors sponsor a community car wash or spaghetti dinner to try and offset just a fraction of the enormous costs involved in saving the child's life. We learn that the family may be forced to sell their home or to declare bankruptcy in order to assure this young victim receives the care he so desperately needs. This would not happen in Canada or Great Britain or France or Sweden or Japan or Germany or Spain or Switzerland or Denmark or any number of other countries throughout the developed world. But it happens in America . . . the most prosperous nation on the planet.

Believe me when I tell you that I understand what I am talking about. At the age of fourteen my son, Grayson, developed a highly aggressive malignant lymphoma diagnosed the morning after he graduated from junior high

143

school. Initially, the prognosis was dismal, but we were fortunate enough to find our way to Michael Link, an exceptional pediatric oncologist at Stanford University. As a result of the tireless efforts of the Stanford researchers, several innovative treatment options were developed and Gray was placed into one of their experimental clinical protocols. The yearlong chemotherapy treatments were brutal and, as you can well imagine, extraordinarily expensive. But fifteen years later, my son is alive, healthy, and free of any residual cancer. My wife and I thank God every day for Michael Link and Stanford University. And I also thank God for my insurance carrier, for even though I am a well-compensated neurosurgeon, without insurance, the financial impact on my family would have been overwhelming.

So I can be counted among the 83 percent of Americans happy with their insurance.[1] My premiums were significant, but I was fortunate enough to earn a salary that allowed me to afford the coverage I needed. However, I remember coming home from Stanford after one of Grayson's cycles of chemo and seeing an announcement in the local paper about a fund-raising dinner to be held at the fairgrounds to benefit a family who had racked up over a quarter of a million dollars in medical bills for their son's leukemia treatment. The glaring inequities of our system were staring me right in the face, just as they do for millions of Americans every day.

We have now reached the breaking point, where forty-seven million Americans have no insurance and where a similar number have insurance that is so inadequate they might just as well have none,[2] or they have a policy that is accompanied by such high deductibles and limited benefits that adequate treatment spells financial ruin. Americans now spend in excess of 17 percent of our gross domestic product on health care, with projections of catastrophic increases in the decades to come that will cannibalize all social programs that currently exist.[3] And we learn that despite such unparalleled expenditures, we are mediocre at best in providing effective care to our citizens when compared to every other industrialized country.[4] We have large companies, such as General Motors, losing their competitive edge as more and more of their profit goes to paying the costs associated with their employees' health insurance. We also have small businesses unable to provide the same benefits to their workers since rates for their premiums are prohibitively high. If those employees must purchase insurance themselves, the costs are even higher and must be paid for in after-tax dollars.

We have insurance companies that have raised premiums beyond the reach of many Americans while providing their stockholders with handsome returns and their executives with obscene compensation packages. They deny policies to those who need them most (with preexisting conditions) and they cancel the policies of their clients who become ill with expensive maladies, while their staffs are awarded bonuses for finding loopholes to deny care. We have pharmaceutical companies that use their innovative talent to simply produce an endless array of "me too" drugs that offer no benefit over those already existing on the market and then charge us three to four times what patients in Canada, Mexico, or Europe pay for the same medication.

American doctors might just as well join the United Auto Workers as they practice assembly line medicine, moving patients through as rapidly as possible and handing them off to midlevel providers such as physician assistants and nurse practitioners. Some of us continue to perform procedures of dubious benefit that have not been proven effective because, as bank robber Willie Sutton replied when asked why he robbed banks, "that's where the money is." And increasing numbers of us refuse to care for patients who present to our emergency rooms, instead opening our own specialty hospitals or diagnostic centers where we can cherry-pick the well insured and abandon the poor to struggling local hospitals. And speaking of hospitals, many of these havens have forsaken their original mission to provide care for the community they serve and instead look to provide admirable returns to the community who invests.

It seems that the only beneficiaries of American medicine are Wall Street money managers, big business executives, and politicians who line their pockets with contributions from the multiple special interests who have the most to gain from preserving the status quo. The trial lawyers, whose fierce battles for potential malpractice victims operate in a dysfunctional system that protects neither the patient nor the medical community, make sure that the Democrats' campaigns are well funded. The insurance and pharmaceutical lobbyists assure Republicans are equally endowed.

But we'll debate and we'll make it look as if we are truly concerned about the issue of health care. As has happened before, we will again allow the debate to be framed by the extremes on the right and on the left, so much so that meaningful and rational discussion will have no seat at the table. We will watch the television news programs on MSNBC, CNN, or Fox News broadcast snippets of "town hall meetings" where the courteous exchange of ideas and information is sacrificed to the vitriolic ranting of the American fringe, many of whom aren't really interested in learning the facts but instead insist on parroting the mindless tirades of their celebrity pundit de jour. We had none other than House Speaker Nancy Pelosi characterizing those who opposed the original Democratic plan as "un-American" or having "swastikas on their shirt sleeves."[5] And we have none other than former vice presidential candidate Sarah Palin characterizing the discussion of advance directives (where patients are given the opportunity to let their doctors and families know what they would want if they became incapacitated) as the establishment of Obama Death Panels that would euthanize her son with Down's Syndrome and her elderly parents.[6] Shame on both of them. Such rhetoric is inflammatory and counterproductive and has no place in the discussion of reforming our health care system. They are supposed to be *leaders* and, as such, the onus is on them to act responsibly and encourage their constituency to do the same.

Although it may serve a political purpose, it serves no constructive purpose for us to mischaracterize what either side is proposing. By doing so we waste precious time responding to inane allegations and counter allegations rather than really discussing the merits of various options. I carefully read through President Obama's plan for reforming health care and was amazed to see it demonized as supporting a "single-payer system," as a governmental takeover of health care, as kicking people out of Medicare, as forcing Americans to fund abortion on demand, as providing full benefits to illegal aliens, as denying care to the elderly, and as creating Death Panels. Give me a break. Look, there is a lot about Obama's plan that I think is naïve and, from a practical viewpoint, unworkable, but we have to start the debate somewhere and if we, as Americans, buy into all of this intentional misinformation, we will never address the complex problems that plague the current system.

We quickly observed all of the special interests showing their true colors and working diligently to make certain their piece of the health care pie was left intact. It was just about three years ago when the president stood on stage with representatives of the American Medical Association, the American Hospital Association, the pharmaceutical industry, the insurance industry, and the like, hands held high, pledging to work together to solve the health care crisis. That is, as long as reform doesn't reduce reimbursement to physicians, Mr. President. That is, as long as you don't cut Medicare funding for hospitals, Mr. President. That is, as long as you don't offer a public option that competes with private for-profit health insurance companies, Mr. President. That is, as long as you promise to continue to forbid Medicare from negotiating for lower medication prices for its members, Mr. President. That is, as long as you promise not to support a national tort reform package capping limits on malpractice awards, Mr. President. That is, that is, that is . . . are you getting it yet, folks?

I attended a town hall meeting in early August of 2009. Our congressional representative, the Honorable Wally Herger, held a meeting with local physicians to discuss health care. I must admit that it was lively, but courteous, and at a minimum brought to the forefront many issues that physicians were in a unique position to discuss. In the open conversation that ensued, the congressman agreed that health care needed to be reformed, although in his words it was "the greatest health care system in the world." (Makes you wonder why it needs reform then, doesn't it?) He went on to decry the manner in which the Democrats and the president tried to ram this reform through at breakneck speed. I had to agree wholeheartedly; something this important takes time to get right, and careful deliberation and debate are essential. But I also understand the thinking in Washington: the longer one waits to pass a bill, the more objections arise, making it important to the president that it was passed before the August recess. I agreed with my congressman that it was more important to do it right than to do it fast. But he went on to say that polls have shown that 80 percent of Americans are happy with their insurance, again suggesting that the problem is not so critical. I wonder how many of those 80 percent were on Medicaid . . . or how many had $10,000 deductibles . . . or how many had a $250,000 lifetime benefit limit . . . or how many were uninsured.

The problem with using such polling figures is that this crisis and this debate are not about the "haves"; they are about the "have-nots." This debate is about the Bob Resnicks (chapter 2) and about the Devon Kramers (chapter 11). Just because my employer or I can currently afford the premium for a generous insurance package doesn't mean the system is working. The system *must* work for the least of our citizens in order for it to be the "best in the world."

Can we really fix health care? Who has the right solutions? What is the best blueprint for meaningful reform? The answer to the first question is easy, for it is not a question of *can*—we *must* fix heath care if we hold out any hope of continuing as a nation of prosperity and providing an admirable quality of life for our children and grandchildren in the generations to follow. It is our responsibility and we are doomed to failure if we simply abdicate our role to the politicians and special interests that got us here in the first place. As to who has the right solutions, the answer is everyone and no one. A multitude of brilliant, well-intentioned individuals from all walks of life have weighed in with opinions on how to best address the many issues that challenge the delivery of health care in America. Many of these ideas are innovative and represent thoughtful, plausible solutions to specific issues related to health care, but none address all the issues adequately. We therefore have a moral imperative to listen to all sides of the debate and extract the best ideas from each contributor. We are compelled, as a great nation, to craft a reform policy that provides each American with the highest level of *effective* care under the practical restraints of what our society can *afford*.

Although I have practiced medicine since my graduation from medical school in 1977, I don't consider myself a health care policy "expert" or purport to have all the answers to reforming our health care system. But I can speak as a physician who has for thirty-five years experienced, alongside my patients, the frustration, anger, and at times, tragedy associated with navigating the barriers our system has placed between patients and their care. In the following pages, I present proposals to address a wide variety of issues that I feel are essential if meaningful, enduring reform is to come. I readily admit that these solutions are not exclusively mine. They are an amalgamation of ideas that has resulted from my own experiences and those of my patients. They have been inspired and fine-tuned by a number of exceptional individuals whose opinions have enlightened and encouraged me. Throughout the countless hours of research I devoted to this work, I have been awed by the insight, dedication, and honesty of the many contributors to this national debate on all sides of the various issues.

So, ladies and gentlemen, fasten your seatbelts and make sure your seatbacks and tray tables are in the upright and locked position, as we prepare to discover just how to fix health care in America . . .

UNIVERSAL COVERAGE: WHO DO YOU THINK YOU ARE, MICHAEL MOORE?

Michael Moore's 2007 documentary film *Sicko* is a wonderful movie. Michael Moore's 2007 documentary film *Sicko* is a terrible movie. And that's the truth! Moore, who has become America's ultimate liberal documentarian, has produced a variety of films designed to address everything from General Motors' corporate destruction of Flint, Michigan (*Roger and Me*), to gun control (*Bowling for Columbine*), to the Bush administration's response to the World Trade Center bombings (*Fahrenheit 9/11*). I have seen most of his movies and to say they are provocative is an understatement. But when I heard he was coming out with a film on America's health care system, I was intrigued. *Sicko* provided Moore with an extraordinary opportunity to catalyze a debate about the perceived failure of the U.S. health care complex. Indeed, he exposed a multitude of shortcomings inherent in our system of delivering care, many of which are chronicled throughout the chapters of this book. Unfortunately, Moore's movie suffered from the same inherent flaw that characterizes all of his documentaries—lack of balance.

There is no mistaking that Michael Moore resides somewhat to the left of Rush Limbaugh, Arlen Specter, Barbara Boxer, Al Franken, and probably even Hugo Chavez. As such, his message suggests that *everything* about American health care is a failure and that *everything* about health care in England, France, or Cuba is absolutely ideal. Although he is lionized by the choir in the far left, Moore loses credibility with not only the far right but many in the political center where this debate must take place. I find it hard to imagine that every single patient in these other countries is delighted with their care or that all doctors who work in the British National Health System drive luxury cars and live in upscale London apartments, while not a single American in the movie seems even remotely happy with any aspect of health care in America.

Moore is a flaming liberal—we all know that—so his message will always be perceived as flaming liberal hogwash, whether it's true or not. And that is the problem with attaching labels to ideas when discussing health care reform. "Socialized medicine" is historically the most commonly used term to define any attempts to achieve health care coverage for all Americans. It was used by the Democrats, as well as the Republicans, to repudiate Harry Truman's attempt to establish a national health plan and, with the Communist menace at America's doorstep, was remarkably successful.[7] Over the past sixty-odd years, the term has been effectively attached to the concept of "single-payer plans," "universal coverage," "national health service," and currently to the "public government funded option," each time with predictable results.

Are these really the same entities? Will their adoption really result in a Communist takeover of our beloved country? Well, the short answer to both questions is no! As a matter of fact, the long answer to both questions is no! But maybe I should elaborate, and an appropriate place to begin is with the concept of "universal coverage." This term is rather straightforward and really it means nothing more than assuring that every individual in the United States has some form of health insurance. It does not dictate what type of insurance, who pays for it, what it covers, or who administers it. Universal coverage simply means everyone has an insurance card.

Each time the debate on health care reform is resurrected, the focus of discussion is always on covering the uninsured or providing universal coverage. OK, this is good, you needn't be afraid. Very few of us would argue that providing health care to everyone is a bad idea, especially in light of the horror stories recounted in this book and others, as well as at the many town hall meetings across the country. So let's not bristle at the term "universal coverage"; don't worry, there will be plenty of things for everyone to loathe about health care reform as we move forward.

The big problem with universal coverage is that all it does is put you on a team. It doesn't necessarily mean you will get a chance to play. As I mentioned in chapter 2, there are plenty of "insured" patients in America who, for all practical purposes, have no access to health care. How often would you see your doctor for preventative care or well-baby checks if your policy had a $10,000 deductible and you had to pay for each visit? If you have a policy that has a $250,000 cap on benefits, you still may lose all you own if your wife develops leukemia and eventually needs a bone marrow transplant, or your son suffers a serious head injury that requires extended care in the ICU and months of rehabilitation. See how easy it is to see a doctor if you are on Medicaid? You're insured, but the reimbursement is so dismal that most physicians won't see you.

In mid-August 2009, I consulted on Laura Cardenez, a thirty-four-year-old woman on Medicaid, who had been progressively losing vision over the course of a year. None of the ophthalmologists in her community would see Medicaid patients, but after several months she got an appointment with a nurse practitioner in one of the local Medicaid Clinics. After fighting for two more months with the Medicaid office in Sacramento, she finally received authorization for an MRI scan, which revealed a large tumor in her pituitary gland at the base of her brain.

My office was contacted by her nurse practitioner, and we arranged to see her two days later. It was obvious she needed surgery as soon as possible, but with tumors such as this, it is important to have a baseline vision examination by an ophthalmologist, as well as a complete endocrine workup to assess the status of her hormonal system. Yet the ophthalmologists reiterated that they did not take Medi-Cal (California's Medicaid Insurance). In addition, the endocrinologist I contacted informed us that the next available appointment for a Medi-Cal patient was ten months away. I eventually got the consultations by begging, cajoling, and threatening, but this exemplifies the barriers that will still be in place despite a system that provides "universal coverage."

Health care reform will not work if we consider the job complete just because everyone has an insurance card. Universal coverage must include universal access or else the plight of patients like Laura Cardenez will continue. It is imperative that our system offers the same benefits for all and that it provides similar reimbursement for physicians so that access is not denied. President Obama can talk about affordable insurance for everyone and, with his formula, indeed get the forty-seven million uninsured an insurance card. But I doubt his plan will get them access. So how can we achieve such lofty goals without spending ourselves into a financial Armageddon?

One idea is the much maligned "single-payer" proposal most often associated with the far left and assured to strike terror in the hearts of all freedom-loving Americans. Ask almost anyone to define "single-payer" and inevitably you will hear the term "socialized medicine." It is important to understand what socialized medicine is and what it isn't if we are going to have meaningful debate about health care reform. In a system of socialized medicine, the government, through taxes, is responsible for all aspects of the delivery of medical care to its population. The government owns and manages all health care facilities such as hospitals, clinics, laboratories, and diagnostic centers.

Physicians, nurses, technicians, housekeepers, hospital administrators, and all other individuals associated with health care are governmental employees and receive their paychecks from the central government, similar to the current Veterans Administration or Military Hospital System. All citizens have the same insurance card and, theoretically, have the same access to care as everyone else. In a nutshell, that is socialized medicine.

As our health care system is currently designed, there are literally hundreds of different insurance companies that operate throughout the United States, all with different benefit packages, all with different premium rates, all with different guidelines as to whom they will and will not insure. Some are government run, like Medicare and Medicaid; some are private and not-for-profit, like the Kaiser Permanente Group; and some are private and for-profit like Aetna, WellPoint, Health Net, and United Health Care. Each of these companies operates differently from one another, and each individual company may operate differently depending upon the states in which they offer policies. Premiums are funded by a variety of sources including employers, individuals, and the government through taxes. Each company has its own set of guidelines to which providers must adhere and each has their own endless array of forms that must be submitted by providers to obtain reimbursement, also unique to each insurance carrier. This creates a massive bureaucratic nightmare for patients and providers that is prohibitively cost inefficient.

In a single-payer system, there are no longer a myriad of different companies—there is only one. That single insurance provider could be a federal program, such as Medicare, or possibly a private, not-for-profit entity that is regulated under federal jurisdiction. In any event, there are many obvious advantages to such a streamlined system. All premiums would continue to be paid by employers or individuals or through federal tax exemptions for low-income families. The resources we now dedicate to Medicare, Medicaid, the VA, and the Military Hospital System could also be channeled through this single entity. Such a system would drastically reduce paperwork and overhead for physicians and their office staffs. No longer would providers have to worry about different guidelines for different insurance companies nor would they be required to master the complex games that are often necessary to navigate the barriers erected by the multitude of players in our current system.

In a single-payer system each American would have the same insurance, the same card, the same benefits, and the same access, all without the endless hassle many commercial insurers now impose upon their beneficiaries. With a single-payer, there would be a single database that would facilitate the sharing of electronic medical records to make certain that when a patient presents unconscious or incapacitated to an emergency room, his or her past history, current medication regimen, and advanced directive wishes (provided by

Obama's Death Panels, of course) are all well known. In addition, that same database could provide us with invaluable information as to the outcomes of the care we provide, helping to assure that treatment is evidence-based rather than profit-based.

We already know that Medicare has the lowest overhead (reported to be less than 3 percent) and the highest percentage of resources devoted to direct patient care when compared to any of the private insurers.[8] In addition, patient satisfaction by Medicare recipients is exceedingly high.[9] On the other hand, commercial, for-profit insurers have overhead expenses that can easily approach 30 percent as they provide jaw-dropping compensation packages to their executives and handsome returns to their primary interest, their stockholders.[10] A single-payer system has no such financial obligations. It won't need a billion dollar advertising budget, nor will it need to employ an army of expensive lobbyists. From a patient point of view and a cost-efficiency perspective, "single-payer" should be a no-brainer.

But just how does the country pay for this new system? According to single-payer advocates, reducing the 25 to 35 percent overhead associated with the private insurance providers could more than pay for universal care. I must admit that I am dubious about such a claim, but according to independent studies published by the Government Accounting Office (GAO) in 1991 and the Congressional Budget Office (CBO) in 1993, sufficient resources are available in the current system to fund such a program by merely reducing those overhead costs to the 3 to 5 percent projected in a single-payer system.[11]

In addition, with universal coverage and universal access, patients with chronic diseases such as diabetes and high blood pressure would be seen earlier in the course of their illnesses. By instituting proper care in a timely fashion, complications such as heart attacks, congestive heart failure, renal failure, and the like would be dramatically reduced, resulting in significant additional cost savings. It is much less expensive to place borderline diabetics on Metformin and encourage a weight loss and exercise regimen than to place them on thrice-weekly kidney dialysis once the disease has progressed. Lastly, as the "negotiator" for 325 million plus patients, the single-payer system would be in an advantageous bargaining position with the pharmaceutical industry and device manufacturers, just like Canada and much of Europe are today. So why do so many voices oppose single-payer when it seems like a logical solution to America's health care woes?

Where do we begin? Aha! Dr. Lobosky, you snake! This is nothing more than *socialized medicine* in single-payer clothing! And that's exactly what opponents will try to tell you, because by affixing the label, they will certainly discourage you from actually looking at what it truly proposes. After all, do you want to be called a socialist (the same as a Communist, fascist, and bicyclist)? But if you remember the definition of socialized medicine we discussed earlier, you can see that single-payer doesn't fit the bill. At least that's what the single-payer proponents want you to believe. Although insurance may be concentrated into the hands of a single entity (and it doesn't need to be governmental, although it would most likely be), the services are all delivered by private, gun-toting, God-fearing, American capitalists. Each doctor still has his own practice to run as he or she sees fit; each hospital is free to operate as they see fit and compete against other hospitals that operate as they see fit. Pharmaceutical companies are free to produce whatever drugs they wish and sell them at whatever price the market will bear. Device companies can develop innovative products and price them at whatever level their competition and the market will allow. So, pay attention here (because soon Rush Limbaugh or Max Baucus will tell you otherwise): *single-payer is not socialized medicine!* The single-payer system is no different from the federal government's NASA program, Department of Defense, or Federal Highway Administration, which contract with *private, for-profit* companies to build their space shuttles, their stealth bombers, and the Interstate 10 corridor between Los Angeles, California, and Jacksonville, Florida.

So if we take the ideologues out of the debate, who else would oppose single-payer? Well, most obviously, the insurance industry, as they stand to essentially lose everything. With single-payer you wouldn't need Blue Cross, Aetna, United Health Care, Kaiser Permanente, Medicare, Medicaid, or any of the hundreds of other insurance providers across America. But you also wouldn't need CEOs making $30 to $50 million a year (see chapter 3) while double-digit rate increases further strap small businesses and individuals. You also wouldn't need that army of claims adjusters whose bonuses are predicated upon the number of patients whose care they can deny and policies they can rescind after becoming ill. Nor would you need all of those faceless benefits clerks who deny the tests, hospitalizations, and procedures requested by the treating doctors merely because they don't align with the guidelines in the voluminous corporate binder that sits upon their desks.

I suspect that Big Pharma would be none too happy with a single-payer system, either. After all, they have already spent millions upon millions of dollars to deny Medicare the right to negotiate medication prices for their 50 million patients. If a 50 million patient base scares them, just think what a 325 million entity would do. (Actually it might force them to bring prices more in line with what they charge patients in Canada, Mexico, or Western Europe.) I am sure we would hear that a single-payer system would create an unfair monopoly, devastate their profits, and reduce their available capital for—all together now—research and development. Without that R & D capital, they would be unable to find a better Viagra or continue the pipeline of "me too" copycat drugs they are currently offering to a grateful America.

In addition, the device manufacturers who provide us with everything from artificial joints to spinal pedicle screws to heart catheters to penile implants would most assuredly share the same concerns as their pharmaceutical brethren. Better bargaining power for the consumer leads to less profit for Wall Street and we can have none of that. If we morph American health care into a single-payer system, these device companies, such as Medtronic, Synthes, Stryker, and the like, will surely warn the public that they will no longer be able to invent "lifesaving" equipment and will rapidly go out of business. More than likely, they would not be able to continue to pay doctors to fly to exotic locales for "education and training" in the use of these devices.

The thought of a single-payer system terrorizes physicians and the hospitals where we treat our patients because although we are free to recommend any treatment we deem necessary and charge any fee we deem reasonable, that single-payer (who now controls approximately 325 million Americans) is also free to deny our recommended treatments and determine what fees they deem "reasonable." We are then free to take it or leave it. Single-payer proponents pledge that all entities involved in American health care will have a seat at the governing table.[12] They envision boards of elected directors who will negotiate fees with doctors and hospitals as well as drug and device manufacturers. They also assure us that physicians', hospitals', pharmaceutical companies', and device manufacturers' representatives will be an integral part of those boards and have significant input as to benefit packages and reimbursement schedules. To take that leap of faith and trust in what the single-payer activists promise is beyond what most of us involved in the delivery of American health care are able or willing to do.

When all is said and done, a single-payer system is nothing more than a monopoly and thus infused with all of the dangers a monopoly represents. Although proponents distinguish between socialized medicine (where everyone associated with health care is a government employee) and their system (where care is delivered by individual contractors), I can't help but view that line of thinking as disingenuous. At the end of the day, even though I run an "independent" medical practice, my paycheck, as well as the paychecks of all other entities, comes from the government, so eschewing the label "socialized medicine" is nothing more than a game of semantics.

I started writing this book without an agenda or a concrete plan as to how we fix our current system. I was more interested in pointing out the weaknesses inherent in American health care and making sure that the average American could understand what those weaknesses were and how they evolved. But as I continued my research and added chapter after chapter, it became obvious that mere criticism without a blueprint for reform would serve no useful purpose and assure my position in the ranks of those who love to complain but offer little constructive substance to the debate. Having reviewed the many different "solutions" to the health care crisis, I have begrudgingly come to the conclusion that from a purely patient care perspective, a single-payer system makes a lot of sense and deserves thoughtful consideration at the very least. But I am convinced that the American people are not ready to accept a single-payer model, despite poll after poll that indicates broad public support.

You can be sure that the politics of health care reform is such that the special interests who oppose such a system will certainly block any meaningful discussion of a single-payer proposal. Max Baucus, the senator from Montana, was charged with developing the Senate's version of health care reform. Senator Baucus is a Democrat, the party of the liberal left and the womb of the single-payer proponents. Yet when Senator Baucus announced the establishment of the Senate bipartisan committee to craft a health care reform bill, he assured us that all options would be on the table for debate—all options, that is, except for a single-payer system. If Senate *Democrats* won't even discuss single-payer as an option, it is hard to envision any scenario where such a plan would get traction. I wonder, is it possible that Senator Baucus—along with hundreds of other Democratic, as well as Republican, lawmakers—receives contributions to his reelection campaigns from those very same interests who oppose a single-payer system? It's just a thought.

So if a single-payer system is not an option, what other proposals are available and what are the chances that they may be enacted? Well, of course, we can simply maintain the status quo, pronounce American medical care as the "best in the world," and continue to let people die as health care expenditures consume more and more of America's resources. That's exactly what happened when the Clinton administration attempted to address the issue in the early '90s, but I really doubt we will see that history repeated today. The dirty little secrets of U.S. health care are now beginning to see the light of day and a sizable portion of the American public is justifiably enraged. That won't stop the special interests from doing their very best to suppress meaningful reform, but we have now gone too far in the debate and, if for no other reason than the political consequences of doing nothing, some type of compromise health care reform is certain to emerge.

Some will argue that the "market" is not the problem in health care; it's the solution. They will tell us that the trouble is too much regulation and not enough competition, assuring us that the answer lies in allowing the market to solve our health care crisis. Is this the same market that gave us the Savings and Loan scandal of the '90s, the accounting scandals of the Enron era, and the subprime mortgage meltdown of our financial institutions of 2008? I find it interesting that when Chrysler, United Airlines, Goldman Sachs, and AIG face financial ruin because of their participation in the "free market," they turn to the government for help. This is the same government they decry as a bastion of overspending inefficiency when someone suggests a "public plan" to cover America's uninsured. When the feds expend billions of dollars to rescue Wall Street, we call it an "economic stimulus package." When those same dollars are used to provide adequate insurance coverage so that low- and middle-class families can receive appropriate medical care, we call it "welfare."

As a practicing physician working in the trenches for almost three decades, I have become convinced that there is absolutely no role for free market policies in the portals of access to American health care. Pay attention here, my capitalist critics (and I am sure there will be plenty of you): I said just the *portals* of access (i.e., insurance companies and hospitals), not all aspects of our current system. I have no problem with the pharmaceutical companies and the medical device manufacturers operating in such a system. They should be free to create their new wonder drugs and innovative tools and then sell them to the system at whatever cost the market will support. If the drugs those free marketers create aren't "wonderful" enough or their tools aren't "innovative" enough, their profits will fall and their businesses will fail. All we will lose are underperforming companies who will be replaced by those who can do better. That is how the market works.

But insurance companies and hospitals are far too important in terms of providing our citizens with access to health care. It is they who determine who gets seen, what gets done, and at what cost. The conflict of interest here should be obvious to all. For-profit insurance carriers and for-profit hospital chains are, by their very nature and definition, in the business to make a profit—their primary responsibility is to shareholders, not patients. They answer to Wall Street and not to the thirty-seven-year-old father of two whose policy they rescinded after he developed lymphoma and required an expensive bone marrow transplant. If our system is to work, it is essential that we eliminate that conflict of interest that drives the for-profit hospitals like Tenet (as we discussed in chapter 6) to value volume over quality. We must also eliminate the for-profit insurance carriers, such as Health Net, who pay bonuses to their employees for finding loopholes that allow them to cancel policies for people who desperately need care the most.

One of the more controversial proposals in Obamacare was the inclusion of a publicly funded insurance entity to provide coverage for those who are unable to obtain it on the open market because of costs or preexisting conditions. This represented a significant step in the right direction that had to be done right if it was to succeed. Simply shifting the uninsured into Medicaid *will not work*, but the new plan proposes lowering eligibility thresholds so that close to twenty million of the uninsured will be shifted into that existing program.[13] Learn from the experience of Laura Cardenez. This is a patient who had insurance, California's Medicaid, was going blind, and still had to wait months to see a doctor (actually a nurse practitioner) in the local Medi-Cal clinic. Then it took two additional months for the clinic to obtain permission from the state to perform an MRI. Yet once the diagnosis of pituitary tumor was revealed, she was told no ophthalmologist would see her and that the next available appointment with an endocrinologist for a Medi-Cal patient was ten months away. Maybe you call that access, but I don't. Let's continue to berate Canada and shake our heads in disgust at the alleged long waits for services for our neighbors to the north while we ignore the identical problem here, sing "God Bless America," and pronounce our system as the *best in the world*.

So shifting a large portion of the uninsured Americans into the Medicaid program will not solve the problem. But there are more access difficulties looming in the current plan that made its way through Congress. There is much talk about paying for the reforms by reducing Medicare reimbursement to physician specialists and hospitals. At current levels, Medicare pays physicians about one half of our standard fees, which forces doctors, as the managed care plans have, to ratchet up the volume of procedures we do to maintain our incomes in the face of rising overhead. If they reduce fees by as much as 30 percent in 2012, as is proposed by the Sustained Growth Rate (SGR) formula, you are certain to see two phenomena emerge. First, thousands of physicians will stop seeing Medicare patients because they just won't be able to afford to. Access for the elderly will evaporate, and more and more Americans, insured Americans mind you, will hear that "the doctor *won't* see you now." Additionally, those physicians who continue to see Medicare patients will be forced to recoup the lost income by doing more procedures and ordering more tests, many of which will be unnecessary or of dubious benefit at best. Thus, solving the problem by reducing reimbursement to providers will only result in less access with little cost savings.

The "public option" was a cornerstone of the Democrats' original reform plans. This idea was designed to address the egregious practices that characterized many of the private insurance carriers. Those who were unable to obtain insurance on the open market because of cost, preexisting conditions, and the like, would be able to purchase insurance from a government-run program at a reasonable price. The plan would compete with private insurance companies and ideally force them to reduce premiums and discontinue their practice of refusing coverage to those with preexisting conditions or canceling the policies of patients who develop expensive illnesses.

The same insurance carriers who stood with President Obama on stage in the summer of 2009 and pledged their support of meaningful reform went berserk! Unfair! It will increase costs! It will cost jobs! It will reduce access! It will result in poor quality! And most importantly, it is nothing more than—are you ready?—*"socialized medicine"*! The special interest troops rallied, President Obama waffled, and like the single-payer system, the public option was taken off the table. I truly find it fascinating that the private insurance companies have no problem whatsoever with a public option for the elderly (Medicare) who are on fixed incomes and are the largest consumers of medical resources. Nor do they have a problem with a public option for the poor (Medicaid) who cannot afford the high premiums they charge. No, they only have a problem with a public option that competes with them for the relatively young, healthy, working population whose premiums are paid by their employers and who are much less likely to access the system. This is the group where the profit is made!

Even if a public option were retained, how we pay for it remains the $64,000 question, or maybe I should say the $2,600,000,000 question. Indeed, as with Medicare, the overhead costs we associate with private, for-profit insurance companies will be significantly less. But if the plan intends to use reduced reimbursement to physicians and hospitals as a way of making up the difference, the same access and overutilization issues I discussed above will certainly ensue. The only way we will be able to fund this "public option" is through more revenue generated by forcing employers who do not provide insurance for their workers to contribute to the fund or asking all Americans to do so (read, taxes!). We must, as a nation, come to the understanding that quality health care is not free and face the fact that every country that provides its citizens with quality universal coverage pays higher taxes than we do in the United States. We now have to struggle with the question of whether quality health care for all is a national priority, and if the answer is yes, we must be prepared to pay for it.

The market-based insurance carriers will have us all believe that a public option is the first step on the slippery slope to a single-payer, government-run system. The U.S. Postal Service certainly isn't a slippery slope for United Parcel Service or Federal Express, unless you mean a slope that slipped them into position as two of the nation's more profitable companies. Instead, the competition among them has made each more efficient and benefited us all. But United Health Group, Aetna, WellPoint, and Health Net will fight a public option tooth and nail. They don't want to compete with an entity that prioritizes patients and not profit. And they have the money to buy a lot of teeth and a lot of nails! By spreading around enough campaign contributions and funding enough television hit ads, the insurance industry made sure the public option evaporated. Most Americans were convinced that the disappearance was in their best interest.

But just look what happened when Scott Brown surprised the country by winning Ted Kennedy's long-held Massachusetts senatorial seat. He announced he would vote against the health care reform plan, assuring the dissolution of the filibuster-proof Congress for President Obama, and thus probably signaled the death knell for a bipartisan reform package. His election was truly a "game changer." And what was the insurance industry's response to Brown's proclamation? Within weeks, Anthem Blue Cross, a subsidiary of WellPoint, announced a 39 percent premium increase in California[14]—a 39 percent increase at a time when many Californians are struggling just to make ends meet in the face of soaring unemployment, plummeting home values, and unprecedented statewide deficits. But I guess we shouldn't be surprised because Anthem had only posted a $2.7 billion profit in the previous quarter.[15] Do you really think they would have had the moxie to initiate such an outrageous premium hike if Scott Brown hadn't been elected?

One of the most difficult tasks facing those who are truly concerned about reforming America's health care system is finding a compromise that keeps the special interest wolves at bay, but accomplishes meaningful and effective reform. The balancing act can be difficult and if reformers become fixed ideologues, America will be condemned to a colossal defeat of reasonable attempts to address the problem (as occurred in 1994). What has emerged is a plan that boasts of reform but in reality fails miserably to accomplish our goals. If we agree that a single-payer system is unrealistic, a public option is untenable, and the status quo is unacceptable, how do we craft a solution that provides universal coverage and universal access while controlling costs?

As a first step, insurance regulations should be federal and not state-based. Insurance carriers should be allowed to compete across state lines and not be bridled with the nightmare of having to play by one set of rules in California and an entirely different set of rules in Ohio. That policy is inefficient and chaotic and contributes to overhead costs. The government should develop federal guidelines that clearly dictate the basic benefit package in every American's health insurance policy. It should cover preventive care, well-baby checks for children, and annual physicals for adults. It must cover the cost for all reasonable treatments that are derived from evidence-based medical studies, including expensive bone marrow transplants.

The playing field should be leveled for all entities that provide health care coverage, and it is encouraging that insurance companies are now forbidden from denying policies or charging higher premiums to patients with preexisting conditions. In addition, the practice of rescinding the policies of those who develop expensive illnesses came to an end. I am amazed that we actually had to pass a law forbidding such egregious corporate behavior. The new plan also removes limits on the amount of care an individual can receive. If you get ill and need care, you will receive what you require.

Those patients who are not covered by their employers can now turn to state-instituted insurance co-ops and have the opportunity to purchase policies at the same rate as General Motors, Microsoft, and AT&T pay for their workers. Insurance is about pooled resources, as well as pooled risks, and it is blatantly unfair for the private carriers to cherry-pick the young and healthy while diverting the poor, ill, and elderly to the current "public options" of Medicare and Medicaid. Insurance companies should truly compete; they can charge what they must and if they can provide their policyholders with high quality at a reasonable cost, they will succeed. However, if they continue to inflate their overheads with eye-popping executive compensation, exorbitant marketing, and lobbying expenses, and create a bureaucratic nightmare for their customers and their providers, they will fail, as they should.

As a form of compromise I believe the "public option" proponents should give these companies an opportunity to play by this new set of rules with the understanding that if, after a finite period of time, progress is lacking, a public option would kick in. Alternatively, the federal government could mandate, as has been suggested by California Senator Dianne Feinstein, that all insurance companies must be "not-for-profit."[16] Such a mandate would set benchmarks for overhead costs as well as executive compensation. This would immediately change the focus of the insurance industry from the generation of profits to satisfy their Wall Street shareholders, to the satisfaction of their patients whose continued enrollment would be critical for their survival.

On June 7, 2011, Blue Shield of California CEO Bruce Bodaken wrote an op-ed piece in the *San Francisco Chronicle* that described the company's new policy of "capping" their profit at 2 percent of revenue. At the end of every year, any net income in excess of 2 percent will be returned to policyholders, physicians, hospitals, and their own charitable foundation. This is an encouraging move but one that will, of course, be eyed with much skepticism. The caveat included is that Blue Shield plans to continue the policy indefinitely, "so long as our board of directors determines that Blue Shield remains financially solvent, with sufficient funds to make the investments needed to stay competitive."[17]

For a system such as this to succeed, everyone must participate. In a single-payer, federally administered program, every legal U.S. citizen would be covered at the moment of their birth. In these alternative scenarios, federal law will have to mandate that everyone purchase a policy. Easier said than done! In his campaign for the presidency, Candidate Obama assured us that as his plan brought down the cost of health insurance, all Americans "would want to participate." However, he never adequately addressed what we would do with those who didn't sign up despite the tremendous opportunity provided by Obamacare. Look, folks, most Americans are hardworking, honest, and responsible. But there remains a sizable population who will continue to forgo health insurance, no matter how reasonably priced, so that they can put in that swimming pool, buy that new car, support their cocaine habit, or spend the potential premiums on a vast array of other priorities.

What happens when those individuals, the nonparticipants, present to the emergency room with their heart attacks or severe head injuries that occurred while driving drunk without their seatbelts? One option would be to simply deny them care. After all, they had the chance to obtain insurance like the rest of us, but made the conscious decision not to. Maybe they should be left to live or die with the consequences of their own choices. As hardened and as cynical as some of us might be, I cannot imagine that we, as a society, could morally sanction such a policy. Throughout this book, I have decried the fate of people who lose all they own as a result of medical catastrophes. But in this scenario, where citizens are given reasonable opportunity to participate and governmental assistance if needed, I have little problem with forcing them to relinquish their homes (and swimming pools) and life savings to pay for the care they now need.

The revamped health care reform plan addresses this issue by levying a tax penalty on those who fail to enroll. That penalty amounts to $95 or 1 percent of an individual's income (whichever is greater) beginning in 2014 and increases to $695 or 2.5 percent of income in 2016. The problem is that $695 or even $1,250 for those at the median income level of $50,000 per year is a miniscule drop in the bucket of care that would be expended on the above victims. Many would simply say, "Go ahead. Fine me $1,250 and then please pay my $185,000 medical bill!" To assure that all citizens share in the benefits of health care reform, we must find a way to assure that all citizens share in the burden, taking into account each American's financial capacity to pay. My suggestion is that when we file our tax returns every April, we provide proof of medical insurance. Those who don't will have the premiums deducted from their tax refunds or be assessed additional taxes to meet the obligation if a refund is not anticipated. In their infinite wisdom, however, in the new bill Congress explicitly stated that failure to pay the assessed penalties would *not* result in criminal prosecution or property liens.[18] Huh? If you don't purchase the mandated insurance, we will punish you with a fine, but if you don't pay the fine, we won't go after you. Now if that isn't a formula for a successful program, I don't know what is.

But if polls are to be believed, America remains schizophrenic on the idea that each of us should be required to have some form of health insurance. In early November 2009, Stanford University and the Robert Wood

Johnson Foundation conducted a survey of 1,502 adults for the Associated Press. When asked if they favored or opposed requiring everyone to have at least some form of health insurance, 67 percent of respondents supported such a measure. Yet when the same group was asked if they supported a law that would fine or tax those who refused to get insurance (unless they were poor), an almost equal number, 64 percent, opposed such a measure.[19] What the pollsters failed to ask was what exactly the respondents would then do to those who decided to skate by while the rest of us paid for health care. We cannot have it both ways! We cannot, as a nation, decide we must require everyone to have insurance, but then turn our backs and shrug our shoulders if they don't. That kind of thinking led to the crisis we now face. If we say no to a fine, no to a tax, and no to simply denying them care, how do we effectively deal with such a crucial issue?

We have to change the perception of health care as a "right" and make sure that the American public knows that right comes with "responsibility." There should be a co-payment attached to every doctor visit. It does not need to be expensive or cause financial pain, but it is an important way of reminding all of us that health care is not free. Hopefully such a policy would force each of us to consider whether that visit to the office of our busy family doctor or expensive emergency room for a runny nose really is necessary. If something is totally free, its value is diminished.

Lastly, we must find a way to compensate physicians and other providers in an equitable manner. As I have reiterated ad nauseam, the outlandish discrepancy in reimbursement between the commercial insurers and the governmental ones, especially Medicaid, creates a system that erects barriers to access and spawns overutilization to make up for the differences. I believe the federal government, in conjunction with *physicians* and medical economists, should set an appropriate fee schedule for medical services across the board. It is no more or less difficult for me to clip an aneurysm in a Medicaid patient than it is in a Health Net patient, therefore I should not be paid less for doing so in the former and more for doing so in the latter. (Now I've done it. I am sure the AMA and the American Association of Neurological Surgeons will be at my door tomorrow to rescind my membership.)

Universal coverage will succeed in improving America's health only if it improves *all* Americans' access. Without reasonable compensation among all the varied health care insurers that goal will not be realized. The anxiety we physicians experience when even considering such a plan as a federal fee schedule is due to the fact that we feel undervalued by the feds as well as the private carriers. We fear across-the-board cuts in reimbursement that might bring fee schedules more in line with Medicaid standards than Blue Cross.

That is why it is so imperative that such a panel have broad representation among private practitioners working in the real world.

Several years ago, I discussed with a number of policy makers the fact that in neurosurgery, elective spinal procedures were reimbursed at much higher levels than lifesaving, middle of the night, complex cranial procedures. I suggested increased reimbursement for trauma care as a way of addressing the growing trend of neurosurgeons opting out of emergency room call schedules. The response was not an acknowledgment that trauma care was indeed undervalued and important. Instead, several panelists opined that spine surgery was probably being overcompensated. And it is that thinking that characterizes much of federal and state policy and what we most dread. But I do think that, like other aspects of health care reform, compromise is possible so that every citizen may have equal access to the brilliant minds and extraordinary technology that define American medicine.

So congratulations! Through a variety of circuitous avenues we have succeeded in providing universal coverage for all Americans. Our work here is now done. I know at times this seemed painful, but it was worth the effort to finally fix America's health care system.

Not so fast, Dr. McDreamy. One of the major problems in addressing health care in America is the belief that insurance reform and universal coverage are the keys to ending the crisis when, in reality, they are only the beginning. If true reform is to succeed, there are many more issues that need be addressed. Far from being done, our work here has just started.

Read on!

EVIDENCE-BASED MEDICINE: YOU KNOW WHAT WORKS. I KNOW YOU KNOW WHAT WORKS. BUT DOES IT REALLY WORK?

After the dust settled on the Great Health Care Debate of 2010, we had hoped to find that we were indeed able to craft a bipartisan compromise that, for the first time in our country's history, assured each American citizen meaningful access to quality health care. It would have been an extraordinary accomplishment for us that could stand beside the many other monumental advances that America has bestowed on its people over the past 235 years. But unfortunately, as noble as this accomplishment is, there is a great potential for this initiative to cost us even more money than we now expend. As I alluded to in the prior section, insuring everyone is only the first step in reforming our system. Now comes the hard part: paying for it.

If equitable universal health insurance (not achievable under the newly devised plan, mind you) were to become a reality, we would essentially add one hundred million more patients into the American health care milieu. Not only will forty-seven million uninsured join the ranks, but those whose access was limited by high deductibles, lifetime benefit caps, and underpaying entities such as Medicaid will now be allowed to truly reap the benefits of American medicine. Relying on premiums alone to offset those increased costs is naïve. We must do better at controlling costs to make sure that what we spend is cost effective as well as therapeutically effective. Without doing a better job of being responsible stewards of all our health care resources, costs will continue to increase and a decade from now the reforms will be pronounced a failure as more and more of our gross national product is cannibalized by the health care system.

Much has been said about the principles of "evidence-based medicine," but many Americans are uncertain what the term actually means. Medical care, whether it be prescribing an FDA-approved medication, taking an over-the-counter "holistic" supplement, undergoing a complex surgical procedure, or receiving weekly chiropractic manipulation, is subject to the biases and experiences of the individual practitioner as well as the patient. Indeed, much of that bias can be related to effective marketing by those entities that stand to profit the most from the use of any given treatment.

If we are now going to pay for an increasing number of interventions for some three hundred million patients, whether those interventions are preventative or therapeutic, it is absolutely imperative that we get our money's worth. Expending resources for treatments that don't work or that are of marginal benefit at best is not only foolish but exceedingly wasteful, and with the added burden of so many individuals, it is no longer affordable. In addition, these treatments may carry significant risk and also may delay the initiation of proper interventions.

But how do we decide what works and what doesn't? We can simply trust the doctor and do whatever he or she advises. After all, physicians have much more education and experience when it comes to medical issues. We can listen to the TV commercials sponsored by the pharmaceutical industry, which advise us what the best available medicines are to treat the illnesses they are convinced we have. After all, they're the scientists who toil long hours to discover the many wonder drugs. We can follow the recommendations of those who hold themselves out as practitioners of "natural healing" and take one of the many herbal or organic compounds. After all, natural must be better. Or we can let *real* science give us the answers.

True science looks at an issue through an objective, unbiased lens. It begins with a postulate or an idea and then sets off to see if that idea is correct by conducting a series of tests called "research." In order for the conclusions of such research to be valid, it is imperative that those conducting the research control all possible variables to assure that the findings are not the result of chance or circumstance. Such a process is painstakingly complex but necessary nonetheless.

For years, the gold standard for such research has been the "randomized, double-blinded, prospective" study. For example, let's say you wanted to know whether a new medication, "Obamarama," was effective at treating high blood pressure. You would first go to a mathematical model and determine the minimum number of patients required to eliminate the possibility that blood pressure variation was a chance event. Next, you would design a study with the proper number of patients and prospectively "randomize" them, meaning that you would randomly assign them to treatment with Obamarama or with a placebo (a simple look-alike pill that has no biological activity). This could be done by merely having each hypertensive patient draw a number from a hat. If it is even, they get randomized to the placebo; if it is odd, they get randomized to the real drug being tested. There has to be a sufficient number of patients to assure that there are relatively equal numbers of men and women, that their ages are equally distributed, that the severity of their high blood pressure is similar, and that other factors such as kidney disease, diabetes, and the like are equally represented in both groups.

But sometimes patients' expectations and those of the researcher can affect outcome. If the patient knows he is getting the placebo, he may decide he won't get better, become frustrated at receiving the nontreatment arm of the study, and become angry with the researcher and the entire project. That frustration could lead to higher blood pressure and become a self-fulfilling prophecy. Additionally, if the test subject knows he received the real medicine, he may be confident it will work and his anxiety level may drop and blood pressure may decline on that basis alone rather than any effect of the medication.

The researchers may have a vested interest in the success of the drug either because they have devoted their lives' work to its development or because (more often) of the potential financial windfall that could follow. As a consequence, they may belittle or minimize side effects and exaggerate or embellish benefits in the test subjects. For this reason, the best scientific studies are "double-blinded," meaning that neither the patient nor the researcher knows who received the real medicine and who received the placebo. At the end of the study, when sufficient numbers of patients have been enrolled that it meets the requirements of mathematical and statistical validity, a Type 1 evidence-based conclusion can be reliably drawn. This is the nature of medical research and the basis of evidence-driven therapies. We can then conclude that "Obamarama" does indeed safely lower blood pressure in hypertensive patients and we can be more confident in prescribing it.

However, not all medical interventions can be so easily evaluated. Consider, for example, spine surgery. The treatment of degenerative spine disease has evolved exponentially over the years and "cutting-edge" treatments have come and gone. Some specialists recommend "conservative" measures for chronic back pain that may include rest, medications, physical therapy, core muscle strengthening exercises, chiropractic manipulation, acupuncture, cortisone injections, and/or biofeedback. Others may recommend a simple "laminectomy" where the roof of the spinal canal is surgically removed, creating more space for the compressed nerves. Still others may recommend a spinal fusion in addition to the laminectomy, where one vertebra is connected to adjacent ones to prevent motion. Even those advocating fusion disagree on whether the fusion should be done with bone alone or be supplemented with screws and rods; whether it should be done from the front or from behind . . . or both.

Attempting to randomize those spine patients into a double-blinded controlled study is impossible unless you are willing to subject patients to a "sham" surgery where an incision is made but no other intervention is performed and compare them with those who received one of the multitude of options noted above. For this reason, many surgical studies require randomizing patients into various treatment options in which neither party is blinded. In addition, these studies are oftentimes "retrospective," meaning that you look at the results of patients you have treated over the years and you report how they fared. But the validity here is questionable since there was no good control (or placebo) group for comparison. Just because a patient did well with a surgery doesn't mean the surgery was the reason. That same person may have done just as well with less expensive, less risky conservative care. But such retrospective analysis can be helpful, although not nearly to the degree as Type I evidence.

Lastly, evidence can be based on individual case reports or the educated "opinions" of so-called experts in the field. Once again, such information can be interesting, stimulate meaningful debate, and assist in crafting treatment options, but it is not science.

Unfortunately, under the current fee-for-service system, most physicians get reimbursed on a case by case, procedure by procedure basis. If I want to increase my income, the only way I can accomplish that is by seeing more patients, ordering more tests, and doing more procedures. This creates, at the very least, a potential conflict of interest, where I would suggest to patients more surgical intervention, as well as more extensive intervention. My fee for seeing a patient and prescribing anti-inflammatory medication and physical therapy for their back pain is much less than if I recommend a laminectomy. My fee for performing a laminectomy is much less than if I performed a fusion as well. And that fee is much less than if I used bone screws and rods for the fusion. And finally, that fee is much less than if I recommended the fusion be performed from the front as well as from behind. So you can easily understand how instrumented spinal fusion has virtually exploded across the United States over the past decade.

That is not to say that most spinal surgery is unnecessary or ineffective. All we can honestly say is that we don't know. As a surgeon, in my heart (hopefully more than in my pocketbook) I know it works. But with the expanding costs of such surgeries over the past ten years, it seems to me we could do a better job of designing studies to prove what my colleagues and I claim to be true. Some years ago, surgery on carotid arteries to prevent stroke was commonplace. Any patient who harbored a "bruit," which is an abnormal whooshing sound over the artery, had an ultrasound performed, and if it showed even mild narrowing, they were recommended to have the artery opened and the plaque removed. Although the surgery is relatively safe, there are a significant number of patients who suffer a stroke or even die as a result of the operation. Several well-designed studies were eventually carried out that showed many of these minor plaques did not require surgery and patients were instead treated with aspirin.[20] The number of carotid endarterectomies dropped and the surgery and attendant risks were offered only to those patients who would truly benefit. This evidence-based data saved the cost associated with unnecessary surgeries and reduced the operative risks to that population of patients.

Patients who experience chest pain, called angina, are usually subjected to a coronary angiogram, where a small catheter is inserted into an artery in the leg and threaded up into the small arteries that supply the heart. Previously, if those arteries were narrowed, doctors routinely recommended open heart surgery, to bypass the obstructed vessels, or an angioplasty, where a small balloon was inserted and inflated to open the artery and a stent placed to keep it patent. These procedures became tremendous revenue generators for the individual physicians as well as the hospitals where they were performed. Yet once again, well-designed studies eventually showed us that many patients do just as well, if not better, by simply taking aspirin along with cholesterol-lowering drugs, thus avoiding the risks of surgical intervention.[21]

More recently, a popular treatment for compression fractures of the spine in osteoporotic individuals has been a vertebroplasty. Here, a large needle is inserted into the softened fractured vertebra and a plastic-like cement is injected to stabilize the spine and relieve the pain. Its use has grown exponentially in the past five years and vertebroplasty has become wildly popular. Yet two recent articles published in *The New England Journal of Medicine* looked at two populations of patients with compression fractures. In one group, the needle was introduced and the cement was injected. In the second group, the needle was once again introduced but no injection of the cement was undertaken, although the machine still made all the appropriate sounds and the smell of the mixing cement permeated the room so that the patients would have no way of knowing if they received the cement or not. Follow-up studies performed several months later showed no significant differences between the two groups either in their amount of pain or in the functional capacity.[22] Not surprisingly, these two articles spawned marked criticism from the two groups who stand to benefit most from vertebroplasty—the physicians who frequently perform the procedure and the companies that sell the technology to do the same.[23] These two papers may not be the final word on the efficacy of vertebroplasty, but at least they have raised the question with two well-designed studies. The onus is now on the critics to refute the evidence-based data with similarly well-designed efforts.

It is imperative that studies such as these be carried out to better delineate what works and what doesn't for a broad range of medical and surgical interventions. In addition, there is no reason that chiropractic care, acupuncture, laser phototherapy, and other treatments that fall outside of the traditionally accepted medical remedies cannot be equally scrutinized, especially if we expect health insurance policies to pay for it. These therapies are expensive and contribute to the overall cost of American health care. As I mentioned earlier, with universal coverage adding millions of patients to our system, we must reduce costs in order for the reforms to succeed. A good start would be eliminating reimbursement for those treatments that are found to be ineffective or only marginally beneficial. That doesn't mean that physicians can't continue to offer the treatment if they are convinced it is helpful despite the science to the contrary. And it doesn't mean that patients can't choose to have such treatments even though the evidence for their efficacy is lacking. All it should mean is that we, as a nation, won't pay for it. If the patients want the treatment, they can pay for it out of their own pocket.

It also doesn't mean such a policy should stifle research into new and innovative treatments; that's what our universities are for. We need to keep looking at better ways to combat chronic diseases and find more effective drugs to assist in such a pursuit. We should not discourage innovation and entrepreneurship, but it is essential that such innovations merit their costs.

Such new therapies should gain traction and adoption as a result of well-designed evidence-based studies and not well-designed marketing strategies.

We would not need to necessarily create an entirely new bureaucratic entity to spearhead such an effort. The National Institutes of Health (NIH), the Institute of Medicine, or any number of other current agencies could be charged with leading such an ambitious undertaking. Each medical and surgical specialty could appoint a panel of well-respected academic researchers to identify the most expensive interventions impacting health care expenditures and to design Type 1 studies (similar to those cited above) and then look objectively, without bias, at the results. As our entire health care system becomes more and more integrated through electronic medical records, researchers should be in a better position to extract important information from that immense data bank. Physicians should not only be encouraged, but compelled, to candidly and honestly report patient outcomes.

Obviously, this will take time, effort, and money and will require a substantial "culture shift" among America's providers. There will be many who will strongly oppose any such effort and decry the creation of "comparative effectiveness institutes" as nothing more than the government's attempt to wrest control of health care from the hands of physicians and place it into the hands of the faceless federal bureaucrats. Undoubtedly, these will be the same individuals who scoff at studies (such as those in *The New England Journal of Medicine* cited above) and simply ignore the science because "they know it works." I am astounded when I see the current health care initiative enacted by Congress discuss comparative outcome studies as an important adjunct to health care reform, but hear that Republicans such as Senator Tom Coburn (see chapter 5) actually introduced an amendment forbidding such data from being used to determine what does and does not get reimbursed.[24] They view it as a form of health care rationing. Are you kidding me? Why bother doing the study if you are not going to use the information to make the system more efficient? This is nothing more than our beloved lawmakers bowing to the pressure of those well-funded special interests, including physicians, and assuring that the final bill is so watered down that meaningful reform will be left behind on the cutting table. In the end, comparative effectiveness research will be generously funded; however, the researchers will be forbidden from suggesting whether a studied treatment be reimbursed or not. Fortunately, Medicare and the commercial insurers will have access to that data and may very well come to those conclusions on their own.

I have now probably succeeded in alienating the majority of my medical brethren and rest assured, I won't be asked to speak at the next AMA convention. But we're just getting started, and if you think my recommendations regarding evidence-based medicine are controversial, you ain't seen nothin' yet!

THE DREADED "R" WORD: THE REASONABLE
RATIONING OF RESOURCES (WHICH "R" DO
YOU THINK IS THE DREADED ONE?)

March 27, 1984 . . . the date probably has no recognizable significance for 99.99 percent of Americans. Yet March 27, 1984, is one of the most important dates in the debate on health care reform and will remain so for generations to come. On that blustery Tuesday morning, Colorado Governor Richard Lamm was giving a speech on the topic of health care in the United States to the Colorado Health Lawyers Association. It wasn't a particularly important policy address and Governor Lamm certainly had no way of knowing that this speech, and one comment in particular, would soon catapult him into the national limelight and forever characterize him as a heinous monster to a large population of American citizens.

Lamm was discussing the enormous cost of health care in the United States and was pointing to the fact that the explosion of technology has allowed physicians to keep patients, many of whom are terminally ill, alive on machines for an indefinite period of time. He was lamenting the fact that such technology was prohibitively expensive and noted that the resources used to provide such care in the face of a dismal prognosis could be much better allocated to covering the uninsured or developing programs to prevent disease among our populace. Lamm correctly pointed out that America's resources were not infinite and suggested that we could not provide everything for everybody. So far, so good, Governor.

But then Richard Lamm spoke the single sentence that will be indelibly associated with him forevermore. While discussing the use of such technology in hopeless situations Lamm opined that *"we've got a duty to die and get out of the way with all of our machines and artificial hearts and everything else like that and let the other society, our kids, build a reasonable life."* Lamm warned that if we continue to provide every treatment to every person regardless of their situation, we would proceed down a course that would bankrupt the country and leave our children and grandchildren with an unserviceable debt.

Two days later, the *New York Times* reported that the Governor of Colorado had advocated that the *"elderly* had a duty to die and get out of the way" and characterized his comments as health care rationing at the expense of the sick and aged.[25] Even though the quote was both incorrect and out of context,

Lamm would never be able to rehabilitate his political reputation and the speech would plague him for the next twenty-five years. What's worse than the unfair demonization of Richard Lamm is the fact that a single sentence assured that the concept of health care rationing would never again be raised by an American politician. Yet without a well-designed policy to assure the reasonable allocation of America's resources to effective treatment options, any attempt at health care reform is destined to fail.

As for Governor Richard Lamm, he just happened to be 100 percent spot on.

First, he was correct that American medical technology is awe-inspiring. We do indeed have remarkable, even miraculous tools at our disposal. From intraoperative MRI scans to robotic surgical suites, we are now able to perform delicate, precise surgery through increasingly narrowed surgical corridors, thus improving accuracy and outcomes while reducing surgical morbidity. In addition, an array of pharmaceutical agents has allowed us to control hypertension, blunt the devastating consequences of diabetes, and effectively combat and even cure some cancers that just a few generations ago were uniformly fatal. But the same technology, the same wonder drugs, indiscriminately applied to every individual without regard to the patient's life expectancy, his or her chance for a reasonable recovery, and most importantly, the quality of his or her remaining life, threatens to bankrupt the entire system, limiting access to such treatments for all of us.

Governor Lamm was justifiably questioning the application of such advanced technology in cases where the outcome is obvious and the use of expensive measures was doing little more than merely postponing the inevitable. His reference to the artificial heart no doubt was in response to the high-profile case of retired dentist Barney Clark, who in 1982 became the first recipient of a fully implantable cardiac pump.[26] America was enthralled with the nightly news reports of this breakthrough technology and the melodrama of Dr. Clark's postoperative course. We, as a country, prayed for Clark's recovery and were devastated when a series of strokes left him wheelchair bound and incapacitated until his death 112 days after his surgery. All of us hoped the artificial heart would work for Barney Clark and then for us when our own hearts fail. But what was not widely discussed on the NBC, ABC, or CBS nightly newscasts were the enormous costs involved in such an endeavor.

Now one certainly should not fault the brave Dr. Clark or his family for trying anything to keep him alive. Nor should we level criticism at the innovative physicians who designed the heart and had the courage to try and break new ground, for it is only through such efforts and such failures that true progress emerges. But what we almost never do is ask if the time we add to *one* life is worth the costs to all others. There are those among us who will argue that if a surgical procedure like the insertion of an artificial heart, or a federal safety regulation like automobile airbags, or a state law such as a 55 mph speed limit saves just one life, then it's worth it. I'm not so sure.

When the U.S. Preventive Services Task Force (an independent panel of medical experts) announced in 2009 that scientific, evidence-based studies demonstrated that mammography needn't be routinely performed under the age of fifty, women across America were outraged![27] Story after story appeared in the press describing how a routine mammogram in a twenty-eight-year-old or a thirty-nine-year-old or a forty-six-year-old led to the early diagnosis of breast cancer and a successful cure. In many of these anecdotal recountings, we heard, "If it saves one woman's life we shouldn't change the policy." If that's the case, why not start screening at puberty to catch that extremely rare tumor in the eighteen-year-old? In the face of our limited resources and a growing population of similarly young but uninsured women who have no access to mammograms, I would respectfully disagree.

We should utilize such technology in a way that would be most effective, and mammography might indeed be indicated in a sixteen-year-old high school student who has a strong family history of the disease. But to perform it routinely on every "insured" woman over the age of forty regardless of risk factors consumes significant amounts of health care resources for little yield other than peace of mind. At the same time, the more money we spend on routine mammography in low-risk populations, the less money we have available to diagnose and treat the disease in high-risk individuals who are unable to afford insurance.

But the panel did not even take cost into account when making their recommendations; they only looked at the science. In a poll done in the weeks following the release of the new guidelines, 84 percent of women said they would ignore the recommendations and still get annual mammograms. In the same poll, 40 percent of the respondents estimated the chance of a forty-year-old woman developing breast cancer in the next ten years to be between 20 percent and 50 percent. Actually, according to the National Cancer Institute, the figure is only 1.4 percent and up to one-third of those cancers have little chance of being fatal. The task force explained that routine mammography in women under fifty leads to a significant number of "false positives," resulting in unnecessary surgical procedures, and that the exposure to radiation has the potential of actually triggering the development of a tumor.[28] But of course, our beloved politicians also chose to once again ignore the science and jump on the public bandwagon of emotion, characterizing the new guidelines as the Obama administration's attempt at health care rationing by refusing to let women get lifesaving mammography.

The truth of the matter is, America, we already ration health care and we have been doing so for years. But we ration it in the cruelest and most unfair of ways—by economic status. If you're wealthy or fortunate enough to be employed in a job that provides health insurance, you get a mammogram whether you need it or not. If you're poor or work for a small company unable to afford health care benefits, you lose, and by the time your breast lump becomes large enough to palpate, the window of opportunity to cure may have already closed. But when the science argues for a more rational way of utilizing mammography, we once again revert to anecdote and emotion and let the science be damned.

And for those of you who still need convincing, may I suggest you look to the state of Arizona, whose legislature passed a law in October of 2010 that discontinued reimbursements for organ transplantations in their Medicaid population? The argument that prompted the change was that survival rates for transplants were too low to justify the expenditure. As a result, a number of Medicaid patients that had been on donor waiting lists were denied the procedure when their name came up and an appropriate donor had been found. They were sent home, the organ was given to the next person on the list with "good insurance," and these Medicaid patients died. The Arizona legislature rationed them right out of the system. In fairness, Arizona should be lauded for actually looking at the data and determining whether continued reimbursement was justified (and recognizing their health care resources are finite), but it seems to me, if the outcomes really don't justify the cost, then the private insurers should be allowed to deny payment in the "well-insured" population as well.[29]

Such controversy is certainly not limited to mammography or women's health, although some would love to characterize the current debate as a sexist disregard for the well-being of American women. Prostatic Specific Antigen (PSA) testing for prostate cancer in males has sparked similar discussions.[30] The bottom line is that we must rely on science, not emotion, to determine how to rationally ration our restricted resources. (Don't you just love alliteration?)

Governor Lamm was also correct when he told the audience that fateful morning that we could not afford to provide every treatment for every patient and still remain a viable economic power. When health care consumes more than 17 percent of our GDP and is projected to increase in the future, one needn't be a Harvard economist to see the writing on the wall. The resources available for health care in the United States truly are finite, and as such, they need to be conserved and utilized judiciously. To do so not only makes economic sense but is the only humane approach to providing care for all Americans. There is not a reasonable soul in Congress who would argue that our ability to support health care is limitless. But it is much more difficult to find a politician who will explain how you utilize those finite resources to provide infinite care. Don't call it rationing if you are afraid of suffering a fate similar to Richard Lamm; but rationing it is, and rationing it must be if we are to succeed in this plan of affordable health care for all to which we pay such lip service.

So just how do we go about rationing care properly? Please, Dr. Know-It-All, why don't you tell us just exactly how it's done? Fine, I will, but you will need to leave your emotions at the door along with all your preconceptions, political affiliations, bleeding hearts, crucifixes, AK-47s, pro-life and pro-choice stickers, NOW and AARP membership cards, Glenn Beck motivational CDs, and testimonials from your neighbor's cousin. You will also have to bring with you the open mind that you haven't accessed since your junior year of college and a selfless commitment to doing what is best for all of us rather than just what is best for you and yours, for in the end it will be the same.

We must allocate (relax, Congressman, you're safe, I didn't use the word "ration") health care resources to those patients in need of the treatments that will succeed in preserving for them not just their lives, but *quality* lives. Obviously, the difficulty lies in determining what a quality life entails, but it is far easier to identify what it isn't than what it is. Most of us would agree that being unresponsive in a nursing home, unable to communicate and being fed by a tube, is not quality. The debate, however, will be taken up by those who feel all life is a gift from God and should be preserved at all costs. We cannot argue that point since it is steeped in religious conviction based on deep faith. The contention can be made that if God wished such a patient to remain alive, He could easily accomplish that without the help of machines or doctors and probably at a much lower price since God has amazing bargaining power that would be the envy of Health Net or Blue Shield.

It is always somewhat easier to discuss "allocation" if the patient is elderly and has lived a full life, although my eighty-eight-year-old mother-in-law and the rest of the Gray Panthers of AARP are now poised to pounce on me. Let me make this clear: I do not feel we should allocate based on age. Allocation should be based on expectation of outcome, whether the patient is ninety-four years or three months old. And here is where the discussion gets really dicey. If that same unresponsive, tube-fed, nursing home resident is an eleven-year-old girl rather than an eighty-seven-year-old man, all of us tend to recoil with the discomfort of such a decision. But the principle must be the same and applied to us all, just as Richard Lamm did in 1984.

It is inherently unfair to direct hundreds of thousands of dollars to the care of individuals in such dire condition while healthy children across

America are unable to obtain immunizations and die from measles pneumonia or a young mother of two succumbs to ovarian cancer for lack of treatment. I fully understand that even raising such points for discussion will open me up to the same outrage bestowed on Richard Lamm and assure my nomination to the new post of Secretary of Obama Death Panels. But we must find an equitable and efficacious way to allocate our limited resources. I am certainly not proposing that we euthanize those unfortunate individuals who are in such a condition, but I also do not feel it is fair for our society to deny others effective treatment because we lack the resources, having allocated them to the above patients. If the families of that child or that elderly man want them sustained beyond reasonable means, then that burden should be theirs, not ours. Let them sell assets. Let their communities hold spaghetti dinners and car washes like many families now do to pay their medical bills. Let them turn to their neighbors, to their church congregations or private philanthropists. I am not advocating that we deny care, but in situations such as those, I contend that we, as a country, cannot afford to pay for it.

If a ninety-four-year-old woman comes into the hospital with a massive heart attack or a major stroke and we deem her chances of survival to be minimal, then once again, we don't deny her a cardiac bypass or a craniotomy to remove her brain hemorrhage, but we make it clear that the financial responsibility for such extreme care lies with her and her family. The argument can be made that only the wealthy will then get the treatments and the poor will not, but it matters little if the outcome for both is inevitable. I would much rather deny futile treatment to America's poor than deny them effective treatment because the well has run dry.

So who determines what reasonable care is and what constitutes futile treatment? I fully realize that we will not be able to predict outcome with 100 percent accuracy and that indeed a given number of individuals who may have benefited from treatment deemed futile will die. I understand that. But we go back to the basic argument that if we save just one life, then it is worthy of all the resources we committed, and if you again agree that our health care dollars are finite, we cannot adhere to such a tenet. Someone will need to determine for which treatments we reimburse and for which we make the individual or their family responsible. To figure that out we must rely on *both* science and the stakeholders in U.S. health care—the American people.

If, in the new system of American health care, we develop a federal electronic medical records network that links all U.S. hospitals and physicians, and if we require both to report outcomes on all patients, we will soon have an unprecedented data bank from which we can extract the statistics necessary to determine which treatments are effective in which individuals. We can then apply that information to our mathematical models and predict outcomes.

I can already hear the voices of suspicion raised that will suggest we cannot trust the federal government and that any results gleaned from the data bank will merely be manipulated by the Democrats or the Republicans to deny costly care. Folks, we cannot continue to justify our inaction by such paranoia. If we all really mistrust the government so much, then we should quit calling ourselves the greatest democracy on the planet and start the revolution.

But once that information is available, through the National Institutes of Health or possibly the Institute of Medicine, we should then turn the data over to a more important task force, what I like to call the "Task Force for Effective Care." It is absolutely essential that such a panel be dominated by physicians, for we are in the best position to interpret the science. But it is equally essential that a broad cross section of Americans have significant representation and input into the decisions emerging from such a body. I anticipate that members will represent the elderly, children, the disabled, soccer moms, the American worker, gays, the poor, the wealthy, the clergy, and a variety of other groups to assure a fair and reasonable consensus. The only requirement would be that these individuals would need to come to the table with that open mind I alluded to earlier; demagogues, ideologues, and politicians need not apply.

As a group, they will represent all Americans and help to determine what our new system will and won't pay for. Such decisions would not be limited to just end of life, futile care concerns. The panel will look at spinal fusions, cardiac bypasses, artificial hearts, vertebroplasties, and yes, even mammograms, and use the science to determine which of those technologies and treatments are efficacious in a given population. We may find that a bypass is a reasonable option in a seventy-four-year-old with hypertension and diabetes but not so in a sixty-eight-year-old who has end-stage emphysema and congestive heart failure. The spinal fusion may be a good alternative in an active fifty-two-year-old with spondylolisthesis (malaligned vertebrae) in addition to his spinal stenosis but unnecessary and ineffective in an eighty-one-year-old with osteoporosis. That doesn't mean we will deny those individuals their bypass or their fusion; they can have it if they wish. They will just have to pay for it themselves.

We often hear pundits and politicians cite horrifically long waiting lists for routine diagnostic procedures such as MRI scans in the Canadian health system. In the United States, on the other hand, if you are insured and strain a back muscle while raking leaves on Saturday, by Monday afternoon you have already obtained a $1,200 MRI. More often than not, the MRI was relatively normal, and if you had just waited a few more days, taken some cheap ibuprofen, and done some stretching exercises, your symptoms would have resolved on their own . . . for much less than $1,200. But instead, your

MRI may have shown some long-standing abnormalities totally unrelated to your current symptoms but prompting a referral to a spine surgeon who now recommends a fusion, with pedicle screws, of course.

That may be why Canada spends much less of their GDP on health care than we do. It may also be related to the fact that they don't have freestanding, physician-owned MRI centers on every street corner as we do here. Do you think it just may be a better policy to define stricter guidelines as to when it is appropriate to order a $1,200 MRI? Guidelines generated by physicians, not the government bureaucrats, and agreed to by a consensus of our citizen representatives? How much money could be saved and how many unnecessary surgeries could be avoided? If you strain your back on Saturday and want your MRI on Monday, then, once again, maybe you should pay for it.

Obviously, this will be a deliberate, time-consuming process. New and innovative treatments will be encouraged and subjected to the same scrutiny as existing ones, using the principles of evidenced-based medicine I discussed in the previous section. Options will be added and deleted, and the task force itself should be a dynamic body with built-in turnover of membership to insure fresh perspectives and prevent empire building. Although such a plan sounds frightening, almost Orwellian, if you really take a breath and consider it objectively, it may be the only way we can make certain that health care will be available for our grandchildren without depleting the multitude of other important national priorities.

And finally, Governor Richard Lamm was right. When all of us reach a point in our journey where a quality life is no longer an option, whether we are old or young, black or white, male or female, rich or poor, we do indeed have a duty to die or at least to stop expecting the rest of society to expend our pooled and limited resources to support us. We need to step aside, embrace our creator, and allow that "other society" about which he spoke to live a reasonable life and have the same chance we did at achieving the American dream. And we should do so with dignity and selflessness; each and every one of us.

Oh, and by the way . . . we all owe Richard Lamm an apology.

TORT REFORM: AND I'M NOT TALKING
ABOUT MAKING A NEW CAKE!

If you want to know what's wrong with the American health care system, you need look no further than the issue of medical malpractice litigation. The medical liability and compensation infrastructure, like all of American health care, is broken, probably beyond repair. The parties responsible for its current state are the same who bear much of the blame for the other failings of our system. Lawyers, physicians, politicians, and patients are all complicit in the evolution and preservation of a tort system that fails miserably in its purported mission to protect and compensate patients who have been injured as a result of medical negligence.

As I discussed earlier in chapter 10, our current medical malpractice system protects neither the American patient nor the American doctor. Indeed, the overwhelming majority of patients who have a legitimate claim of malpractice never file suit and only one out of fifteen victims of true medical negligence ever receives compensation.[31] On the other hand, evidence clearly suggests that a sizable majority of malpractice claims that eventually are filed have no valid basis.[32] Lastly, injured patients who prevail in a malpractice trial find that well over half of their settlement goes to their attorney, the multiple "expert" witnesses, and the courts.[33] So everyone wins except the doctor or the injured patient.

Now the majority of my colleagues and most Republican lawmakers will tell you that tort reform is one the most important issues contributing to the current health care crisis; indeed it is. They will tell you that fear of frivolous lawsuits leads to the practice of defensive medicine where unnecessary tests that inflate the cost of American health care are performed merely to "cover your ass"; and indeed it does. But you can search throughout the literature and discover figures all over the board, depending upon the source. Recently, the Congressional Budget Office studied the issue of tort reform that included capping noneconomic losses (i.e., pain and suffering) as we do in California, and estimated that such reform would result in a cost savings of over $5 billion per year. Not a great amount when you consider a $2.5 *trillion* expenditure, but $5 billion here and $5 billion there and soon we're talking real money![34]

In addition, a significant number of physicians, especially in my field of neurosurgery, are dropping off of emergency room call schedules and citing the fear of malpractice suits as the cause. Increasingly, they are also giving up their cranial surgery privileges, meaning that even if their hospitals force them to take call, they can't cover the emergency room because they don't have surgical privileges to do so. In my discussions with neurosurgical colleagues and malpractice defense attorneys, it is clear that the vast majority of malpractice cases filed against American neurosurgeons are related to *elective spinal surgery*, not neurosurgical cranial emergencies. But lo and behold, we aren't dropping our elective spine surgery privileges. Go figure.

On the other hand, those wonderful knights in shining armor, America's trial lawyers, contend that malpractice reform will do nothing more than allow bad doctors to practice bad medicine and will severely limit an injured patient's access to legal representation. After all, what attorney in his or her right mind would take on a case where the maximum reward for the intangibles of pain and suffering was a mere $250,000 to $500,000? By capping noneconomic losses, the trial bar contends that many attorneys would not find the potential rewards worth the effort, even though no one has suggested placing a similar cap on tangible economic concerns, such as lost earning potential, lifelong supportive care, and future medical costs.

And the public, under a barrage of television and print marketing ads by those same trial lawyers, are convinced that just maybe they could hit the lottery and that their MRSA (methicillin-resistant Staphylococcus aureus) wound infection in their 390-pound, diabetic, nicotine-filled body is really the fault of their surgeon, the hospital, or hopefully both, since more defendants equals deeper pockets. And by the way, they will be quick to inform you that *their* pain and suffering is worth much more than $250,000 as they take another hit of medical marijuana and wash down their OxyContin with the last gulp of their Jack Daniels, while blaming their loss of consortium on their postoperative depression rather than their disgusting physical appearance. (Wow, sorry, folks, a lot of pent-up anger there, I guess.)

And although many Republicans, like the rest of the lawyer bashers, feel that tort reform is the key to health care reform, the Democrats completely and shamelessly ignore the entire issue. Traditionally, America's trial lawyers have nurtured and supported Democratic candidates, and in return, the party of the working class has made sure that their benefactors were well taken care of.[35] Heck, they even had a vice presidential candidate who made his millions suing obstetricians in North Carolina.[36] So it is not surprising that the House and Senate bills on health care reform did little or nothing to address the medical malpractice crisis. Once again, we will have a broad coalition of physician groups and most Republicans standing in opposition to any reform bill, however reasonable, because of the Democrats' unwillingness to include meaningful steps to fix a system that all of us know is ineffective.

If members of either party were truly concerned about average Americans instead of only those who support their reelection campaigns (be it the trial lawyers or the AMA), then they would craft a solution to medical liability that seeks to fairly compensate all victims of a medical misfortune while protecting physicians from frivolous lawsuits and the lottery mentality that characterizes the current system. As in other arenas of health care reform, we must reject the idea of "profit motive" and replace it with "justice motive."

As I alluded to in chapter 10, it is unfair to a defendant physician when guilt or innocence is determined by a panel of lay people with little background or understanding of the complex medical issues inherent in a malpractice case. I have repeatedly called for evidence-based medicine to be the backbone of health care reform, and I feel it is just as important that evidence-based justice form the backbone of tort reform. The problem with physician calls for malpractice reform is that they usually focus on protecting doctors but do nothing to address protecting patients. The same is usually characteristic of Republican plans as well. And as far as the trial lawyers are concerned, to them malpractice reform is little more than removing caps on pain and suffering, which would increase their incomes but do little to assist that majority of patients who are injured and don't realize they are the victims of malpractice or to protect physicians from frivolous lawsuits. Like everything else in our convoluted system, all parties must accept responsibility for the failings and create innovative solutions that address everyone's concerns, not just their own.

More and more American hospitals are beginning to incorporate honesty and apology as tools in confronting potential malpractice events. For years, every hospital has employed a risk manager who reviews all patient complaints and adverse events. Certainly that individual could identify those cases where mistakes by the medical, nursing, or pharmaceutical staff injured a patient, resulted in a prolonged hospitalization and/or additional charges, or otherwise contributed to an unfavorable outcome whether the patient realized it or not. The risk manager and the physician, nurse, or pharmacist involved might then simply explain to the patient what transpired, apologize for the mistake, and offer to remedy the situation in a mutually agreeable manner. Although on the surface such a practice appears risky and could potentially expose the hospital and its staff to unwanted scrutiny, those institutions, such as the University of Michigan, that have incorporated the practice into their policies have reported marked reductions in malpractice claims.[37] And there would be no law forbidding a physician in practice outside of a hospital from handling difficulties that arise in his or her office in a similar manner.

As for those patients who still decide to file a lawsuit, why not set up a specific "malpractice review council" in each jurisdiction made up of highly respected practicing or retired lawyers and physicians who could review the merits of a given case and recommend equitable compensation if they deem malpractice has indeed occurred? Such a body would be able to bring to the table not only a keen sense of the law but a clear understanding of the intricate and detailed medical issues of a case. If either the plaintiff or the defendant challenges the panel's recommendation, they would be free to pursue the case in court but must be responsible for all associated costs, including the other party's attorney's fees, if they lose. And in court, the case would be tried in front of a judge, who would be less susceptible to the emotional trappings of such cases, rather than before a jury whose random selection could not guarantee a panel with the medical sophistication and sentimental impartiality required to ensure fairness to both parties.

Beyond that, it is imperative we insure that the lion's share of any malpractice judgment end up in the hands of the injured parties, namely, the patients, and not their attorneys or their conga line of hired gun experts who will testify to anything, anywhere, at any time for a fee. I would propose that a minimum of 75 percent of any malpractice judgment must go to the plaintiff. We also must admit that pain and suffering, the intangible noneconomic factors, does indeed result from malpractice, but limiting such subjective variables to $500,000 does not seem unreasonable.

Lastly, physicians need to be encouraged to bring down the wall of silence that most of us, including myself, maintain. We bemoan the fact that many plaintiffs' experts are the so-called hired guns who show up at trial after trial rather than engaging in the true practice of medicine. Yet most of us are loath to testify on behalf of an injured patient even when we know that malpractice has clearly occurred. We fear being shunned by our colleagues and what's more, we fear that we could be next and those same colleagues would no longer feel obligated to maintain that silent wall. So we let the "guns" do the job. At the very minimum, the courts should require that an expert medical witness be actively engaged in the practice of the specialty that is in question.

We fail to report the physicians among us who clearly practice below the standard of care, in other words, the surgeon on staff that we would never allow to operate on our family but whom we let operate on some anonymous patient that turns up on the next week's morbidity and mortality report. Physicians have a collective responsibility to assure that our communities are protected from the rare "bad apple" that puts everyone at risk and defines malpractice in our towns. That culture of shared accountability must be nourished in medical school and residency training and perpetuated in the communities in which we practice. Physicians must commit themselves to integrity and candor when it comes to patient care. Mistakes will be made; physicians are only human. But a mistake is not malpractice. Failing to admit it, failing to disclose it to the patient, and failing to learn from it is.

AN OUNCE OF PREVENTION IS WORTH
$2.6 TRILLION OF CURE ... OR IS IT?

Most of us who are middle-aged or older can remember the hackneyed adage "An apple a day keeps the doctor away," which was ingrained into America's psyche as a way to promote healthful nutrition and prevent disease. Many of our mothers took such advice to heart and packed our lunches with fresh fruit and vegetables, hoping to keep us well and avoid visits to the local family doctor or pediatrician. My, how times have changed! Today that apple most likely is covered in caramel, dipped in chocolate, and washed down with a venti peppermint white chocolate mocha from Starbucks that contains 700 calories, 27 grams of fat, and 74 grams of carbohydrates.[38] Today's young consumers probably arrived at the café by car rather than walking or riding their bikes as we did. And after school, they probably settled down in front of the television to watch the latest installment of *Family Guy* or *The Simpsons* until they began their crusade to better yesterday's score on the latest and most realistic video game whose virtual imagery makes you feel as if you actually are exercising.

With such activities so commonplace across the American landscape, it should so come as no surprise that we now have almost twenty-five million fellow citizens with diabetes and another fifty-seven million who are on the verge.[39] According to the American Diabetes Association, in 2006, diabetes became the seventh leading cause of death across the United States, accounting for more than 72,000 deaths and contributing to over 233,000 more.[40] In addition, as a result of their diabetes, many of these patients will suffer heart disease, stroke, hypertension, blindness, neuropathy, and the like. In 2005 alone, over 175,000 Americans began chronic renal dialysis related to diabetes-induced kidney failure.[41] And just how much does this single, for the most part, preventable disease cost us? If you believe the American Diabetes Association and National Institutes of Health, the number now exceeds $200 *billion* annually![42]

Similarly alarming figures can be cited for a multitude of other maladies, such as heart disease, stroke, emphysema, cancer, and trauma. Certainly not all of these diseases are preventable, but many of them are, and the benefits of prevention in terms of longevity, quality of life, and cost of care should be obvious to everyone regardless of one's educational background or political affiliation. Politicians on both sides of the aisle frequently mention "preventative care" as if it were the panacea to solving our current health care crisis. It does seem intuitive that if we had fewer Americans with diabetes, then we would have fewer Americans utilizing resources to treat the myriad of complications associated with the disease. At $300 to $400 per treatment, it doesn't take a math whiz to appreciate what the 180,000 diabetics on thrice-weekly dialysis cost our health care system or figure out better ways to spend that money if even half of those cases of renal failure could be prevented. Certainly, cost savings for these services would be real, but it also costs money to prevent disease and encourage healthy lifestyles.

If we wish to see the World Health Organizations indices reflect better on American health care, it is essential that we change the way we look at health. Traditionally, the American health care system has emphasized treatment—better technology, better drugs, more innovative surgery, consumer-friendly hospitals, and so on. Maybe it's time we focused more on keeping our citizens healthy and preventing those very same diseases that require all of the breathtaking technology, wonder drugs, robotic surgeries, and public relation gimmicks to encourage patients to come to our hospitals in the first place. Although such a culture shift may bode well for the American patient, I am not sure it would be as beneficial to American physicians and American hospitals. As I have stressed earlier, our system financially rewards performance of procedures over preventing illness, and it will no doubt be exceedingly difficult, if not impossible, to change such an ingrained attitude.

Imagine, if you will, spending money on health club memberships for employees to exercise and lose weight rather than on cardiac bypasses or coronary angioplasties. Imagine funding innovative physical education programs in schools while emptying the vending machines of high-calorie snack foods and soft drinks and replacing them with nutritious alternatives. Maybe the epidemic rise in childhood obesity would be curbed and the number of juvenile diabetics and hypertensives would plummet. Imagine making sure that all American children received their vaccinations so that in the twenty-first century we would not have to place three-year-olds on ventilators in the ICU to manage their measles pneumonia or whooping cough. Imagine programs that assisted Americans in their quest to finally quit smoking, programs that were accessible to everyone and not just those with the means to afford them. I would venture a guess it would be less expensive than treating the lung cancer or emphysema that will oftentimes victimize these patients if they continue to smoke. Imagine instructing workers in proper lifting techniques and providing assistive devices on the job to prevent the millions of work-related back injuries each year. Once again I suspect it would be less expensive than all the missed days from work, the twenty-five chiropractic treatments per month, or the expensive spinal surgical procedures that have exponentially mushroomed over the past decade. Imagine . . . well, you get my point so I'll stop for now, with my apologies to the late John Lennon. But do imagine . . .

The goal of health care reform should be the promotion and preservation of the well-being of every American citizen, as well as the development of innovative and effective treatment options for those who become ill. Too often the debate focuses on providing insurance coverage to everyone or on preventing government interference in health care or on controlling spiraling costs. But at the end of the day the bottom line is keeping Americans healthy. Doing so is going to require a Herculean effort to change American culture and, unfortunately, that effort will be accompanied by significant resource expenditures.

To accomplish the goals of reducing heart disease, obesity, diabetes, stroke, and cancer, we will somehow have to convince our population to turn off their TVs, unplug their Xboxes, and drag their lazy, overweight carcasses off the couch and to the park or gym. Nutritionists will need to take a leading role in trying to influence Americans to eat healthier and in more reasonable proportions and to reduce the intake of high-calorie junk food that dominates the U.S. diet. Exercise physiologists will be required to develop effective fitness programs that can be integrated not only in the schools but in the workplace as well so that access to such important activities is not limited to those who can afford a health club membership. Just as insurance coverage for getting ill has been tied to employers, prevention efforts must be as well in order to work. And like it or not, the only entity that can truly accomplish such widespread and culture-changing efforts is the federal government.

It will cost money . . . maybe lots of money. The feds will need to provide grants to develop and test the programs and most likely offer tax incentives to employers to implement them. The schools must be mandated to integrate such programs into their curricula, but in order to succeed, this effort cannot become just another of the government's many already un-funded mandates. We need to pay more than lip service to prevention efforts, and we cannot expect that private insurance carriers or private industry will lead the way. After all, with most for-profit insurance companies, the goal is "profit" and not the health of their patients. They don't need to expend large amounts of their investors' potential returns on preventing diabetes or heart disease, as most of the expensive consequences of such early neglect will not significantly manifest themselves until patients near Medicare age when they are jettisoned from the rolls of the private carriers and left to the responsibil-ity of the "government" option. As I mentioned earlier, it's funny how the private carriers decry the public option when it comes to competing for rela-tively young, healthy populations who utilize fewer resources, but welcome the public option to care for the older, sicker (and obviously less profitable) segments of our society.

We have seen in this country a remarkable drop in automobile-related deaths and injuries as more and more Americans utilize seatbelts, newer cars are equipped with air bags and antilock brakes, and individual states get serious about impaired drivers by lowering acceptable blood alcohol levels and toughening the consequences of drunk driving.[43] Increasingly, state leg-islatures are restricting the use of cell phones and other distractive devices in hopes of bringing the death and injury rates down even further.[44] But much of prevention strategy in the arena of injury does bring into conflict the concept of individual freedoms versus the right of the society to protect itself from the costs associated with such injuries.

A good example of this is the mandated use of motorcycle helmets. In the spirit of full disclosure, I must admit that as a neurosurgeon I realized early in my career that despite the remarkable technology at our fingertips and the dedicated skills of the ICU staffs, our ability to reverse the devastating effects of head and spinal cord injury was significantly limited. Thus, I have dedicated a good portion of my professional life to the prevention of brain and spinal cord injury in my own community and on the national stage as well. At times this has put me in direct conflict with various groups who sincerely value the right of the individual to make decisions regarding their own well-being and are justifiably concerned with "big brother" government intruding on their lives.

In the early '90s, California was embroiled in a public debate regarding the passage of a law requiring motorcyclists to wear a protective helmet. Civil libertarians and the lobbying group ABATE (A Brotherhood Against Totalitarian Enactments) opposed such legislation on the basis of its infringement upon the right of the motorcyclists to make their own decisions regarding their safety. Biker after biker decried the proposed law as interfering with the pleasure of feeling the wind rush through their hair as they sped down the many beautiful California highways that we Left-Coasters are privileged to enjoy. Some argued that wearing a helmet was actually more dangerous as it impeded vision and reduced hearing, although the science in support of such claims was ridiculously flawed.

While lobbying in support of the law, I acknowledged that personal choice and individual freedom was indeed a cornerstone of American life and not one to be ceded capriciously. Yet I pointed out that a multitude of well-designed studies supported the fact that helmets did indeed save lives and reduced the severity of brain injury.[45] Now they didn't reduce the number of accidents, nor was there any evidence that they increased accident rates because of restricted hearing or vision. All they did was reduce the chances that, in the event of an accident, the rider would suffer a devastating brain injury.

I countered the argument about individual choice and personal freedom by pointing out that in the 1980s, 82 percent of all motorcyclists treated in California emergency rooms were either uninsured or covered by Medi-Cal, our state Medicaid program.[46] These figures were similar in other states as well. I went on to argue that along with an individual's "right" to choice was their "responsibility" for the consequences of such choices. If they chose not to wear a helmet and suffered a significant brain injury as a result of that choice, it was blatantly unfair to expect me as a physician or the public to pay for the consequences of their poor choice. Therefore, I suggested that if the legislature did not wish to pass such a law that they should require every motorcyclist to carry at least $1 million in insurance. If the injured individual was uninsured and chose not to wear a protective helmet, then we should be allowed to leave them on the pavement and suffer the consequences of their "choice." Of course, I explained that in a reasonable and progressive society, that would never be an option, so they had no choice but to enact this law. Thanks to the efforts of many like-minded groups the law was passed and soon California found head injury death rates from motorcycle accidents had declined by almost 40 percent.[47]

Lest you think I favor the restriction of individual choice in all activities related to injury, I will share with you another situation that actually put me at odds with many prevention groups I have worked with over the years. When California congressman and entertainer Sonny Bono suffered a fatal head injury when he lost control and skied unhelmeted into a tree at Heavenly Valley in 1998,[48] I was the medical director of the National Injury Prevention Foundation, known at the time as ThinkFirst. I was contacted by an NBC news crew that was doing a story on the accident. They asked whether I supported a federal law mandating the use of protective helmets while skiing. I think my answer surprised them as well as many of my colleagues in the injury prevention arena. I carefully explained that although I thought the use of helmets was indeed an excellent idea while skiing, I did not support a law mandating such. The Bono death created a lot of media coverage because of who he was, as well as the fact that Michael Kennedy, the son of Robert F. Kennedy, had died just the week before in a similar accident in Aspen, Colorado.[49] But the number of skiers who die of head injuries each year is relatively small, and as a result, I did not feel that the numbers or the economic consequences justified legislation restricting the individual's choice to wear a helmet or not. As I spoke about when discussing health care rationing and comparative effectiveness research, although I value the life of every individual, I do not subscribe to the tenet that if a law or an intervention saves just one life then it should be enacted. As we move on in preventative care, it is important that we do so while still safeguarding Americans' rights to individual choice, whether it involves combating obesity or reducing motor vehicle deaths.

It seems intuitive that a reduction in the major risk categories should result in significant health care savings. Lowering cholesterol and promoting regular exercise should lead to a reduction in heart disease and a savings of the resources required to care for its victims. Combating obesity should help us preserve much of the $218 billion we spend annually on diabetes and its complications. Colonoscopy screening can detect potentially cancerous polyps, which can be removed prior to their malignant transformation into colon cancer, saving both lives and the expensive treatments necessary if they progress undetected. But again, all of this costs money.

Indeed, if we are successful in reducing risk factors in our population, life expectancy will only increase and that mushrooming cohort of individuals who would have died from heart disease or diabetes a generation earlier will still be around to "consume" health care resources for years to come. This is admirable and is to be considered one of the success stories of health care reform, but once again as the population of elderly, non-income-contributing citizens expands, so will the cost to care for them. To assume that preventative strategies will save money in the long run may not be as accurate as our congressmen and senators would like us to believe. Prevention will help us to control costs but will also add to them.

An oft-quoted study appearing in *The New England Journal of Medicine* in 2008 by Joshua Cohen and his colleagues surveyed approximately 600 articles that looked at the cost effectiveness of preventative care and concluded that although some preventative measures do indeed save society money, the vast majority do not.[50] These measures most certainly improve the health and quality of life of the population, but the authors correctly pointed out that the politicians engaged in the health care debate were misleading the public by suggesting preventative strategies would result in significant health cost savings.[51]

One study went so far as to explain how smoking cessation programs and attempts at reversing obesity would actually increase health care costs for society by extending the lives of these individuals. Statistics revealed that smokers died an average of seven years earlier than nonsmokers, usually as a result of lung cancer, emphysema, or heart disease. Obese people died on average four years earlier than healthy, thin nonsmokers. Although there are costs associated with treating these patients as their tobacco- and obesity-induced conditions progress, in the long run it is less expensive than the costs of health care in that same population if they lived an additional four to seven years.[52]

So let's not kid ourselves that prevention is the answer to the health care crisis. Like everything else, it is only one piece of an intricate mosaic designed to improve the health of all Americans. Prevention will not be easy given American culture; nor will it be cheap. An apple a day may not keep the doctor away forever and an ounce of prevention may not be worth a pound of cure.

But it may be worth a bit more than that supersized Big Mac with cheese.

REVERSAL OF FORTUNES: MOVING THE MONEY FROM THE POCKETS OF CONGRESS TO THE HOSPITAL BEDS OF AMERICA'S PATIENTS

"Congress shall make no law respecting an establishment of religion, or prohibiting the free exercise thereof; *or abridging the freedom of speech*, or of the press; or the right of the people peaceably to assemble, and to petition the Government for a redress of grievances."

I seriously doubt that when James Madison drafted the First Amendment in 1789, or when the first United States Congress ratified it in mid-December two years later, that they did so with the explicit purpose of making certain that wealthy individuals, labor unions, or dominant industries would be able to donate unlimited amounts of money to politicians through lobbying firms or political action committees (PACs). Knowing what I do about our American forefathers, I suspect they would cringe at the very idea that political influence could be bought and paid for by the sectors of society with the means to do so. Yet, that is exactly what occurs every day across America and it is done in the name of the First Amendment.

The reason that the Patient Protection and Affordable Care Act is doomed to failure is the same reason that many other important initiatives that significantly impact average citizens also fail. Americans and their elected leaders operate in a corrupt system that legalizes, under the First Amendment protection, the buying and selling of influence through campaign contributions, PACs, "independent" television ad campaigns, and the like. We hypocritically decry the rampant corruption of governments in India, Pakistan, Afghanistan, and Iraq but allow PhRMA, the AMA, the American Bar Association, America's Health Insurance Plans (AHIP), and the American Hospital Association to donate millions of dollars to the reelection campaigns of American politicians. We actually sit there silently while the recipient swears that such gifts have absolutely no impact on the important votes affecting the donors. Who are they kidding?

How is it that when an Afghan businessman wants a permit to erect a new office building and he provides a monetary "gift" to the commerce minister to make certain the permit is awarded, it is called corruption? But when Schering-Plough donates $50,000 to the Democratic Senatorial Campaign Committee (as discussed in chapter 4) and twenty-four hours later, Senator Robert Torricelli (who just happens to be chairman of that committee) introduces a bill to extend the company's patent on Claritin, it is not condemned as corruption.[53] I would like someone to explain to me the difference.

The pharmaceutical industry did not distribute millions in campaign contributions during the 2010 election cycle because they thought the candidates were all exceptionally bright, talented progressives with good hair. They did it to make sure that when the new health care bill passed it would not allow Medicare, with its fifty million plus patients, to bargain for reduced drug costs like the private insurance companies do. They did it to make sure the new bill would not allow the reimportation of medicines from Canada or Mexico. And guess what? It worked.

The insurance industry, through the AHIP, didn't donate millions in campaign contributions and PAC support because the recipients were shining examples of fair-minded leaders who diligently considered all sides of important issues. They did it to make sure that a government-sponsored public option that would compete with them for the newly mandated insured Americans would never see the light of day. And guess what? It won't.

There is a reason that the trial lawyers in this country provided millions to primarily support Democratic candidates in the past election cycle and it wasn't because they were all brought up to be good Democrats like their mothers and fathers. They did it to ensure that any new health care initiative would not contain significant tort reform measures that might threaten the cash cow they call medical malpractice. And guess what? It doesn't.

America's physicians tend to be a generous bunch, and to prove that, they provided politicians with millions of dollars through their lobbying arm, the American Medical Association. But they didn't do it because they were concerned about their congressmen's health. They did it so that Congress would once again delay the draconian cuts in Medicare reimbursement mandated by the Sustained Growth Rate (SGR) initiative that were scheduled to go into effect on January 1, 2010. And guess what? The cuts were delayed. And while my colleagues and I breathed a collective sigh of relief, none of us really expected otherwise.

Do you really think that the scenarios described in the previous paragraphs were coincidental? Do you really believe Nancy Pelosi or Joe Lieberman or Max Baucus when they look you in the eye and tell you with a straight face that the millions of dollars they have received from health industry lobbyists had no influence on their decisions regarding where to compromise on the new health care bill? I certainly don't. Maybe you believe the Republicans like John Boehner, Mitch McConnell, or that gentleman of the House, South Carolina's own Joe "You Lie" Wilson, when they tell you that the health care bill is nothing more than socialized medicine and their opposition to it is their way of looking out for all Americans? Well again, I certainly don't.

Look at any of the sites that list campaign contributions to politicians and their PACs and see how much money was donated by the poor, by Medicaid recipients, by the Medicare program, by the uninsured, by individuals who were forced to file for bankruptcy after their cancer treatments ruined them financially, or by those unfortunate individuals who lost their jobs and their insurance coverage. I am sure I don't have to tell you what you will find. But that is why you don't see their interests protected and why the compromises to ensure passage of the Patient Protection and Affordable Care Act are always compromises affecting them.

This isn't only about health care. We are in the midst of one of the most devastating economic crises since the Great Depression, yet when congressional help came, it came quickly and it came to AIG, to CitiBank, and to a host of other traditionally generous donors who in turn used the money to dole out obscene bonuses to the very individuals responsible for the meltdown. All while the unemployment rate remains high and average Americans continue to gasp for air as they struggle to somehow survive this financial catastrophe. We're told that the economic bailout was necessary; that some financial institutions were too large to let fail. That may be. But there is also a sector of ordinary, hardworking Americans that is too large to let fail, but they do and they will.

Americans, all of us, deserve what we are getting. We have allowed our political system to become nothing more than a well-lubricated machine promoting graft and corruption and sanctioning the buying of our elected representatives' votes. I understand that I may sound cynical, but all of America is becoming cynical, as poll after poll reveals our dissatisfaction with Congress and our lack of confidence in their ability to truly represent us. But cynicism alone solves nothing. If we earnestly want to change the direction in which America is heading, it is time that we cease characterizing our democracy as the greatest on the face of the earth. A democracy is not great that deprives its poor of adequate health care or rewards its wealthiest with bailouts during economic hard times while ignoring the victims of their avarice and mismanagement.

We need to take our cue from Howard Beale, the aging television anchor in the 1976 hit movie *Network*, who proclaimed that he was "mad as hell and wasn't going to take it anymore." If we sit idly by and allow the status quo to be maintained by all those special interests that benefit from the current system, then nothing will ever change. We'll continue to see major issues determined by the checkbooks of the power brokers rather than the needs of American citizens. We'll continue to see politicians spend the lion's share of their time chasing the money to fill their reelection campaign chests rather than representing those who elected them. And ten years from now, twenty years from now, we will see that health care in America hasn't changed.

It's easy and convenient to lay blame for the failure of the current health care reform efforts at the feet of the Republicans, for their role in this entire process has been nothing more than proclaiming our current system the best in the world, characterizing any Democratic initiative as "socialized medicine," and suggesting that medical malpractice reform will solve all the ills. During the February 25, 2010, health care summit convened by President Obama to try and jump-start the debate after Scott Brown's election, House Speaker John Boehner (who was actually House Minority Leader at the time) *actually said* that medical malpractice and defensive medicine were the biggest cost drivers of runaway health care costs.[54] Are you serious, Congressman? What have you been smoking? The impartial Congressional Budget Office estimated that tort reform would reduce health care spending by *one half of one percent* . . . and that's the biggest cost driver?[55] Finally, the Republicans are committed to doing everything in their power to assure meaningful change doesn't happen. That is the best way they could hand Barack Obama and his party an embarrassing setback, improve upon the victories they won in the midterm elections, and keep their sugar daddy supporters happy. Winning back the House or the Senate was much more important than assuring all Americans have access to affordable quality health care.

But the real blame lies with the Democrats, and actually, with the liberal arm of the Democratic Party. Now before I go further you should probably know that I would best describe myself as a "moderate Democrat," although my conservative friends think I am a liberal and my liberal friends think I'm a Nazi. Despite the fact that I am a registered Democrat, I frequently vote across party lines depending on the quality of the candidate and I tend to avoid "ideologues" on either end of the political spectrum. I find the far right too self-absorbed with their own best interests and too wedded to ideological slogans to thoughtfully engage in objective discussions on most major issues. And I find the far left to be bleeding hearts who see themselves as defenders of the poor and saviors of society with little interest in the role of personal responsibility and the consequences of one's actions—to them, everyone's a victim.

But in this debate on health care, the liberals actually had it right, or at least closer to right than any other faction, be it the Blue Dog Democrats or Tea Party Republicans. Now I say that only after almost three years of reading everything I could get my hands on from all over the political map. When it comes to health care, many Americans actually *are* victims—victims of a system that denies them access, ruins them financially in the event of a serious illness, and rewards the profiteers who call the shots in the free enterprise model of medicine we now have.

With the historic election of Barack Obama and the feeling of pride and unity that accompanied his elevation to the presidency, there was, for the first time in recent memory, a golden opportunity to finally address the national disgrace we call American health care. President Obama campaigned on the issue and he told Americans clearly what his vision was for health care reform. Universal coverage, insurance reform, a public option for those who could not afford insurance through the commercial carriers, taxing the "Cadillac" plans to help pay for the poor, allowing Medicare to negotiate prices for prescription drugs, promoting comparative effectiveness research . . . These were all openly revealed to an American public that listened and then swept him into office. The perfect storm was forming for the liberals where a filibuster-proof Congress and a left-leaning, immensely popular president could overcome the long-standing barriers to finally realizing true heath care reform.

Then they folded, both the Democrats and the president.

They allowed the Republicans to take control of the debate. They allowed the Rush Limbaughs and the Glenn Becks of the world to define the battle, and most Americans preferred to sit on the sidelines, ingest whatever Fox News or MSNBC fed to us, and pick sides. We followed the cheerleaders rather than the quarterback and the result was predictable. The rush to pass a health care bill was far too frantic. Politicians on both sides were asked to vote for a measure they didn't have time to read or debate, and to secure rapid passage, provision after provision was compromised away on the altar of special interests. And each time the president compromised, the liberal left cringed, held their noses, and acquiesced.

Soon there was nothing left but a skeleton of the original plan. But Big Pharma was placated, the insurance industry was placated, the trial lawyers were placated, the AMA was placated, and America's poor lost. Even then, unsavory backroom deals were made to pay for the Medicaid burdens in Nebraska and Louisiana in order to secure the votes of their representatives.[56] And how about that "Cadillac" tax? Well, it remained, but labor and other special interests were appeased. Whatever happened to the President Obama who promised us transparency and an end to backroom politics?

And where was the liberal wing of the Democratic Party? Well, we could certainly hear them complain, but their influence was not be found as they shook their heads in disgust and wept softly with each concession. It seemed to me that House Speaker Nancy Pelosi and Senate Majority Leader Harry Reid were more interested in passing *a* health care bill than passing the *right* health care bill. At the end of the day, I am sure they envisioned standing next to the president at the White House ceremony, hands joined and held high, extolling the Democrat's victory in finally reforming health care when all they and their colleagues really accomplished was the selling out of America's disenfranchised, the same individuals they professed to champion.

The passage of a meaningful package of reform required strong leadership and both the president and the Democratic Congress showed they were not up to the task. For the president's part, he should have drawn a line in the sand early on and made it clear that certain provisions (such as the public option) were not open to compromise, vowing to veto a bill that excluded them. On the other hand, once the White House began to cave to the special interests in hopes of securing their support, Congress should have said an emphatic *NO* to the many compromises that gutted the bill of important provisions. Instead what resulted is so watered down that it will fail to resolve the problems, and a decade from now, we will be devoting even more than 17 percent of our GDP to health care. Still millions of Americans will continue to have little or no access to that care despite having a bright, shiny insurance card. Politically, President Obama would have been better off to use his bully pulpit to push through the bill rather than hand it off to Pelosi and Reid to carry. He should have reminded the Republicans, as well as the entire nation, that he was overwhelmingly elected espousing the health reform package of "Obamacare," and instead of courting the special interests he should have exposed them and their congressional minions for what they were. That way, if the bill went down to defeat, it would be the Republican and the Democratic toadies who would get the blame. But instead, it is now going to be viewed as President Obama's failure. What's more ironic is the fact the new plan is labeled "Obamacare" even though it bears little resemblance to the plan he shared with us during the presidential campaign.

But there is even a bigger tragedy in this current fiasco. In 1994, the Clinton administration tried unsuccessfully to address the deficiencies in American health care and they failed miserably, resulting in a midterm election reversal (similar to what we have recently experienced) that had a profound effect on the remainder of the Clinton presidency. A decade from now, when the failures of this proposed bill become evident, there will be calls for reform, but no reasonable politician will touch health care with a ten-foot pole. Additionally, it will be much longer than sixteen years before the American public can stomach the effort to rally around health care reform, as they look back at the battle of 2010, realize the futility of their endeavor, and have little enthusiasm for taking up arms once again. And a large population of Americans will continue to suffer under the "greatest health care system in the world."

It's time for all Americans to become a Howard Beale. It is time for all of us to stand up to our elected leaders and tell them emphatically we are mad as hell and we are not going to take it anymore. If this country is to right itself again, "we the people" need to wrest control of the country back from the privileged few. We need another Thomas Jefferson, Abraham Lincoln, or Martin Luther King. If we are ever going to see meaningful and effective reform in health care, education, the financial system, or any number of other important issues that affect the lives of all Americans, we need to start by reforming the very political system that has essentially paralyzed our ability to address them.

We need to establish term limits, not only for the presidency as we now have, but for the House and Senate as well. Government service was not created to be a lifelong career, for innovation and progress require fresh ideas, which, in turn, require fresh faces. As esteemed as long-serving senior legislators may be, the vision of Strom Thurmond or Robert Byrd (both who were still serving in their nineties and obviously quite feeble) being wheeled into the Senate for a crucial vote should be sufficient to convince all of us that term limits are a necessity in a vibrant democracy.

Politicians should *serve*, *impact* society, and then *move* on. I would propose two six-year terms in the Senate and three four-year terms in the House. Two-year congressional terms simply mean that a U.S. representative does nothing but run for reelection from the moment he or she arrives in Washington. In turn, this means that as soon as they walk through the threshold of the Capitol, the race to capture the big money to finance their campaigns begins and the influence peddling ensues. None of them should receive significant amounts of money from any source and we should limit, as we do, direct contributions. But for us to call ourselves the world's greatest democracy, it is absolutely imperative that we forbid the indirect contributions where the majority of big money is exchanged and close the loopholes that allow the wealthy and the powerful to buy influence unavailable to the common man. No individual nor corporation nor labor union should be allowed to give more than $1,000 in support of a candidate, either directly or indirectly through issue ads that benefit the candidate or "hit pieces" directed at the candidate's opponent.

It is also prudent for us to set an absolute limit on what a candidate may spend on his or her campaign. This would prevent a Bill Gates, a Warren Buffet, or a Rupert Murdoch from self-financing a campaign that could theoretically buy all the media air time in a given market, essentially shutting out the less well-heeled candidate. You want to run for the U.S. Senate? Fine. You can spend up to $20 million; it can be your own $20 million, or it can be gifts from individuals as long as no one person gives you more than $1,000. I doubt if a grand is going to buy anyone enough influence to get a public option insurance plan included or excluded. Running for president? Fine. You can spend up to $100 million, as long as no gift is in excess of $1,000.

And while we're on the subject of the presidency, why not simply elect a candidate to a single seven-year term? We all know it takes a good year or two to get comfortable in that office, so why not let him or her spend the rest of the time improving the lives of average Americans rather than chasing money and making compromises for the sake of reelection? If you're a lame duck from day one, there is no pressure to pay attention to the polls and see what's popular. Just do the job we elected you for and lead! But lead courageously.

Our campaigns have devolved into nothing more than meaningless sound bites and attack ads, which at best mislead and at worst deceive. There should be state and federal "truth in advertising" commissions made up of trusted individuals from all political affiliations that would review all television, radio, and print campaign spots to determine the veracity of the information presented. If it is determined that the spots are false or deceptive, then they don't run, similar to what the FTC now does with product ads. Our elections ought to be based on reasoned *debate*, not on false Madison Avenue marketing ploys. Debate!

Every Sunday for the eight weeks prior to a presidential election, the candidates should square off and debate a different topic—health care, the economy, jobs, the environment, national defense, the BCS College Football Championship format, whatever, but tell us what you really think so we can be better informed as to whether we want you to lead. And in these debates, *answer the freaking question!* When we ask what you would do about unemployment, don't use the question as a segue to tell us how your opponent is soft on crime or is a misogynistic pro-lifer. Tell us what you would do about unemployment. Really, folks, how hard can this be? Campaign reform isn't brain surgery.

This will be a tough sell. Remember the First Amendment. And reform will only result from a grassroots uprising by citizens from every walk of life who are truly dedicated to the democracy envisioned by our forefathers some 235 years ago. It will be made even more difficult by the recent U.S. Supreme Court decision in January 2010, which overturned the many statutes limiting political contributions by corporations and labor unions.[57] Once again, under the umbrella of "free speech," the court granted the wealthy power brokers unlimited ability to shape the political landscape. The cheers and hoots from Wall Street and corporate boardrooms across America were deafening. It is time for all of us to fight back, to say no. It is time for that visionary to emerge and lead that battle to essentially amend the First Amendment and return the power to the people . . . all of the people.

OH, JUST ONE THING MORE OR TWO OR TEN . . .

We aren't quite done yet as there are still a few loose ends that we need to address if "Loboskycare" is going to work. It seems to me that a reasonable place to start is with our friends in the pharmaceutical industry. As I explained in chapter 4, our pharmaceutical giants are among the most successful corporate enterprises in America, but they have lost their focus. Instead of devoting their substantial resources to discovering innovative drugs that will cure cancer or combat the devastation of Alzheimer's disease, they use the lion's share of their riches to produce an endless parade of "copycat" drugs that are no better than those already on the market. By doing so they are able to simply skirt the patent laws so that instead of one or two medicines available for the heartache of gastro-esophageal reflux disease, we now have a half a dozen. I understand that drug companies are in the market to make money and there is no moral imperative to use their talents to ease society's suffering, but let's not be complicit in their mission.

I also understand that developing a successful drug and bringing it to market costs a lot of money, although the evidence suggests it may not be the $800 million price tag that PhRMA wants you to believe. If profit was my main goal, I too would be less than motivated to do the work required to discover a genuinely innovative and lifesaving drug if my competitors could alter a few molecules and sell it on the open market. As a result, I propose two major changes in the way the FDA approves a new drug. First, in order for a new medicine to be brought to market, clinical studies must clearly demonstrate *significant* benefit when compared to what is already currently available rather than just when compared to a placebo. That would eliminate many of the "me too" drugs that now flood the shelves of pharmacies across the country. Such a law would have the additional benefit of removing incentives to use research and development money to create those "me too" drugs and freeing capital for the quest to produce truly valuable new medicines.

Secondly, if a company is going to throw millions of dollars of their own money into such research then they should reap the rewards of their labors. Why not extend pharmaceutical patents an additional five to seven years before the generics are allowed to replicate the drugs and cut into the original manufacturer's profit? I realize there is a danger that Pfizer, for example, could find the cure for diabetes and as the only patent holder extort obscene amounts of money from the needy patients. But certainly, societal pressures and governmental incentives might be able to offset such a risk.

Next, there is absolutely no rational argument to prevent Medicare from using its massive market share to negotiate prices with the large pharmaceutical firms, just like the many for-profit commercial carriers do. Although PhRMA wants you to believe it would decimate their R & D budgets, why doesn't it decimate them when Aetna, Health Net, WellCare, and Kaiser do the same? This would help reduce the monopolistic risks I described above, at the same time eliminating the need for American citizens to travel to Canada or Mexico for affordable medications. Good-bye to the drug trains and hooray for the elderly who will no longer have to choose between their food and their heart medicines.

Enough already with direct-to-consumer advertising (DTC) by the drug companies! Through slick ads and celebrity spokespersons they have convinced us all that we are sick with an array of fabricated maladies that they have the pill to cure. They run these ads for one reason alone—to circumvent the medical professionals who are more skilled than the public at determining what works and what doesn't. They hope to convince you as best as they can to "ask your doctor if Boniva is right for you" so that you pressure him or her to write that prescription at your next visit.

Congress should rescind the law that allows DTC advertising (and leave New Zealand as the only developed country in the world who allows the practice[58]) and stop the drug companies from insinuating themselves between patient and physician. Opening the floodgates to DTC advertising in 1997 has done nothing to improve America's health; instead it has only resulted in massive increases in the number of prescriptions written and launched the profits of the pharmaceutical giants. In addition, we will be spared the discussion of erectile dysfunction in front of our children and grandchildren and will no longer have to listen to a sixty-second commercial with fifteen seconds of hype and forty-five more of rapid-fire recitation of side effects. Lastly, and maybe most importantly, the billions of dollars the industry spends each year on these ads could be put to better use funding their research labs and clinical trials.

Finally, in their quest for new and innovative medicines, pharmaceutical companies perform painstaking research to assess not only the efficacy of a new drug, but its safety as well. During the course of clinical trials, side effects and drug interactions are carefully monitored. Despite such scrutiny, there are instances when a drug that has been approved by the FDA and has been on the market for an extended period of time is found to have a complication or side effect that was not apparent during the initial clinical testing. At times, these untoward effects have proven to be fatal. But that information was not available until we had years of experience with the drug. Therefore, we should immunize the pharmaceutical industry from litigation over these newly discovered side effects. They developed this medicine in good faith and should not be punished for something they did not know or have reason to anticipate. Of course, if these complications were indeed known by the company and that knowledge withheld from the FDA, then that same immunity would be forfeited.

And one more thing . . .

I have been disheartened, but not surprised, by the response of organized medicine in this health care reform debacle. Whether it is the AMA, the American College of Surgeons, my own specialty organization (the American Association of Neurological Surgeons), or the state and county medical societies, the focus is always to point fingers at someone else and refuse to admit physicians' culpability in our current crisis. Our leaders stood up with President Obama and pledged to help craft meaningful reform, but as soon as the lights dimmed and the cameras stopped rolling, they scurried to make sure *our* interests were the ones preserved.

Yes, we agreed with reforming the insurance industry, but once again opposed any attempt at the establishment of a public option. We joined the chorus of "socialized medicine" to frighten Americans, yet didn't offer viable alternatives for those unable to afford insurance through the private sector. And yes, we demanded tort reform, telling Congress that malpractice was forcing many specialists out of business and costing the system billions of dollars in the practice of defensive medicine. But for us tort reform consisted of merely capping pain and suffering to protect ourselves, and little was discussed about how to protect patients from those rare practitioners who really do cause harm.

It is understandable that our own special interest groups should have our special interests at heart. But that is why this entire attempt at reform has failed. Physicians must start looking at health care reform in broader terms, not only what works for us, but equally important, what works for patients. We pay lip service to the importance of patient care, but when you look at our proposals, it becomes obvious that the economic well-being of physicians and the autonomy of the practice of medicine are our first priorities. The success of physician practices and the well-being of our patients do not have to be mutually exclusive.

Physicians are loath to admit our complicity in the failure of the system. As I have discussed throughout this book, physicians are refusing to provide emergency room care for the population they serve with an alarming frequency. We oftentimes cite "malpractice exposure" as the primary cause. Yet in my home state of California, the problem is just as acute, despite having one of the nation's most favorable malpractice reform laws in effect since the mid-1970s. That just doesn't add up. So patients suffer unconscionable delays while ER docs try to transfer them to a community where care is available. And each year more and more of those patients suffer permanent injury or die as a result of the unnecessary delays. But I have read little from organized medical societies that propose we require physicians to serve the emergencies of their communities. It's not our problem.

Additionally, and justifiably, physicians will tell you they refuse ER coverage because of poor reimbursement, as many of those patients are either uninsured or poorly insured through Medicaid. By initiating universal health care (hang on, not socialized medicine), by increasing physician reimbursement to reasonable levels for all insurance plans (including Medicaid), and by providing comprehensive malpractice reform, we would eliminate those barriers to ER coverage. Once those impediments are abolished, emergency room call responsibility should be mandatory for a physician wishing to obtain a license to practice medicine.

To enhance their incomes many physicians have opened their own free-standing surgery hospitals, clinical laboratories, MRI and CT scan centers, as well as dialysis suites. They then "cherry-pick" the healthy and well insured to treat or test at their facilities and slough off the poor and complicated to their local hospitals. They tell you that it improves quality of care by increasing competition with the local hospitals, but in reality, all it does is economically hurt the community hospitals and increase the incomes of the physician/investors. My personal opinion is that we should forbid physicians from owning such facilities, as the potential conflicts of interest (cherry-picking and overutilization of testing) are obvious.

But if we are going to allow doctor/entrepreneurs to compete with community hospitals, then at the very least we must level the playing field so that such facilities are subject to the same regulations as their competition. They should be required to accept all patients, regardless of insurance status, and there should be stricter rules about referring patients to facilities they own. I have no problem with a physician in Los Angeles owning an MRI scanner in San Francisco since his or her patient base would not be located there. If that San Francisco MRI center was more efficient and demonstrated superior quality, it should be profitable for its owner in Los Angeles and not just because it was accepting only the well-insured or filling its schedule with referrals of dubious indications from the owners/investors.

And one more thing . . .

While we're on the subject of doctors, we need more of them. A lot more. Our population has been increasing but we have not opened a new medical school in decades. We are poised to thrust more than forty-five million more Americans (previously uninsured) into a system that was straining to provide access for those already enrolled. Most importantly, as I explained in chapter 9, the culture of medicine has changed dramatically over the past twenty years and I don't think that Washington policy makers or the American public realizes it. Today's physicians are not willing to work one hundred hour weeks (as their predecessors did) and sacrifice their families and personal lives for their professional ones. They want to be doctors but they also want to be husbands and fathers, wives and mothers. They want to be soccer coaches and they want to sing in the church choir just like everyone else. So they seek balance and they work fewer hours, which means more time with their families but also less access for their patients. So we need more of them and we need them now! It is imperative that the government (there's the government again) moves quickly to establish new medical schools and begin infiltrating communities across the United States with a cadre of new practitioners to provide the needed care.

Listen to almost any voice addressing the physician shortage and you will hear a cry for medical schools to turn out more and more primary care doctors and less specialists. Well, it may not surprise you that I disagree. Primary care, especially when provided by family physicians, general internists, or pediatricians, usually involves caring for common maladies such as uncomplicated hypertension or diabetes, sore throats, earaches, runny noses, annual physicals, and well-baby exams. All of these services, as well as preventative measures, such as immunizations and lifestyle counseling (weight reduction, smoking cessation, etc.), are critical to keeping Americans healthy.

But when that hypertension becomes refractory to the usual medications and the diabetes involves more than oral hypoglycemic drugs or simple insulin regimens, those patients are more often than not referred to specialists for their care. As more Americans have become hypertensive and obese and diabetic at earlier ages, those diseases have become more complex, their management has become more involved, and the need for specialty input has increased. Since more and more primary care physicians have been forced to dramatically increase the volume of patients they see in order to insure their incomes keep pace with their rising overhead, they are less able to devote the necessary time to more complex patients and more inclined to remand them to the care of the specialist. The unfortunate truth is that the Marcus Welbys of the world are disappearing quickly and many primary care practices are simply becoming "triage" centers; if you really need care you are sent to the specialist, and if you need to be hospitalized you are sent to the "hospitalist."

To address the "primary care shortage" that has gripped American health care for the last several decades, our system has evolved or adapted. Now it is common for that same primary care, that same triage service to be performed by a physician assistant (P.A.) or a nurse practitioner (N.P.). Theoretically, these health care providers work under the supervision of a licensed physician and early on they did so in the offices of that proctor. But over time their scope of practice has expanded and the oversight has diminished to the point that many of these "non"-physicians essentially run independent practices. Indeed, I see many patients in my own office who refer to their P.A. as "doctor" (and I seriously doubt if the P.A. expends much effort correcting the misconception). These patients have had an exam completed, an MRI performed, and a referral to a neurosurgeon arranged without ever once seeing a primary care physician. Surprisingly, the quality of the examination, the indications for the MRI, and the appropriateness of the specialty referral are similar to those I receive from primary care physicians. Many of my colleagues in medical and surgical specialties confirm the same observation, and I am unaware of any study that presents evidence to the contrary.

The one big difference is that it costs a lot less to train a physician extender (P.A. or N.P.) than it does to train a physician. It also costs a lot less to pay a physician extender than it does to pay a physician. So my question is simple: if a physician assistant or a nurse practitioner can provide essentially the same services that a licensed physician can, *and* if the quality of the care provided is similar, *and* if the cost is significantly less, then why not begin turning out droves of well-trained physician extenders to provide America's primary care and leave those extra slots in U.S. medical schools for the specialists who will be increasingly called upon to provide definitive care? Let's train less primary care physicians but make sure that they take a more active role in really supervising the extenders. It makes sense from both a manpower perspective and an economic perspective as well.

I am sure these proposals will enrage my primary care colleagues. Why not add them to my list? As my wife proofread earlier chapters in this book, she advised me that if it ever got published we would be forced to relocate to a new community. After reading this part, she has had a change of heart. She is now convinced we will need to move to a new country.

Not that the American Academy of Family Physicians would mind.

And one more thing . . .

Speaking of other countries, much has been made of how a revised American health care system will deal with the millions of illegal aliens who reside uninvited in the United States. The average American does not wish to see his or her tax dollars used to pay for the medical care of individuals who are in this country illegally. Such a view is certainly reasonable. However, the numbers characterizing the current cost to our system are as elusive as the illegal aliens themselves; if it were easy to identify those who are here illegally, it would be much easier to address the problem. My experience has been that undocumented individuals are far less likely to access the health care system for fear of discovery. When they do seek access, it is usually for a more serious problem that has progressed because of lack of attention or an emergency such as an auto accident. These circumstances, in turn, are usually much more costly.

So although we cannot state with certainty how big the problem really is or how much the care of undocumented individuals costs us, it is probably safe to say that the impact is not inconsequential. The answer as to how we can best address the issue of health care for illegal immigrants is as complex as the answer to addressing illegal immigration itself. Immigration policy in the United States has for decades been a schizophrenic exercise. The U.S. economy relies on the relatively inexpensive labor provided by the millions of undocumented workers who cross our borders and fill jobs that many

Americans are unwilling to take. Thus, for years, a blind eye was turned to those who arrived from Mexico, China, and much of Latin America. This was essentially the U.S. Immigration Service's own version of "Don't ask. Don't tell."

But every once in awhile (usually during election years) the illegal alien issue is paraded in front of the American public. Those same workers who wash dishes in the back of small restaurants, serve as nannies to our children, or pick the fruits and vegetables that we put on our table become scapegoats for our economic woe du jour. Those on the right respond by wanting to form posses, round up the varmints, and deport them back to their countries of origin. They form vigilante groups to patrol our borders and propose constructing long barriers (has anyone heard of the Berlin Wall?) from California to Texas that will keep the undesirables out. Those on the left decry such policies and, with their bleeding hearts on their sleeves, weep at the thought of breaking up families and returning them to the poverty they left behind. The left resists when others suggest that individuals provide proof of citizenship before accessing the rights enjoyed by Americans and labels such policies as racist. Yet few of these compassionate liberals seem willing to open their wallets and actually pay for that same care they feel our country is morally obligated to provide.

Once again, folks, you can't have it both ways. It serves no useful purpose and usually does more damage to enact a law and then not enforce it. But further discussion on general immigration policy is beyond the scope of my effort here. Those of us in the middle are equally clueless as to the answer and would just as soon not have to deal with it. But, of course, that won't stop me from proposing a solution to the issue of health care for undocumented individuals.

The answer came to me as the result of my personal experience as a patient in a foreign country several years ago. I was invited to be the keynote speaker at an International Trauma Prevention Conference in Turin, Italy. I arrived the day before the conference began but was too early to get into my hotel room, so I left my luggage and grabbed a cab to a museum I was looking forward to visiting. After purchasing my ticket, I anxiously bounded up the white marble staircase toward the first floor of exhibits. Unfortunately for me, I missed one of the steps and fell forward, striking my face squarely on the beautiful marble, which was soon covered in an expanding pool of blood.

Needless to say, I had created quite a spectacle within my first hour in Turin. I tried to calm the screaming women in my less than fluent Italian and was quickly attended to by the museum staff, who summoned an ambulance that drove me to the nearest emergency room. I was soon evaluated by a beautiful Italian ER physician (I decided then and there I loved Italy's medical system) who ordered X-rays and CT scans that confirmed that I had broken my nose. She summoned a plastic surgeon who repaired my facial lacerations and an ENT specialist who determined I would need surgery to repair the nasal bones once the swelling went down. He filled my nose with packing, placed me in nasal splint, and wrote me a prescription for pain medications. The next morning I gave my address to the crowd of dignitaries sporting two black eyes and speaking with a nasal twang that would make even the best country and western singer envious.

Oh, and by the way, when I finished with the ER, I handed them my Visa card praying that the cost of care would not exceed my generous limit. It was courteously returned to me with the revelation that it would cost me nothing. You heard me correctly: nothing. I was informed that I was a guest in their country and in their system (another one of those horrific quasi-socialized medicine havens, no doubt) everyone is covered. I spent some time talking with the doctors who told me that if I was diagnosed with cancer or some chronic disease that didn't require immediate attention, I would be expected to return home for my care, but that an emergency was an emergency. I was speechless and grateful, but as I regained my senses and offered the staff my heartfelt "grazie," I thought how different it would be if the tables were turned. It seemed to me that the Italians' approach was so, I don't know, *kind* and so *charitable*.

If a physician from Italy had come to the United States, slipped on the stairs ascending the Lincoln Memorial, and suffered the same injuries as I had, he would have been taken by ambulance to the nearest hospital and probably received the identical treatments that I had received in his country. But there would have been one big difference. Before leaving the emergency room he would have been presented a bill, probably in the neighborhood of $10,000 (remember he was not enrolled in the Blue Cross PPO Plan so had to pay "retail") for the care he received and he would not have been allowed to board his flight home until arrangements were made to settle his account. He would then return home and relate his experience with the "best medical system in the world."

I realize that this story has nothing to do with illegal aliens; I was visiting Italy legally. But I think it holds the key to how we should treat everyone who must access our system of health care—with kindness and compassion. Americans have always displayed our ingrained humanity and we shouldn't abandon it now. But we must also be practical and again realize that as compassionate as we wish to be, our resources remain finite. So I would propose we treat all aliens, legal or not, as I was treated in Italy. We cannot allow people to die as a result of life-threatening maladies or suffer needlessly in times of true emergencies. We should treat them with the best that we have to offer, and if they are unable to pay for it, then we can do nothing but absorb the cost.

But as to those nonemergent issues that arise, well, again, we should be like the Italians and tell those "visitors," legal or not, they must access their own health care system to address those problems unless they have the means to pay for it here. I know it may sound heartless to deny well-baby checkups to children or antihypertensive medicines to old men, but until we, as a nation, responsibly address the issue of illegal immigration, I see no other choice. Capisce?

Before I forget, one more thing . . .

Quality health care is expensive. It always will be, no matter what reforms we enact. Because of the tremendous costs involved in providing that care, we, as a society and as individuals, must be responsible stewards of the resources made available to fund our health care system. All of us—from the doctors who direct the care, to the hospitals where the care is delivered, to the pharmaceutical companies and device manufacturers whose products support the care, to the insurance firms that manage the care, and to the millions of patients who access the care—all of us have a shared responsibility to assure that American health care is efficient, compassionate, and based on sound scientific evidence.

If we are to offer such care to all Americans, there is no room for wasteful practices, entrepreneurial gouging, or most importantly, outright fraud. Although the costs of fraud are difficult to know with certainty, testifying before the Senate Judiciary Subcommittee on Crime and Drugs, Malcolm Sparrow of Harvard's Kennedy School of Government estimated losses between \$100 and \$500 billion per year.[59] This is an expenditure we can ill afford to absorb. Such fraud is perpetrated by a wide cross section of criminals representing every sector in American health care, including physicians, allied health professionals, hospitals, equipment suppliers, pharmaceutical companies, and yes, even patients. Fraudulent billing practices in the Medicare and Medicaid programs have been around since their inception in the mid-1960s, and as the programs have grown, so have the number of schemes to bilk the system. When you realize that Medicare alone processes over 4.5 million claims each day and pays out almost \$1 billion daily in reimbursement for beneficiary care, it becomes apparent that tracking the integrity of such claims can be daunting.[60]

Health care fraud can occur in a myriad of ways but most often results in billing for services or equipment that were never provided to the patients, oftentimes by entities who aren't really providers in the first place. Commonly, the criminals (sometimes physicians and sometimes not) will simply obtain a list of patient Medicare or Medicaid numbers and file claims for reimbursement even though the patients whose numbers were submitted were never seen.

Others open phony storefront operations that purport to provide Medicare recipients with durable medical equipment (DME) such as canes, wheelchairs, walkers, and the like. Many of these businesses have an address but no inventory, or have a P.O. Box as a place of business. In South Florida alone, of the 1,581 DME providers, 25 percent had no staff and were not operating during their posted business hours.[61] Once again, they obtain Medicare/Medicaid billing numbers and patient IDs and off they go. Physical therapists, speech therapists, and occupational therapists have also been implicated in such deceptive practices. A Houston, Texas, clinic was recently shut down after it was discovered they were providing Medicare patients with "arthritis kits," consisting of a knee brace and heating pad, at more than $3,000 a pop.[62]

Home health services have become fertile ground for wasteful and outright fraudulent activities as our population has aged. Home health services provide nursing care, physical therapy, nutritional support, and other needed amenities for patients who return home after prolonged hospitalizations. The home health nurses will visit the patients' homes, assess their needs, and recommend specific treatments, medical equipment, and other items to assist patients and their families. Needless to say, the opportunity is ripe for unscrupulous providers to order unnecessary services or equipment that benefits no one but the home health agency itself. Because of the large number of retirees who live in South Florida, the region has become one of the nation's hotbeds for Medicare fraud and home health abuses are rampant. At a recent Medicare Fraud Summit, Health and Human Services Secretary Kathleen Sebelius hinted at the scope of the problem when she revealed that over *90 percent* of Medicare home health recipients in Dade County, Florida, receive more than *$100,000* in home health services annually.[63] When compared to other regions of the country, that number is astronomical!

At the same summit meeting, U.S. Attorney General Eric Holder told of two hospital executives from Los Angeles who were convicted of having the neighborhood's homeless patients admitted to their facilities under false pretenses.[64] These individuals were hospitalized for no other reason than inflating their censuses so that they could bill Medicare and Medicaid for undesired and unnecessary services—a nice way to improve their spreadsheets and elevate their standing with corporate honchos and, of course, their Wall Street investors. And at times, patients themselves are more than happy to join the team. By selling their Medicare numbers to scam artists or even accessing certain clinical services they do not need, they receive a kickback to enrich themselves at the expense of the very system designed to care for them, all the while costing taxpayers untold billions of dollars in waste that could have been much better directed for legitimate medical services.

Even more disturbing were the recent indictments of the nationally prominent Small Smiles Centers, a consortium of some seventy dental clinics across the country purportedly established to provide needed care for low-income children, many on Medicaid. On the surface it would seem to be an honorable enterprise, as many of these children have no access to dental care in their communities. Department of Justice officials charged the clinics with performing unnecessary dental procedures on the unsuspecting children, including painful tooth extractions, and billing the Medicaid system for the cost. The investigation resulted in a $24 million settlement.[65] The financial malfeasance in this case is bad enough, but the undue suffering of these young patients is unconscionable.

This type of activity represents only the most egregious of practices. More subtle and more difficult to address are the billions wasted on procedures of dubious clinical indications other than enhancing the provider's income (lab tests, MRI scans, spine surgery, joint replacement), duplication of tests, defensive medicine, and the distribution of unnecessary medical equipment just because it is covered by Medicare. I am sure everyone has seen the TV commercials for motorized wheelchairs encouraging the viewer to "call this number" and promising that they can provide you with this wonderful conveyance at no cost to you. They will even file the Medicare paperwork for you. I just wonder how many of those expensive mobile chairs have been sent to Medicare recipients who really didn't need or require them. Using "creative" coding practices, these companies are able to move their products to countless individuals who would probably be much better off if they got out of their chairs in the first place and did a little exercise. Is this fraud? It's hard to say and much harder to prove because indeed there are patients who would benefit from their use. But I contend that such determinations should be initiated by the treating physician and not be the result of direct-to-consumer marketing while watching *Seinfeld* reruns.

Fraud is certainly not limited to the federally administered programs of Medicare and Medicaid. The entire workers' compensation system provides another opportunity for waste and deception. There is a population of physicians and attorneys whose entire income is generated by the evaluation of workers' compensation patients. The system was created to protect and care for individuals who are injured as a result of on-the-job activities. It was meant to be a form of "no-fault" insurance designed to protect the employer from time-consuming and costly litigation, while making certain the patient received the care he or she required. It has morphed into a battleground between the carriers who deny treatment at every turn and the patients who at times embellish their injuries in hopes of improving their settlements.

In my practice group we have recently chosen to stop seeing workers' compensation patients, as the struggle to obtain authorization for treatment of the legitimately injured worker has become exhausting. In California, the hassle far exceeds the benefit for the treating physician. Not infrequently, by the time authorization has been obtained, the patient's condition has worsened, the outcome is less successful, and the patient is unhappy.

But in general, the fraud here usually presents in two forms. First is the army of worker's compensation independent medical examiners (IMEs) who are charged with examining the patient, reviewing the tests, and determining if treatment is warranted or if long-term compensation is appropriate. Most of these physicians are dedicated to doing a good job of evaluating the patient, without bias, and making recommendations that are fair to both parties. Others simply run "comp mills" that generate multipage reports without ever laying a hand on the patient. I have reviewed ten- to fifteen-page documents from these individuals that describe rather detailed motor, sensory, and reflex examinations and MRI interpretations. However, when I discuss the report findings with the patients, I am surprised to learn that they were never examined and that the MRIs they brought with them were never looked at by the doctor. Indeed, when I review the IME's "independent" interpretation of the MRI scan, I find it uncannily similar (and usually identical) to the written report of the radiologist. That, my friends, is fraud.

On the other side are those who suffer injuries but yet have complaints disproportionate to their physical and radiological findings. Take, for example, Michelle Brand, a thirty-four-year-old woman who was legitimately injured in her job as a cafeteria worker and suffered a ruptured disk in her low back. Prior to reparative microsurgery, each time she presented to my office she did so in a wheelchair propelled by her boyfriend. She tearfully recounted her intolerable pain and inability to walk more than ten feet. At surgery a moderate-sized fragment of disc, which was compressing the nerve going down her right leg, was removed. I expected a quick and complete recovery.

Instead, Michelle returned to see me still in the wheelchair, still alleging an inability to return to work and demanding that I extend her disability for another month. This prompted a follow-up MRI scan that looked pristine, without a trace of the previous disk fragment. I was perplexed, as the objective neurological deficits prior to surgery had completely resolved. And I remained perplexed until nine days later when I received a video from her workers' compensation carrier that showed her walking briskly through the mall, lugging three large bags of merchandise and tossing them effortlessly into the trunk of her car. The carrier also informed me that Michelle had an airline ticket for a trip to Hawaii leaving in ten days.

When I asked Michelle to come in for a follow-up visit, she again returned in the wheelchair, her eyes red and cheeks moist, grimacing in pain. But rather than examine her, I simply wheeled her and her boyfriend into my private office and placed the DVD from the insurance carrier into the computer. Michelle was awestruck, then embarrassed, then enraged. She rose from the wheelchair (a feat I had not seen since watching Oral Roberts on TV as a child), let out with a few choice expletives, and stormed out of my office. That, my friends, is fraud.

Finally, health care fraud can be perpetrated by the suits in corporate boardrooms across America with equal skill and cunning. In the largest health care fraud case ever recorded, the pharmaceutical giant Pfizer recently paid out $2.3 billion dollars to settle a case involving illegal kickbacks and off-label drug marketing.[66] And Pfizer's corporate competitors, Eli Lilly and Merck, no doubt doing their best to keep pace, each settled similar federal suits for $1.4 billion and $58 million respectively.[67]

For decades, the financial resources to combat health care fraud have been sorely lacking, making entities such as Medicare or workers' compensation nothing more than a candy store of opportunity for the criminal element. Some FBI sources have found that the returns are so enormous and the risk of detection so low that many organized crime rings have shifted their focus from illegal drug trafficking to health care fraud, with good reason. It is high time that the crime fighters of the Department of Justice and the Department of Health and Human Services get serious about fraud, not only its detection but also its prevention. The good news is that help may be on the way.

Back in 2005, Congress rejected a budget request of $300 million to combat fraud, despite data from the Office of the Inspector General that found that for every dollar expended in the fight against health care fraud, $17 were recovered—not a bad trade-off, if you ask me.[68] But two years later, the Bush administration established several Medicare Fraud Strike Forces, created using agents from both the Department of Justice (DOJ) and Health and Human Services (HHS), to target specific regions in the United States where fraud was rampant. Directing efforts in Florida, California, Texas, and other states, they began successfully exposing and prosecuting a growing number of health care fraud cases, resulting in the incarceration of hundreds of criminal perpetrators and the recovery of billions of dollars in Medicare payments and fines.[69]

It appears the Obama administration is locked in as well. The 2009 fiscal year budget for combating fraud was approximately $200 million and increased 50 percent to $300 million in 2010.[70] In May 2009, Secretary Sebelius and Attorney General Holder announced the formation of a joint HHS and DOJ initiative called the Health Care Fraud Prevention and Enforcement Action Team (HEAT) to build on the success of the Bush administration's Medicare Strike Force teams.[71] In 2009, convictions for false claims fraud skyrocketed to 580 and the DOJ recovered over $2.2 billion under the False Claims Act.[72] More encouraging is the fact that the budget to clamp down on these parasites is slated to increase even further in 2011 to $561 million.[73] These efforts should put criminals on notice that the government is finally serious about curbing the crime of fraud in health care. It appears there's a new sheriff in town.

And one last thing . . . Really, I promise.

Technology is truly awe-inspiring and American technology ranks among the world's best. It has allowed us to diagnosis diseases that a generation ago eluded detection. It has led to safer interventions, to more complete tumor resections through minimally invasive surgical pathways, and to shorter hospital stays with better outcomes. We are truly blessed as doctors and as patients to have such tools at our disposal. But technology also drives, to a great degree, the high cost of medical care in this country, especially when it becomes technology applied for technology's sake.

Physicians who utilize such tools must bear the responsibility for using such advances judiciously. We must also be willing to rely on time-honored procedures that, although less technologically "advanced" and with less potential for "marketability," are equal in efficacy to the more expensive high-tech endeavors. Everyone clamors for their "laser surgery" after reading the glossy ads that appear in airline in-flight magazines. It then takes a significant effort for practitioners to explain to their patients the difference between science and marketing. For some surgeries the laser has a distinct advantage, but for many others, the only difference between the laser and the scalpel is the price.

Computers are being integrated into all aspects of American health care, both in the operating room as well as in the physician's office. In remote regions of the country where access to a physician or physician extender is limited, patients can now visit a provider online. They can relate their history and using laptop-mounted cameras show the doctor their rash. They can even apply a stethoscope to their heart so that the cardiologist five hundred miles away can listen to its rhythmic beating. All of this is great application of technology and should be pursued with abandon.

I have been intrigued by the number of pundits, be they politicians or policy wonks, who have focused attention on electronic medical records (EMR) as one of the keys to solving America's health care crisis and controlling runaway costs. I figured that Bill Gates or the late Steve Jobs sent corporate moles to infiltrate the campaigns of each presidential candidate and, while everyone was asleep on their well-appointed bus or private plane, subliminally suggest that the adoption of EMRs was the answer they were looking for.

For as long as anyone can remember, a patient encounter, whether it be in a physician's office or in a hospital, was recorded in a paper chart known as the medical record. Each time the patient returned, that same chart was accessed and information added. You can only imagine the size of some of these charts accumulated over years of interaction. The law requires that such documents are preserved for a minimum of seven years and this is true even for X-rays and laboratory tests. The amount of storage required to house such information is enormous. In addition, such information is not very portable and a physician seeing a patient in his office does not have access to the records of that same patient's recent admission to the hospital. And two weeks earlier when that patient presented to the emergency room in a diabetic coma, the ER physician had no access to that patient's history, as it was stored in the office of his primary care provider.

With the application of computers in medicine, hospitals began storing records electronically and freeing up the space that was previously cannibalized by the tons of paper charts that held the medical stories of thousands upon thousands of patients. Over time, physicians began to see the light and started modernizing their office charts as well. Not only does this save money on storage space, but more importantly, with the click of a mouse, the most important information regarding each and every patient can be immediately relayed not only to the local emergency room, but to virtually any hospital or physician in the world with access to a computer. When I kissed the marble with my nose in Italy, if I had been taken to the ER unconscious, they could have contacted my hometown hospital who would quickly scan my record and forward it on.

So EMRs are a good idea. They can improve safety by making unfamiliar providers aware of a patient's allergies and medications, alerting them to preexisting conditions, and even (with all due respect to Sarah Palin) letting them know if the patient had an advanced directive regarding the care they wished to receive if they were incapacitated. Theoretically, medical errors would be reduced since patients would be less likely to receive a medication to which they were allergic or which interacted unfavorably with a medication they were currently taking. And yes, the EMR might prevent the initiation of CPR on a terminally ill ninety-two-year-old woman who would not want her life prolonged. Or it might prevent doctors from placing a patient on a life support system who had specifically directed those who care for him to never do so. Or it might be able to honor the religious beliefs of a Jehovah's Witness who would refuse blood products under any circumstance.

However, for such safeguards to work, it is imperative that all the EMR systems available on the market have the ability to "communicate" with one another. If Doctor Jones has the Brand X EMR System in his office and his community hospital has installed Brand Y, they may not be able to share that important information the system was designed to facilitate. The other obstacle to the adoption of an EMR system is the cost. Physicians can find themselves spending $50,000 to $100,000 to incorporate a reliable EMR system in their practices. With the rapid changes in technological advances today, many doctors are wary of expending such a capital outlay only to find it obsolete in three or four years.

I would propose that we move toward a "National EMR Network" that seamlessly connects all physicians and hospitals across the United States and its territories. A task force of financially disinterested experts could sit down and assess the pros and cons of all EMR systems currently available or in development and award the contract not necessarily to the lowest bidder, but to the creator of the best system. The government then would bear the cost of installing such a system into all physician offices and care facilities across America. Let's face it; the cost of such a program will be substantial. So although EMRs may indeed save the system money by reducing medical errors and eliminating duplication of tests, I seriously doubt it will have the financial impact on health care costs that so many politicians and proponents promise.

But imagine how much safer and more efficient it would be if, as occurs in several other developed countries already, each citizen had in a wallet or on a bracelet a thin flash drive that could be slipped into the USB port on a computer in any emergency room in America and immediately make the treating doctor as knowledgeable of that patient's medical history as his or her own family doctor. It may indeed be expensive and it may not save much money in the long run, but it just might save lives.

And isn't that really what health care reform is all about?

Epilogue

$\mathscr{I}$ began writing this book over three years ago. It started out as nothing more than a catharsis, a way of cleansing my soul of the cynicism that I found insinuating itself into both my personal and medical psyches. I had been a doctor since 1977, and even through the travails of managed care, declining reimbursement, and suffocating paperwork that evolved during my career, I still loved my job. I found great joy and satisfaction in my interactions with my patients, and I was stimulated by the advances in technology that offered my patients better treatments and helped to transform many of their lives.

But all that changed when our local medical community went through a crisis of its own, a crisis that tore at the very fabric of collegiality that we had all enjoyed for so many years. I became disheartened as colleagues were filled with pessimism and bile. I was saddened and ashamed when physicians of incomparable skill and unquestionable devotion to quality patient care began opting out of on-call ER responsibilities and leaving our community of patients under the care of "locum tenens" practitioners who neither lived in our community nor had an emotional investment in their care. They were shift workers who came in, provided care, picked up their checks, and went on their way. The practice of medicine was not supposed to be like this, especially not in our community.

In my disenchantment and despair, I found my own attitude changing. No longer did I look forward to my daily schedule of patients nor the interesting challenges their maladies presented me. This feeling was so foreign; I could not recognize nor understand it, but my wife could. Her advice was simple: "Get your fire back! You need to do so for yourself, but more importantly, for your patients." She reminded me that I had always loved to write, since my days as editor of my high school newspaper, and suggested that I write as a way of understanding what went wrong and how it could be fixed. So I started to write.

As I began examining what forces were responsible for the breakdown of our own medical staff in particular and for the growing chasm between doctors and their patients in general, I soon realized that our experience was not unique but had been repeated in community after community across our nation. It was just our turn. It dawned on me that this was not a problem of uncaring doctors or ungrateful patients. The overwhelming majority of physicians were truly committed to quality care; they toiled endlessly on behalf of their patients and they were determined to make them whole. And patients still wanted to trust their doctors and place their health, and at times their lives, in their hands. Patients understood how difficult the road to a medical career could be and appreciated the effort and dedication required to attain that goal. No, the problem was neither the individual doctor nor the individual patient; the problem was the *system*.

And so my focus changed and I began to explore the system in which we practice the art of medicine. I began to delve into the history of the various components that make up and drive medical care and I became fascinated with how each began and, more importantly, with how each evolved. And as I did, I became enlightened and finally began to understand just how America's health care system had arrived at its current state of dysfunction. I began to see the light and was determined that my patients, that *all* patients, should see it, too.

But life does not occur in a vacuum and by luck (or by fate), at the time I was writing this book, the politics of the 2008 presidential election began to take center stage. Not surprisingly, the issue of American health care rose to the forefront. Since I had already developed an understanding of our system both from a historical perspective as well as from the personal perspective of a community practitioner, I was fixated on the proposed solutions offered by the various candidates. And when Barack Obama was elected president on that historic November evening, I was filled with the same hope that millions of other Americans shared. I was ready to see if he would succeed and truly reform our broken system.

I remained engaged throughout the year and a half of acrimonious debate, paying close attention to the special interests I knew would try to abduct the bill and preserve the status quo. I did not agree with all that President Obama had proposed. As someone who practices every day in the trenches, I knew some of his plan to be impractical and destined to fail. But I had hoped that bipartisan cooperation would result, in the end, in a bill that would truly save American health care. But as the debate began to shift from the center to the extremes on the right and on the left, and as more and more important components of the bill were sacrificed on the altar of the special interests, I knew that successful reform was doomed.

This book is intended not only to educate, but to inspire. Somewhere among us there must exist leaders with selfless intent and great charisma who can lead all of us in the middle to revolt—to revolt against a system that allows the overt sale of political influence, that breeds political intolerance and makes meaningful reform of almost any institution virtually impossible. I was intrigued as the Tea Party phenomenon grew and heartened that maybe, just maybe, it might be the platform for reasoned debate and rational discourse. Yet, as I have seen it emerge, I am afraid that we are spawning just another political movement dominated by extremism, an antigovernment extremism, unlike liberal or conservative extremism, that believes all government is bad and will not allow that sometimes it is the only solution to an issue imbued with interests that conflict.

The recent health care debate was far too important for us to allow it to be dominated by the far right or the far left and framed by politicians who were in the back pockets of the special interests or the TV pundits so many of us turn to for guidance. I suggest to all of you that this debate was a battle for our nation's collective soul and will define, both to ourselves and to the world, who we are as a people for decades to come. This debate is not about being a Democrat or a Republican or a Tea Partier. It is not about Nancy Pelosi or Sarah Palin. It is not about Glenn Beck or Keith Olbermann. Nor is this debate about those of us with a job that provides coverage, nor about those with other forms of insurance that guarantee us quality care. It's not about Americans who say they are happy with their insurance or those of means who can afford to access the many miracles American medicine has to offer.

As I said earlier, this debate is not about the "haves"; it's about the "have-nots." This debate is about those who for years have been denied health care coverage because they had a preexisting condition and actually needed coverage the most. It's about hardworking Americans stuck in a job they hate because if they leave, they stand to lose the insurance that is covering the chemotherapy for their wife battling breast cancer. It is about those American families who now stand to lose everything they own because their young child has developed leukemia and needs a bone marrow transplant that costs far beyond the paltry coverage offered by their employer. It's about senior citizens who are forced to choose between paying for their blood pressure medicines and paying their heating bills. It's about the thousands of Americans who are forced to travel abroad to obtain the medical care they need because it is not affordable for them here.

What we must all understand is that every one of us is one closed factory away from being one of those have-nots. Every one of us is one more premium increase away from having our employer no longer able to afford insurance, thus making us a have-not. And as a country, if a decade from now we find we are spending 20 percent or more of our GDP on health care and are no longer able to adequately fund our schools or Social Security, we will become a nation of have-nots.

The time has come for all of us—Democrats, Republicans, Independents, and Tea Partiers alike—to stand up and to demand more: to demand more from our health care system, to demand more from our doctors, to demand more from our hospitals, to demand more from the companies that create our medicines and medical devices, to demand more from the legal profession, and to demand more from our politicians. But most of all, the time has come for us to demand more from ourselves. Each of us looks upon our wonderful country with a profound sense of pride. With good reason, we hold America up to the world as a great and noble nation. Here's the chance for us to prove it.

Acknowledgments

Creating a book requires much more than an author putting his or her thoughts to paper. My experience writing this one has taught me that pressing a series of keys on a word processor is probably the easiest part of the task at hand. In the words of former first lady and current secretary of state Hillary Clinton, "It takes a village." And I am fortunate that my village is populated by a multitude of family, friends, colleagues, and scholars who have assisted me along the journey.

I greatly appreciated the constant input of so many of my closest friends who listened to me drone on ad nauseam about this project and enlightened me with their perspectives on the many issues I address throughout the book. I found their candid remarks about my own opinions helpful beyond measure. They forced me, time and again, to reassess my interpretation of the information, which in the end, I believe, resulted in a more balanced presentation of the data. My 8:24 Saturday morning golf partners—Jim Boice, Dave Valponi, Will Bono, and Ben Cannon—tolerated my unrestrained banter about health care these past three years as we sauntered along the links and they gave me a varied perspective that oftentimes properly tempered my zeal. I am especially indebted to Ben, who along the way read each and every chapter as it unfolded and reassured me that the final product was worth my effort.

My partners and our staff at Northstate Neurosurgical Associates have provided unwavering support for this project, and I am buoyed by their anticipation of finally seeing it come to fruition. My medical assistant, Patty Chamberlain, was a reliable sounding board who represented the population of soccer moms I was hoping to reach with my message. Her effusive responses to each completed section reinvigorated my joy in writing, but most of all, I appreciated the way she would laugh at all the subtle jokes and innuendos I would bury within the pages.

My longtime friend and favorite lawyer, Dave Dimitruk, provided invaluable insight in reviewing my chapter on medical liability as well as reviewing for me the details of the many contracts whenever I asked. The persistent interest in the book by "Dog" and his wife, Vicki, has been a source of constant encouragement throughout this process. Dr. Michelle Mello from Harvard Law School was a wonderful source of information on the medical malpractice issue, and I benefited beyond words from her willingness to respond to my e-mails and point me in the right direction.

My brother-in-law, Mark Merryfield, and his staff provided me with all of the financial data on the pharmaceutical and insurance companies, as well as their CEOs. Their mining of that data was a godsend for me. Dave Sayer was kind enough to help me understand the ins and outs of the insurance industry and direct me to the sites that not only answered my initial questions about health insurance but helped me ask better questions as the work progressed. Dev Corbin enlightened me with a drug rep's perspective of my chapter on the pharmaceutical companies. Her unabashed defense of certain practices and unbiased admission of some of the industry's shortcomings helped me see both sides of a complex business.

Matt Meuter, a professor in the Business College at Chico State University (whom I have known since he was a student), provided me with a "business"-oriented response to the work. I learned a lot from Matt and found his critique of the book to be insightful and illuminating. Matt Jackson was another of the chosen few that I asked to review the manuscript and provide feedback. His candor and his unwavering support have propped me up on more than one occasion. I also must thank Hank and Madeline McGowan, who carefully poured through the book and provided me with valuable insight, as well as Brent Roden, who painstakingly scrutinized every word.

The office staff of the California Medical Association was indispensable in helping me to understand some of the varied laws and regulations that govern medicine and frustrate physicians. They freely provided me with information on everything from the federal Emergency Medical Treatment and Active Labor Act (EMTALA) to state laws mandating translators in physicians' offices. Katie Orrico, organized neurosurgery's own legislative superstar, has always kept me posted on federal health care issues and was a treasure of information during the debate on the Patient Protection and Affordable Care Act.

I owe a debt of gratitude to my agent, Bob Diforio from the D4EO Literary Agency, for taking a chance on a first-time, relatively unknown author simply because Bob believed in the book and felt that it was important to get the message out in hopes of effecting a change. Suzanne Staszak-Silva, Melissa McNitt, and Kimberly Ball Smith at Rowman & Littlefield were most responsible for assuring my book would see the light of day, and I will be forever grateful to them and their staff for shepherding the work through from manuscript to final product.

My baby sister, Julie Harman, is one of the most creative people I know and she has assisted me in this project in a myriad of ways. It is somewhat sobering to realize that even though I am a neurosurgeon, I am considered the "underachiever" of the family, yet having her and my younger brother, Greg, as siblings, I am forced to face that fact.

And while I am on the subject of family I must thank my three children, Hollie, Kimberly, and Grayson, for not only sharing their input and support along the way but for being the reason I wrote this book. My daughters' husbands, Jeff Harris and Marc Castleman, married into the family but I still love them as sons and appreciate the encouragement and interest they both provided along the way. Changing the way we deliver medical care is necessary for two good reasons: Rilyn Avery Harris and Emerson Keely Harris, my granddaughters. I owe it to them to make sure every American has affordable access to the wonders of American medicine. Hopefully this book will help to do just that. My mother-in-law, Mary McLing, provided valuable insight into the plight of our seniors. I will always be grateful for her candor.

Good marriages require nurturing and hard work. I have been blessed for the past thirty-nine years to have by my side a woman of incomparable beauty, intellect, compassion, optimism, and grace. From the moment we met, I knew Diana was special and I have been the beneficiary of her many gifts from that moment on. She is the one who worked hard to put me through medical school, who selflessly filled the roles of both mother and father at times when my career called me away. She has kept me humble (with good reason) and yet makes me feel like the most fortunate man alive. It was indeed Diana who suggested I write this book and who refused to allow me to give it up when time and again my frustration compelled me to do so. She was quick to let me know when what I wrote was unfair or could be hurtful and would always suggest a better way to make my point. This book is as much her creation as it is mine.

Notes

PROLOGUE

1. The Emergency Medical Treatment and Active Labor Act of 1986, 42 U.S.C. §1395dd (1986).

CHAPTER TWO

1. "Strong American Schools," The National Academy of Science, The Organization for Economic Cooperation and Development, Post Secondary Education Opportunity, *Sources* (2007).

2. Lynne Sladky, "One-Third of Students Need Remedial College Math, Reading," *USA Today*, May 11, 2010, www.usatoday.com/news/education/2010-05-11-remeddial-college_N.html.

3. World Health Organization, *World Health Report* (Geneva: World Health Organization, 2006).

4. Ibid.

5. Ibid.

6. Ibid.

7. Ibid.

8. Ibid.

9. Ibid.

10. Ibid.

11. Ibid.

12. Ibid.

13. Ibid.

14. Ibid.

15. Ibid.

16. Ibid.

17. Centers for Medicare and Medicaid Services, U.S. Department of Health and Human Services, "National Health Expenditure Data," www.cms.gov/NationalHealth ExpendData/02_NationalHealthAccountsHistorical.asp#TopOfPage.

18. World Health Organization, *World Health Report 2000* (Geneva: World Health Organization, 2000).

19. Phillip Musgrove, "Judging Health Systems: Reflections on the WHO's Methods," *The Lancet* 361, no. 9371 (May 2003): 1817–20, doi: 10.1016/S0140 -6736(03)13408-3.

20. Phillip Musgrove, in discussion with the author, April 23, 2010.

21. Phillip Musgrove, "Health Care Rankings," *The New England Journal of Medicine* 362, no. 16 (August 22, 2010): 1546–47.

22. J. K. Rajaratnam et al., "Neonatal, Post-neonatal, Childhood and Under 5 Mortality for 187 Countries, 1970–2010: A Systematic Analysis of Progress Towards Millennium Development Goal 4," *The Lancet* 6736, no. 10 (May 24, 2010): 60703–9, doi:10.10.16/S0140; M. C. Hogan et al., "Maternal Mortality for 181 Countries: A Systematic Analysis of Progress Towards Millennium Development Goal 5," *The Lancet* 375, no. 9726 (May 8, 2010): 1609–23, doi:10.1016/ S0140-6736(10)60518-1.

23. "47 Million Americans Without Health Insurance, Census Report," *Medical News Today*, August 29, 2007.

24. David U. Himmelstein, M.D., Deborah Thorne, Ph.D., Elizabeth Warren, J.D., Steffie Woolhandler, M.D., M.P.H., "Medical Bankruptcy in the United States, 2007: Results of a National Study," *American Journal of Medicine* 122, no. 8 (August 2009): 741–46, doi:10.1016/j.amjmed.2009.04.012.

25. Neal Conan, "Medical Tourism and the Costs of Traveling for Care," *Talk of the Nation*, National Public Radio, March 8, 2007.

26. Ibid.

27. Patrick Marsek, in discussion with the author, July 10, 2007.

28. Mark Tutton, "Medical Tourism: Have Illness, Will Travel," CNNHealth .com, March 26, 2009, www.cnn.com/2009/HEALTH/03/26/medical.tourism.

29. Dawn Frantangelo, *NBC Nightly News*, May 15, 2007.

30. Marcia Angell, *The Truth About the Drug Companies: How They Deceive Us and What to Do About It* (New York: Random House, 2004).

CHAPTER THREE

1. Jonathan Cohn, *Sick: The Untold Story of America's Health Care Crisis and the People Who Pay the Price* (New York: Harper Collins Publishers, 2007); Jill Quadagno, *One Nation, Uninsured: Why the U.S. Has No Health Insurance* (New York: Oxford University Press, 2005); Norma Nielson, "Health Insurance," *Microsoft Encarta Online Encyclopedia*, 2007; Melissa Thomasson, "Health Insurance in the United States," eh.net, April 18, 2003, eh.net/encyclopedia/article/thomasson.insurance.health.us;

Melissa Thomasson, "From Sickness to Health: The Twentieth Century Develop-
ment of U.S. Health Insurance," *Explorations in Economic History* (July 2002): 39;
"The History of Blue Cross Blue Shield," BlueCross BlueShield Association Website;
Gareth Marples, "History of Insurance," the historyof.net; Michael F. Makover,
Mismanaged Care: How Corporate Medicine Jeopardizes Your Health (Amherst, NY:
Prometheus Books, 1998).

2. Ibid.
3. Ibid.
4. Ibid.
5. Ibid.
6. Ibid.
7. Ibid.
8. Ibid.
9. Ibid.
10. Ibid.
11. Ibid.
12. Ibid.
13. Ibid.
14. Ibid.
15. Ibid.
16. Ibid.
17. The Wage and Price Stabilization Act of 1942, 50 U.S.C. §901 et seq. (1942).
18. Nielson, "Health Insurance"; Thomasson, "Health Insurance in the United
States"; Thomasson, "From Sickness to Health"; Marples, "History of Insurance."
19. Ibid.
20. David Blumenthal, M.D., M.P.P., and James Morone, Ph.D., "The Lessons
of Success: Revisiting the Medicare Story," *The New England Journal of Medicine* 359
(2008): 2384–89.
21. Ibid.
22. The Health Maintenance Organization Act of 1973, 42 U.S.C. §300e (1973).
23. Ibid.
24. Nielson, "Health Insurance"; Thomasson, "Health Insurance in the United
States"; Thomasson, "From Sickness to Health"; Marples, "History of Insurance."
25. Ibid.
26. Cohn, *Sick.*
27. Bob Egelko, "Court Limits Health Insurance Policy Cancellations," *San Francisco Chronicle*, December 26, 2007.
28. Victoria Colliver, "Health Net Fined for Deception: Lying About Bonuses to
Cost Insurer $1 Million Penalty," *San Francisco Chronicle*, November 16, 2007.
29. Annual Reports filed with the United States Securities and Exchange Commission, provided by Mark Merryfield, Senior Vice President for Morgan Stanley,
Laguna Niguel, California.
30. Ibid.
31. Ibid.

32. Russell Turk, M.D., "The Doctor Is In: How Health Insurers Hinder Health Care Reform," dailyfinance.com, October 7, 2009, www.dailyfinance.com/2009/10/07/the-doctor-is-in-taking-aim-at-health-insurance-companies-hold/.

CHAPTER FOUR

1. Kevin Brown, *Penicillin Man: Alexander Fleming and the Antibiotic Revolution* (Stroud, UK: Sutton, 2004); Andre Maurois, *The Life of Sir Alexander Fleming: Discoverer of Penicillin* (New York: Dutton, 1959); Wikipedia on Alexander Fleming, en.wikipedia.org/wiki/Alexander_Fleming.

2. Ibid.

3. Brown, *Penicillin Man*; Maurois, *The Life of Sir Alexander Fleming*; Wikipedia on Alexander Fleming; Ralph Lardau, Basil Achilladelis, and Alexander Scriabine, *Pharmaceutical Innovation: Revolutionizing Human Health* (Philadelphia: Chemical Heritage Press, 1999).

4. S. Hadzovic, "Pharmacy and the Great Contribution of Arab Islamic Science to Its Development," *Med Arh.* 51, nos. 1–2 (1997): 47–50; Wikipedia on the pharmaceutical industry, en.wikipedia.org/wiki/Pharmaceutical_industry.

5. Lardau, Achilladelis, and Scriabine, *Pharmaceutical Innovation*; Merrill Goozner, *The $800 Million Pill: The Truth Behind the Cost of New Drugs* (Berkeley: University of California Press, 2004).

6. Goozner, *The $800 Million Pill*.

7. Ibid.

8. Lardau, Achilladelis, and Scriabine, *Pharmaceutical Innovation*; Goozner, *The $800 Million Pill*; *The Columbia Encyclopedia*, 2001–2008, s.v. "mustard gas."

9. Lardau, Achilladelis, and Scriabine, *Pharmaceutical Innovation*; Goozner, *The $800 Million Pill*; *The Columbia Encyclopedia*, s.v. "mustard gas;" "Disaster at Bari: December 1943," RSA.org, November 2008, www.rsa.org.nz/review/art2003 november/article_3.htm.

10. Lardau, Achilladelis, and Scriabine, *Pharmaceutical Innovation*.

11. Wikipedia on the pharmaceutical industry.

12. Marcia Angell, *The Truth About the Drug Companies: How They Deceive Us and What to Do About It* (New York: Random House, 2004).

13. Robert Pear, "Research Cost for New Drugs Said to Soar," *New York Times*, December 1, 2001.

14. Joseph A. DiMasi, Ronald W. Hansen, and Henry G. Grabowski, "The Price of Innovation: New Estimates of Drug Development Costs," *The Journal of Health Economics* 22 (2003): 151–85.

15. "Rx R&D Myths: The Case Against the Drug Industry's R&D Scare Card," *Public Citizen Congress Watch*, July 2001, www.citizen.org/documents/ACFDC.PDF.

16. Ibid.

17. The Bayh-Dole University and Small Business Patent Act of 1980, 35 U.S.C. §§ 200–212 (1980).

18. Goozner, *The $800 Million Pill*; Angell, *The Truth About the Drug Companies.*

19. Goozner, *The $800 Million Pill*; Angell, *The Truth About the Drug Companies*; Martha Raffaele, "Merck to Pay $58 Million to Settle Vioxx Ad Claims," *San Francisco Chronicle*, May 31, 2008; Lindsey Tanner, "Reports Raise Questions on Vioxx Trials," *San Francisco Chronicle*, April 16, 2008.

20. Raffaele, "Merck to Pay $58 Million to Settle Vioxx Ad Claims"; Tanner, "Reports Raise Questions on Vioxx Trials."

21. Tanner, "Reports Raise Questions on Vioxx Trials"; Joseph S. Ross, M.D., M.H.S., et al., "Guest Authorship and Ghostwriting in Publications Related to Rofecoxib: A Case Study of Industry Documents from Rofecoxib Litigation," *The Journal of the American Medical Association* 299, no. 15 (2008): 1800–1812, doi: 10.1001/jama.299.15.1800; Bruce M. Psaty, M.D., Ph.D., and Richard A. Kronmal, Ph.D., "Reporting Mortality Findings in Trials of Rofecoxib for Alzheimer Disease or Cognitive Impairment: A Case Study Based on Documents from Rofecoxib Litigation," *The Journal of the American Medical Association* 299, no. 15 (2008): 1813–17, doi:10.1001/jama.299.15.1813.

22. Alex Berenson, "Lilly Discussing Fine to Settle Drug Probe," *San Francisco Chronicle*, January 31, 2008.

23. Goozner, *The $800 Million Pill.*

24. James T. Robinson, "Changing the Face of Detailing By Motivating Physicians to See Pharmaceutical Sales Reps," *Product Management Today*, November 2003.

25. Julie Appleby, "Analyzing the Side Effects of Drug Ads," *USA Today*, March 4, 2008.

26. Appleby, "Analyzing the Side Effects of Drug Ads"; Julie Appleby, "Drug Ads Push Rx Requests Higher," *USA Today*, March 3, 2008.

27. Julie Snider, "Kaiser Family Foundation/Harvard School of Public Health Survey," *USA Today*, March 3, 2008.

28. "Retail Prescription Drug Sales 1995–2009," www.census.gov/compendia/statab/2011/tables/11s0155.pdf.

29. Goozner, *The $800 Million Pill*; Angell, *The Truth About the Drug Companies.*

30. Goozner, *The $800 Million Pill*; Appleby, "Analyzing the Side Effects of Drug Ads"; Appleby, "Drug Ads Push Rx Requests Higher"; "Retail Prescription Drug Sales: 1995–2009."

31. Angell, *The Truth About the Drug Companies.*

32. Ray Moynihan and Alan Cassels, *Selling Sickness: How the World's Biggest Pharmaceutical Companies Are Turning Us All Into Patients* (New York: Nation Books, 2005).

33. Angell, *The Truth About the Drug Companies.*

34. Goozner, *The $800 Million Pill*; Angell, *The Truth About the Drug Companies.*

35. Appleby, "Drug Ads Push Rx Requests Higher."

36. Angell, *The Truth About the Drug Companies.*

37. Ibid.

38. Ibid.; Charles Babcock, "Patent Fight Tests Drug Firm's Clout, Claritin Maker Goes All Out in Congress," *The Washington Post*, October 30, 1999.

CHAPTER FIVE

1. OpenSecrets.org, www.opensecrets.org.

2. "Retail Prescription Drug Sales 1995–2009," www.census.gov/compendia/ statab/ 2011 /tables/11s0155.pdf.

3. "About Billy," pharma.org, www.pharma.org/about_billy.

4. Paul Blumenthal, "The Legacy of Billy Tauzin: The White House-PhRMA Deal," The Sunlight Foundation (blog), February 12, 2010, sunlightfoundation.com/ blog/2010/ 02/12/the-legacy-of-billy-tauzin-the-white-house-phrma-deal/.

5. "Viewpoint: Price Negotiation Would Dramatically Lower the Cost of Prescription Drugs for Medicare Beneficiaries," The National Committee to Preserve Social Security and Medicare, April 2006, www.ncpssm.org/news/archive/vp_pricenegotiation/; Dean Baker, "The Savings from an Efficient Medicare Drug Plan," Center for Economic and Policy Research, Washington, D.C., January 2006, www.cepr.net/ documents/efficient_medicare_2006_01.pdf.

6. "Max Baucus," OpenSecrets.org, www.opensecrets.org/politicians/summary .php?cid=N00004643&cycle=2012.7.

7. John Heilemann and Mark Halperin, *Game Change: Obama and the Clintons, McCain and Palin, and the Race of a Lifetime* (New York: Harper Collins, 2010).

8. OpenSecrets.org.

9. Ibid.

10. "Max Baucus," OpenSecrets.org.

11. OpenSecrets.org.

12. Peggy Peck, "AMA: After One Year Increase, AMA Membership Declines Again," *MedPage Today*, June 25, 2007, www.medpagetoday.com/MeetingCoverage/ AMA/6006.

13. Vince Galloro, "An Insider's Guide to the Health Care Debate," *Modern Healthcare*, November 4, 2009, www.modernhealthcare.com/article/20091104/ REG/311049952/-1.

14. OpenSecrets.org; "Visualizing the Health Care Lobbyist Complex" (as featured on NPR's *All Things Considered*, July 22, 2009); The Sunlight Foundation (blog), July 22, 2009, sunlightfoundation.com/projects/2009/healthcare_lobbyist_ complex/.

15. The Emergency Medical Treatment and Active Labor Act of 1986, 42 U.S.C. §1395dd (1986).

16. The Federal Civil Rights Act, 42 U.S.C. §1981 et seq. (1991); Executive Order 13166, "Improving Access to Services for Persons with Limited English Proficiency"; 65 Fed.Reg. 50, 121 (August 16, 2000); Dymally-Alatorre Bilingual Services Act, California Government Code §7290 (1973).

17. "Tom Coburn, M.D., United States Senator from Oklahoma," coburn.senate .gov/public/?p=biography.

18. Ibid.

19. Ibid.

CHAPTER SIX

1. Stephen Klaidman, *Coronary: A True Story of Medicine Gone Awry* (New York: Simon and Schuster, 2007).

2. Ibid.

3. Ibid.

4. Ibid.

5. Ibid.

6. Ibid.

7. Ibid.

8. Ibid.; "$395 Million Payment to Settle Unnecessary-Surgeries Suit," *New York Times*, December 22, 2004.

9. Klaidman, *Coronary*; "National Medical Settlement," *New York Times*, March 9, 1994.

10. Guenter B. Risse, *Mending Bodies, Saving Souls: A History of Hospitals* (New York: Oxford University Press, 1999).

11. Ibid.

12. Ibid.

13. Ibid.

14. Ibid.

15. Ibid.

16. Ibid.

17. Ibid.

18. Ibid.

19. Quoted in Robert Kuttner, "Columbia/HCA and the Resurgence of the For-Profit Hospital Ownership and Increased Medicare Spending," *The New England Journal of Medicine* 335 (August 1, 1996): 363.

20. Ibid.

21. Jay Hancock, "Medicine May Finally Be Facing Its Own Enron Moment," *Baltimore Sun*, March 7, 2010.

22. Klaidman, *Coronary*.

23. Elaine Silverman, M.D., M.P.H., Jonathan Skinner, Ph.D., and Elliott Fischer, M.D., M.P.H., "The Association Between For-Profit Hospital Ownership and Increased Medicare Spending," *The New England Journal of Medicine* 341, no. 6 (August 5, 1999): 420–26.

24. P. J. Devereaux et al., "Payments for Care at Private For-Profit and Private Not-For-Profit Hospitals: A Systems Review and Meta-Analysis," *Canadian Medical Association Journal* 170, no. 12 (June 8, 2004): 1817–24, doi: 10.1503/cmaj.1040722.

25. Steffie Woolhandler, M.D., M.P.H., and David U. Himmelstein, M.D., "When Money Is the Mission: The High Costs of Investor-Owned Care," *The New England Journal of Medicine* 341, no. 23 (August 2, 1999): 1768–70; Steffie Woolhandler, M.D., M.P.H., and David U. Himmelstein, M.D., "The High Costs of For-Profit Care," *Canadian Medical Association Journal* 170, no. 12 (June 8, 2004): 1814–15.

26. Woolhandler and Himmelstein, "The High Costs of For-Profit Care."

27. Ibid.

28. "For-Profit Hospitals Costlier and Less Efficient: Harvard Study Shows Bureaucracy Takes 26% of Hospital Budgets," *Public Citizen*, March 12, 1997, www .citizen.org/ publications/release.cfm?ID=6609.

29. Maggie Mahar, "Do Non-Profit Hospitals Deserve Their Tax Breaks?" The Health Care Blog (blog), June 20, 2006, www.thehealthcareblog.com/the_ health_care_blog/2006/06/do_nonprofit_ho.html.

30. Ibid.

31. Ibid.

32. Ibid.

33. Elizabeth Fernandez, "Hospitals, Patients Clash on Privacy," *San Francisco Chronicle*, May 27, 2008.

34. Ibid.

CHAPTER SEVEN

1. Jill Quadagno, *One Nation, Uninsured: Why the U.S. Has No Health Insurance* (New York: Oxford University Press, 2005); David Hoskins, "Cold War Politics Forced Truman's Hand," Workers World (blog), August 19, 2009, www.workers .org/ 2009/us/health_care_0827/.

2. David Kestenbaum and Chana Joffe-Walt, "How Should Medicare Pay Doctors?" *All Things Considered*, National Public Radio, February 26, 2010.

3. David Schactman, "Specialty Hospitals, Ambulatory Surgery Centers and General Hospitals: Charting a Wise Public Policy Course," *Health Affairs* 24, no. 3 (2005): 868–73, doi: 10.1377/hlthaff.24.3.868; Rachel C. Wilson et al., "When Entrepreneurship and Ethics Collide: The Case of Physician-Owned Specialty Hospitals," *The Journal of Applied Management and Entrepreneurship* 13, no. 1 (January 2008): 68-83; "Medicare-Referrals to Physician-Owned Imaging Facilities Warrant HCFA's Scrutiny," General Accounting Office (GAO) Report to the Chairman, Subcommittee on Health, Committee on Ways and Means, U.S. House of Representatives, October 1994; Seth A. Strope, M.D., et al., "Physician Ownership of Ambulatory Surgery Centers and Practice Patterns for Urological Surgery: Evidence from the State of Florida," *Med Care* 47, no. 4 (April 2009): 403–10.

4. "Statement of the American Hospital Association Before the EMTALA Technical Advisory Group," October 26, 2005, www.aha.org/aha/testimony/2005/051026-tes -aha-emtalatag.pdf.

5. Jack Resneck, Jr., M.D., Shira Lipton, M.D., and Mark J. Pletcher, M.D., M.P.H., "Short Wait Times for Patients Seeking Botulinum Toxin Appointments With Dermatologists," *Journal of the American Academy of Dermatology* 57, no. 6 (December 2007): 985–89, doi:10.1016 /j.jaad.2007.07.020; Natasha Singer, "Botox Found Quicker to Get Than a Mole Check," *San Francisco Chronicle*, August 29, 2007.

6. Singer, "Botox Found Quicker to Get Than a Mole Check."

7. Richard A. Deyo, M.D., M.P.H., "Back Surgery—Who Needs It?" *The New England Journal of Medicine* 356, no. 22 (May 31, 2007): 2239–43.

8. John Carreyrou, "Senators Request Probe of Surgeons," *Wall Street Journal*, June 9, 2011, online.wsj.com/article/SB10001424052702304778304576373592455703056.html.

9. William E. Boden et al., "Optimal Medical Therapy With or Without PCI for Stable Coronary Disease," *The New England Journal of Medicine* 356, no. 15 (April 12, 2007): 1503–16.

CHAPTER EIGHT

1. "Biography of Alex Rodriguez," JockBio.com, jockbio.com/Bios/ARod/ARod_bio.html.

2. Jason Reid, "Texas-Sized Deal. Baseball: Rodriguez's Contract with the Rangers Gives Him the Highest Salary of Any U.S. Athlete," *Los Angeles Times*, December 12, 2000.

3. "Physician Salary Surveys," physiciansearch.com, physiciansearch.com/physician/salary.html.

4. "Physicians' Real Income Continues to Fall," *Managed Care Magazine*, July 2006, managed caremag.com/archives/0607/0607.compmon.html; Ha T. Tu and Paul B. Ginsburg, "Losing Ground: Physician Income, 1995–2003 (Tracking Report No. 15)," Center for Studying Health Systems Change, June 2006, hschange.org/CONTENT/ 851/.

5. Marcy Tolkoff, "Exclusive Earnings Survey: How Are You Doing?" *Medical Economics*, October 20, 2006.

6. Monica Langley, "Why $70 Million Wasn't Enough," *Wall Street Journal*, October 20, 2006.

7. Ibid

8. J. Rose, "Wall Streeters Fear for 6-Figure Bonuses," *San Francisco Chronicle*, September 2, 2007.

9. Adam Shell, "Cash of the Titans: Criticism of Pay Grows," *USA Today*, August 30, 2007.

10. Mark R. Laret, Chief Executive Officer of the University of California, San Francisco Health Care System (lecture, 2007 Society of Neurological Surgeons Conference, San Francisco, California, May 7, 2007).

11. Full-page advertisement sponsored by the Mills-Peninsula Health Services, *San Francisco Chronicle*, March 21, 2008.

12. "Sammy Sosa," Baseball-Reference.com, baseball-reference.com/players/s/sosasa01.shmtl.

CHAPTER NINE

1. The Association of American Medical Colleges, "U.S. Medical School Applicants and Students: 1982–83 to 2009–10," www.aamc.org/data/facts/ charts1982to2010.pdf.

2. Patient and Physician Safety and Protection Act of 2001, H.R. 3236, 107th Cong. (2001); Patient and Physician Safety and Protection Act of 2002, S. 2614, 107th Cong. (2002).

3. "Report of the Accreditation of Graduate Medical Education (ACGME) Work Group on Resident Duty Hours," ACGME, Chicago, July 11, 2003.

4. K. Matheson, "Patient Mortality Not Affected By Residents' Work-Hour Restrictions," *San Francisco Chronicle*, September 5, 2007; Kevin G. Volpp, M.D., Ph.D., et al., "Mortality Among Hospitalized Medicare Beneficiaries in the First 2 Years Following ACGME Resident Duty Hour Reform," *The Journal of the American Medical Association* 298, no. 9 (September 15, 2007): 975–83, doi: 10.1001/jama.298.9.975; Kevin G. Volpp, M.D., Ph.D., et al., "Mortality Among Patients in V.A. Hospitals in the First 2 Years Following ACGME Resident Duty Hour Reform," *The Journal of the American Medical Association* 298, no. 9 (September 15, 2007): 984–92, doi: 10.1001/jama.298.9.984.

5. "The Physician Workforce: Projections and Research into Current Issues Affecting Supply and Demand," U.S. Department of Health and Human Services, Health Resources and Services Administration (HRSA), December 2008, bhpr.hrsa.gov/healthworkforce/ reports/physicianworkforce/female.htm; Catherine Arnst, "Are There Too Many Women Doctors?" *Bloomberg Businessweek*, April 17, 2008, businessweek.com/magazine /content/08_17/b4081104183847.htm.

6. The Association of American Medical Colleges, "U.S. Medical School Applicants and Students."

7. "The Next Four Decades—The Older Population in the United States: 2010–2050," The U.S. Census Bureau, May 2010, www.census.gov/prod/2010pubs/p25-1138.pdf.

8. Robert Steinbrook, M.D., "Medical School Debt—Is There a Limit?" *The New England Journal of Medicine* 359, no. 25 (December 18, 2008): 2629–32, doi.10.1056/NEJMp 0808520.

9. The Health Maintenance Organization Act of 1973, 42 U.S.C. §300e (1973).

10. Eva S. Schernhammer, M.D., Dr.P.H., and Graham Colditz, M.D., D.P.H., "Suicide Rates Among Physicians: A Quantitative and Gender Assessment (Meta-Analysis)," *The American Journal of Psychiatry* 161 (December 2004): 2295–2302.

11. Richard A. Cooper, Thomas E. Getzen, Heather J. McKee, and Prakash Laud, "Economic and Demographic Trends Signal an Impending Physician Shortage," *Health Affairs* 21, no. 1 (January 2002): 140–54, doi: 10.1377/hlthaff.21.1.140.

12. "The Next Four Decades—The Older Population in the United States: 2010–2050."

13. James Merritt, Joseph Hawkins, and Phillip Miller, *Will the Last Physician in America Please Turn Off the Lights?* (Irving, TX: Practice Support Resources, The MHA Group, 2004).

14. James A. Hallock, Stephen S. Seeling, and John J. Norcini, "The International Medical Graduate Pipeline," *Health Affairs* 22, no. 4 (July 2003): 94–96, doi: 10.1377/hlthaff.22.4.94.

15. Ibid.

16. Ibid.

17. Merritt et al., *Will the Last Physician in America Please Turn Off the Lights?*
18. Ibid.
19. Luis R. Leon, Jr., M.D., R.V.T., et al., "The Journey of Foreign-Trained Physicians to a United States Residency: Controversies Surrounding the Impact of This Migration to the United States," *Journal of the American Medical College of Surgeons* 206, no. 1 (January 2008): 171–76, doi:10.1016/j.jamcollsurg.2007.06.311.
20. The Association of American Medical Colleges, "U.S. Medical School Applicants and Students."

CHAPTER TEN

1. Milan Korcok, "U.S. Malpractice Premiums Soar Again," *Canadian Medical Association Journal* 166, no. 9 (April 30, 2002): 1195.
2. *Bodine v. Enterprise High School*, Case No. 73225, Shasta County Superior Court (1982).
3. Health Coalition on Liability and Access (HCLA), Protect Patients Now, protect patientsnow.org; "Medical Liability Reform—NOW!" American Medical Association, October 19, 2005.
4. Health Coalition on Liability and Access (HCLA), Protect Patients Now, protectpatientsnow.org; "TV Spot Starting Today in Nevada Features Victim of Medical Liability Crisis," *PR Newswire*, April 21, 2003.
5. Health Coalition on Liability and Access (HCLA), Protect Patients Now, protectpatientsnow.org; "Federal Medical Liability Reform," American College of Obstetricians and Gynecologists 2004 Survey, Alliance of Specialty Medicine, July 2005.
6. Health Coalition on Liability and Access (HCLA), Protect Patients Now, protectpatientsnow.org.
7. Denise Grady, "Caesarean Births Are at a High in U.S.," *New York Times*, March 23, 2010.
8. World Health Organization, *World Health Report* (Geneva: World Health Organization, 2006).
9. "Malpractice Crisis Blamed; Fewer U.S. Seniors Match to OB/GYN Residency Slots; the Fill Rate of This Group Falls to 65.1%," *OB/GYN News*, April 2004.
10. "Medical Liability Reform—NOW!" American Medical Association; "AMA Survey: Medical Students' Opinions on the Current Medical Liability Environment," American Medical Association, November 2003.
11. David E. Bernstein, "Breast Implants: A Study in Phantom Risks: Research Memorandum No. 5," The Manhattan Institute for Policy Research, April 1995, www.manhattan-institute .org/html/research_memorandum_5.htm.
12. *Daubert v. Merrell Dow Pharmaceuticals*, 509 U.S. 579 (1993).
13. Bernstein, "Breast Implants: A Study in Phantom Risks."
14. *Daubert v. Merrell Dow Pharmaceuticals*, 509 U.S. 579 (1993).
15. Sherine E. Gabriel et al., "Risk of Connective Tissue Diseases and Other Disorders After Breast Implantation," *The New England Journal of Medicine* 330, no. 24 (June 16, 1994): 1697–1702.

16. E. C. Jankowsky, L. L. Kupper, and B. S. Hulka, "Meta-Analysis of the Relation Between Silicone Breast Implants and the Risk of Connective Tissue Disease," *The New England Journal of Medicine* 342, no. 11 (March 16, 2000): 781–90; S. Edworthy et al., "A Clinical Study of the Relationship Between Silicone Breast Implants and Connective Tissue Disease," *The Journal of Rheumatology* 25, no. 2 (February 1998): 254–60.

17. "The High Cost of Medical Lawsuit Abuse," Doctors for Medical Liability Reform, Protect Patients Now, protectpatientsnow.org.

18. Health Coalition on Liability and Access (HCLA), Protect Patients Now, protectpatientsnow.org.

19. "The High Cost of Medical Lawsuit Abuse," Doctors for Medical Liability Reform, Protect Patients Now, protectpatientsnow.org.

20. Ibid.

21. "American Association of Neurological Surgeons and Congress of Neurological Surgeons 2004 Survey," Federal Medical Liability Reform, Alliance of Specialty Medicine, July 2005.

22. Doctors for Medical Liability Reform, "The High Cost of Medical Lawsuit Abuse," Protect Patients Now, protectpatientsnow.org.

23. The California Medical Injury Compensation Reform Act of 1975, California Business and Professions Code §6146, California Civil Code §§3333.1, 3333.2, California Code of Civil Procedure §667.7.

24. "Trial of Errors Led to 3 Wrong Brain Surgeries," Health Care on msnbc.com, December 14, 2007, www.msnbc.msn.com/id/22263412/ns/health-health_care/t/trail-errors-led-wrong-brain-surgeries/.

25. Maura Lerner and Josephine Marcotty, "Monday: Wrong Kidney Removed from Methodist Hospital Cancer Patient," *The Star-Tribune*, March 18, 2008.

26. "Veteran Has Wrong Testicle Removed, Files Claim," Men's Health on msnbc.com, April 5, 2007, www.msnbc.msn.com/id/17964480/ns/health-mens_health/t/veteran-has-wrong-testicle-removed-files-claim/.

27. David M. Studdert, LL.B., Sc.D., M.P.H., et al., "Claims, Errors and Compensation Payments in Medical Malpractice Litigation," *The New England Journal of Medicine* 354, no. 19 (May 11, 2006): 2024–33.

28. Troyen Brennan, M.D., J.D., M.P.H., Colin Sox, B.A., and Helen Burstin, M.D., M.P.H., "Relation Between Negligent Adverse Events and the Outcomes of Medical Malpractice Litigation," *The New England Journal of Medicine* 335, no. 26 (December 26, 1996): 1963–67.

29. Kathleen Pender, "High End Escorting—Big Pay and Huge Risks," *San Francisco Chronicle*, March 13, 2008.

CHAPTER ELEVEN

1. Centers for Medicare and Medicaid Services, U.S. Department of Health and Human Services, "National Health Expenditure Data," www.cms.gov/NationalHealth ExpendData/02_NationalHealthAccountsHistorical.asp#TopOfPage.

2. Ken Terry, "Health Spending Hits 17.3 Percent of GDP in Largest Annual Jump," The CBS Interactive Business Network (BNET), February 4, 2010, www.bnet.com/blog/healthcare-business/health-spending-hits-173-percent-of-gdp -in-largest-annual-jump/1117.

3. World Health Organization, *World Health Report* (Geneva: World Health Organization, 2006).

4. "Accidental Death and Disability: The Neglected Disease of Modern Society," Committee on Trauma and Committee on Shock, Division of Medical Sciences, National Research Council, 1966.

5. "The History of Emergency Medicine," The American Board of Emergency Medicine, www.abem.org/PUBLIC/portal/alias__Rainbow/lang__en-US/tabID__3573/DesktopDefault.aspx.

6. P. E. Collicot, "Advanced Trauma Life Support (ATLS): Past, Present, Future—16th Stone Lecture, American Trauma Society," *Journal of Trauma* 33, no. 5 (November 1992): 749–53.

7. "The History of EMS," The Wisconsin EMS Association, www.wemsa.com/history.htm.

8. "9-1-1 Origin and History," The National Emergency Number Association, www.nena.org/?page=911overviewfacts.

9. "The History of EMS," The Wisconsin EMS Association.

10. The Emergency Medical Treatment and Active Labor Act of 1986, 42 U.S.C. §1395dd (1986).

11. Milan Korcok, "U.S. Malpractice Premiums Soar Again," *Canadian Medical Association Journal* 166, no. 9 (April 30, 2002): 1195.

12. Health Coalition on Liability and Access (HCLA), Protect Patients Now, protectpatientsnow.org.

13. Committee on the Future of Emergency Care in the United States Health System, Board on Health Care Services, and the Institute of Medicine, *Hospital Based Emergency Care: At the Breaking Point, Future of Emergency Care Series* (Washington, DC: National Academy Press, 2007).

14. Andis Robeznieks, "Docs on the Do Not Call List," *Modern Healthcare* 37 (May 28, 2007): 26–29.

15. Committee on the Future of Emergency Care in the United States Health System et al., *Hospital Based Emergency Care: At the Breaking Point.*

16. Ibid.

17. Ibid.

18. Ann S. O'Malley, Debra A. Draper, and Laurie E. Felland, "Hospital Emergency On-Call Coverage: Is There a Doctor in the House? (Issue Brief No. 115)" (Washington, DC: Center for Studying Health System Change, November 2007).

CHAPTER TWELVE

1. The Centers for Disease Control and Prevention (CDC), *Obesity and Overweight for Professionals: Data and Statistics—U.S. Obesity Trends*, 2008, www.cdc.gov/

obesity/data/trends.html; Allen K. Sills, M.D., "The Measure of Obesity: A Look at the Data," *American Association of Neurological Surgeons* 17, no. 2 (2008): 8–9; Carolyn Lochhead, "Obesity's Heavy Toll on Medical Expenses," *San Francisco Chronicle*, August 16, 2009.

2. The Centers for Disease Control and Prevention, *Obesity and Overweight for Professionals*; Jeffrey Kluger, "How America's Children Packed on the Pounds," *Time*, June 23, 2008, 66–69.

3. Kluger, "How America's Children Packed on the Pounds."

4. Ibid.

5. National Institute of Diabetes and Digestive and Kidney Diseases (NIDDK), *National Diabetes Statistics, NIH Publication No. 08-3892* (Bethesda, MD: The National Institutes of Health [NIH], June 2008).

6. Ibid.

7. Ibid.

8. Ibid.

9. Martha N. Gardner, Ph.D., and Allan M. Brandt, Ph.D., "The Doctor's Choice Is America's Choice: The Physician in U.S. Cigarette Advertisements, 1930–1953," *American Journal of Public Health* 96, no. 2 (February 2006): 222–32.

10. Surgeon General's Advisory Committee on Smoking and Health, *Smoking and Health: Report of the Advisory Committee to the Surgeon General of the Public Health Service (Public Health Service Publication No. 1103)* (Washington, DC: United States Public Health Service, Office of the Surgeon General, 1964).

11. "Cigarette Smoking Statistics—National Health Interview Survey (NHIS), 2008, National Center for Health Statistics," American Heart Association, americanheart.org/presenter.jhtml?identifier=4559.

12. The Centers for Disease Control and Prevention (CDC), *Economic Facts About U.S. Tobacco Production and Use* (Atlanta, GA: The Centers for Disease Control and Prevention [CDC], 2009).

13. "Annual Smoking-Attributable Mortality, Years of Potential Life Lost and Economic Costs—United States 1995–1999," *Morbidity and Mortality Weekly Report (MMWR)* 51, no. 14 (April 12, 2002): 300–303.

14. "Fact Check: Smokers May Not Cost Society Lots of Money After All," FoxNews.com, April 8, 2009, www.foxnews.com/story/0,2933,513196,00.html.

15. "NIAAA Launches COMBINE Clinical Trial—Eleven Universities to Test Behavioral and Pharmacological Treatment for Alcoholism," *NIH News*, March 8, 2001.

16. "Alcohol Statistics," DrugRehabs.org, www.drug-rehabs.org/alcohol-statistics .php; "Health Costs of Alcohol," The Marin Institute, www.marininstitute.org/ print/alcohol_policy/health_care_costs.htm.

17. The National Institute on Drug Abuse (NIDA), *Magnitude: Drug Abuse Is Costly* (Bethesda, MD: The National Institutes of Health [NIH], United States Department of Health and Human Services, October 25, 1999).

18. Ibid.

19. The California Compassionate Use Act of 1996 (Proposition 215), California Health and Safety Code §11362.5 (1996).

20. California Vehicle Code §27803.

21. National Highway Transportation and Safety Administration (NHTSA), *Motorcycle Helmet Use in 2009—Overall Results*, DOT HS 811 254 (Washington, DC: United States Department of Transportation, December 2009).

22. Bruce A. Lawrence, Wendy Max, and Ted R. Miller, *Costs of Injuries Resulting from Motorcycle Crashes: A Literature Review*, DOT HS 809 242 (Washington, DC: National Highway Transportation and Safety Administration [NHTSA], United States Department of Transportation, 2002).

23. The Rehabilitation Act of 1973, 29 U.S.C. §794 (1973); The Americans with Disabilities Act of 1990, 42 U.S.C. §§12101 et seq. (1990).

24. California Health and Safety Code §120990.

CHAPTER THIRTEEN

1. The Gallup Annual Healthcare Survey, November 11–14, 2007, www.gallup.com/poll/102934/majority-americans-satisfied-their-own-healthcare.aspx.

2. Carmen DeNavas-Walt, Bernadette D. Proctor, and Jessica Smith, *Income, Poverty and Health Insurance Coverage in the United States: 2006* (Washington, DC: United States Census Bureau, United States Department of Commerce, August 2007).

3. Ken Terry, "Health Spending Hits 17.3 Percent of GDP in Largest Annual Jump," The CBS Interactive Business Network (BNET), February 4, 2010, www.bnet.com/blog/ healthcare-business/health-spending-hits-173-percent-of-gdp-in-largest-annual-jump/1117.

4. World Health Organization, *World Health Report* (Geneva: World Health Organization, 2006).

5. "In a Tight Spot, Pelosi Calls Health Care Critics Un-American," FoxNews.com, August 10, 2009, www.foxnews.com/politics/2009/08/10/tight-spot-pelosi-calls-health-care-critics-american/.

6. Celeste Katz, "President Obama Fires Back at Sarah Palin Post Claiming His Health Plan Would Create a Death Panel," *New York Daily News*, August 8, 2009.

7. "This Day in Truman History, November 19, 1945, President Truman's Proposed Health Program," Harry S. Truman Library and Museum, www.trumanlibrary.org/. anniversaries/healthprogram.htm.

8. "A Summary of the 2010 Annual Reports," Social Security and Medicare Boards of Trustees, United States Social Security Administration, www.ssa.gov/oact/trsum/index.html.

9. Mark Blumenthal, "Who's Afraid of Public Insurance? Health Care Consumers Give Medicare Higher Marks Than Private Plans," NationalJournal.com, June 29, 2009, www.nationaljournal.com/njonline/who-s-afraid-of-public-insurance--20090629.

10. Ezra Klein, "Administrative Costs in Health Care: A Primer," *Washington Post*, July 7, 2009; "Single-Payer FAQ," Physicians for a National Health Program (PNHP), pnhp.org/facts/single-payer-faq.

11. "Single-Payer FAQ," Physicians for a National Health Program (PNHP).

12. Ibid.

13. The Patient Protection and Affordable Care Act of 2010, Public Law No. 111-148 (2010); Staff of Washington Post, *Landmark: The Inside Story of America's New Health Care Law and What It Means for Us All* (Philadelphia: Perseus Books Group, 2010).

14. Victoria Colliver, "Anthem Blue Cross Raises Premiums," *San Francisco Chronicle*, February 16, 2010.

15. Jake Tapper, "White House Presses Anthem Blue Cross on Rate Hike," ABCNews.com, February 16, 2010, abcnews.go.com/GMA/white-house-presses-anthem-blue-cross-rate-hike/story?id=9784888.

16. Senator Dianne Feinstein, *A History of the Medical Insurance Industry*, Floor of the U.S. Senate, November 2, 2009.

17. Bruce Bodaken, "Blue Shield Will Cap Profits," *San Francisco Chronicle*, June 7, 2011.

18. The Patient Protection and Affordable Care Act of 2010, Public Law No. 111-148 (2010); Staff of Washington Post, *Landmark: The Inside Story of America's New Health Care Law.*

19. Ricardo Alonso-Zaldivar and Trevor Tompson, "Americans Fear Health Care Law's Costs, Poll Finds," *San Francisco Chronicle*, September 17, 2009.

20. Cathy A. Sila, M.D., Randall T. Higashida, M.D., and G. Patrick Clagett, M.D., "Management of Carotid Stenosis," *The New England Journal of Medicine* 358, no. 15 (April 10, 2008): 1617–21; Executive Committee for the Asymptomatic Carotid Atherosclerosis Study, "Endarterectory for Asymptomatic Carotid Artery Stenosis," *The Journal of the American Medical Association* 273, no. 18 (1995): 1421–28.

21. William S. Weintraub, M.D., et al., "Effect of PCI on Quality of Life in Patients with Stable Coronary Disease," *The New England Journal of Medicine* 359, no. 7 (August 14, 2008): 677–87; William E. Boden et al., "Optimal Medical Therapy With or Without PCI for Stable Coronary Disease," *The New England Journal of Medicine* 356, no. 15 (April 12, 2007): 1503–16.

22. Rachelle Buchbinder, Ph.D., et al., "A Randomized Trial of Vertebroplasty for Painful Osteoporotic Vertebral Fractures," *The New England Journal of Medicine* 361, no. 6 (August 6, 2009): 557–68; David F. Kallmes, M.D., et al., "A Randomized Trial of Vertebroplasty for Osteoporotic Spinal Fractures," *The New England Journal of Medicine* 361, no. 6 (August 6, 2009): 569–79.

23. Christopher Bono, M.D., et al., "Newly Released Vertebroplasty RCTs: A Tale of Two Trials," North American Spine Society Press Release, October 13, 2009; James N. Weinstein, D.O., M.S., "Balancing Science and Informed Choice in Decisions about Vertebroplasty," *The New England Journal of Medicine* 361, no. 6 (August 6, 2009): 619–21.

24. Nina Owcharenko and Bob Moffit, "Senate HELP Amendment Highlights," National Review Online, August 10, 2009, www.nationalreview.com/critical-condition/48516/senate-help-amendment-highlights/nina-owcharenko.

25. "Governor Lamm Asserts Elderly, If Very Ill, Have 'Duty to Die,'" *New York Times*, March 29, 1984.

26. "Affairs of the Heart: Searching for a Substitute," PBS's *Scientific American Frontiers* (web feature), www.pbs.org/saf/1104/features/substitute.htm.

27. Rob Stein, "Task Force Urges Cutting Back on Mammograms," *San Francisco Chronicle,* November 17, 2009; U.S. Preventive Service Task Force, "Screening for Breast Cancer: U.S. Preventive Services Task Force Recommendation Statement," *Annals of Internal Medicine* 151 (November 17, 2009): 716–26; Victoria Colliver, "Anger, Shock at New U.S. Mammogram Guidelines," *San Francisco Chronicle,* November 17, 2009; Alice Park and Kate Pickert, "The Mammogram Melee: How Much Screening Is Best?" *Time,* December 7, 2009.

28. Liz Szabo, "Women Insistent on Cancer Screening: Poll Finds Support for Mammograms," *USA Today,* November 24, 2009.

29. Jane E. Allen, "Two Dead Since Arizona Medicaid Program Slashed Transplant Coverage," ABC News/Health, January 6, 2011, abcnews.go.com/Health/News/arizona-transplant-deaths/story?id=12559369.

30. Correspondence, "Prostate-Cancer Screening," *The New England Journal of Medicine* 361, no. 2 (July 9, 2009): 202–206.

31. David M. Studdert, LL.B., Sc.D., M.P.H., Michelle M. Mello, J.D., Ph.D., and Troyen A. Brennan, M.D., J.D., M.P.H., "Medical Malpractice," *The New England Journal of Medicine* 350, no. 3 (January 15, 2004): 283–92; Paul C. Weiler, *A Measure of Malpractice: Medical Injury, Malpractice Litigation and Patient Compensation* (Cambridge: Harvard University Press, 1993).

32. Weiler, *A Measure of Malpractice.*

33. David M. Studdert, LL.B., Sc.D., M.P.H., et al., "Claims, Errors and Compensation Payments in Medical Malpractice Litigation," *The New England Journal of Medicine* 354, no. 19 (May 11, 2006): 2024–33.

34. Patricia Murphy, "Tort Reform Could Save Health Care $54 Billion, Says CBO," PoliticsDaily.com, December 10, 2009, www.politicsdaily.com/2009/10/12/tort-reform-could-save-health-care-54-billion-says-cbo/.

35. "Agribusiness: Top Contributors 2009–2010," OpenSecrets.org, www.opensecrets.org/indus.php.

36. "Edwards' Malpractice Suits Leave Bitter Taste," *The Washington Times,* August 16, 2004.

37. Richard C. Boothman, J.D., et al., "A Better Approach to Medical Malpractice Claims? The University of Michigan Experience," *Journal of Health and Life Sciences Law* 2, no. 2 (January 2009): 125–59.

38. Starbucks.com, www.starbucks.com/menu/catalog/nutrition? drink=all#view_control=nutrition.

39. National Institute of Diabetes and Digestive and Kidney Diseases (NIDDK), *National Diabetes Statistics, NIH Publication No. 08-3892* (Bethesda, MD: The National Institutes of Health [NIH], June 2008).

40. Ibid.

41. Ibid.

42. Ibid.

43. Associated Press, "Traffic Deaths Plummet to Lowest Level in 60 Years," *New Haven Register,* September 10, 2010.

238   *Notes*

44. Governors' Highway Safety Association, *Cell Phone and Texting Laws*, www.ghsa.org/html/stateinfo/laws/cellphone_laws.html.

45. National Highway Traffic Safety Administration, *Traffic Safety Facts, Laws: Motorcycle Helmet Use Laws*, Report no. DOT HS-810-887W (Washington, DC: U.S. Department of Transportation, 2008); Daniel C. Norvell and Peter Cummings, "Association of Helmet Use with Death in Motorcycle Crashes: A Matched Pair Cohort Study," *American Journal of Epidemiology* 156, no. 5 (2002): 483–87, doi: 10.1093/aje/kwf081.

46. "Q & A: Helmet Use Laws. U.S. Roads," *Auto and Road User Journal*, June 4, 1997,

www.usroads.com/journals/aruj/9706/ru970601.htm.

47. Ibid.

48. Bernard Weinraub, "Sonny Bono, 62, Dies in Skiing Accident," *New York Times*, January 7, 1998.

49. Tom Kenworthy, "Michael Kennedy Dies in Accident on Aspen Slopes," *Washington Post*, January 1, 1998.

50. Joshua T. Cohen, Ph.D., Peter J. Neumann, Sc.D., and Milton C. Weinstein, Ph.D., "Does Preventative Care Save Money? Health Economics and the Presidential Candidates," *The New England Journal of Medicine* 358, no. 7 (February 14, 2008): 661–63.

51. Ibid.

52. Pieter H. M. van Baal et al., "Lifetime Medical Costs of Obesity: Prevention No Cure for Increasing Health Expenditure," *Public Library of Science Medicine Journal* (February 2008).

53. Marcia Angell, *The Truth About the Drug Companies: How They Deceive Us and What to Do About It* (New York: Random House, 2004); Charles Babcock, "Patent Fight Tests Drug Firm's Clout, Claritin Maker Goes All Out in Congress," *The Washington Post*, October 30, 1999.

54. Glenn Thrush, "No Clear Winner in Seven Hour Gabfest," *Pittsburgh Post-Gazette*, February 26, 1010.

55. Patricia Murphy, "Tort Reform Could Save Health Care $54 Billion, Says CBO," PoliticsDaily.com, December 10, 2009, www.politicsdaily.com/2009/10/12/tort-reform-could-save-health-care-54-billion-says-cbo/.

56. Associated Press, "Sen. Landrieu Defends Medicaid Deal for La.," msnbc.com, February 5, 2010, www.msnbc.msn.com/id/35242193/ns/politics-health_care_reform/.

57. "Supreme Court Removes Limits on Corporate, Labor Donations to Campaigns," FoxNews.com, January 21, 2010, www.foxnews.com/politics/2010/01/21/supreme-court-sides-hillary-movie-filmmakers-campaign-money-dispute/.

58. Angell, *The Truth About the Drug Companies*.

59. Statement of Malcolm K. Sparrow, Professor of the Practice of Public Management and Faculty Chair of the Executive Program on Strategic Management of Regulatory and Enforcement Agencies at the Harvard Kennedy School, U.S. Senate on the Judiciary, Subcommittee on Crime and Drugs, May 20, 2009.

60. Remarks of Health and Human Services Secretary Kathleen Sebelius, National Health Care Fraud Summit, Bethesda, Maryland, January 28, 2010.

61. Bill Frogameni, "Task Force Strikes Hard at Medicare Scams," *Christian Science Monitor*, March 25, 2008.

62. K. Kennedy, "More Than 30 Arrested in Medicare Fraud Sweep in Houston, Boston, New York and Louisiana," *Dallas Morning News*, July 30, 2009.

63. Remarks of Health and Human Services Secretary Kathleen Sebelius, National Health Care Fraud Summit, Bethesda, Maryland, January 28, 2010.

64. Remarks of Attorney General Eric Holder, Jr., National Health Care Fraud Summit, Bethesda, Maryland, January 28, 2010.

65. Ibid.

66. Remarks of Acting Deputy Attorney General Gary Grindler, National Health Care Fraud Summit, Bethesda, Maryland, January 28, 2010.

67. "Lilly Discussing Fine to Settle Drug Probe," *San Francisco Chronicle*, January 31, 2010; Martha Raffaele, "Merck to Pay $58 Million to Settle Vioxx Ad Claims," *San Francisco Chronicle*, May 31, 2008.

68. Jay Weaver, "Criminals Bilk Medicare of Billions Each Year," *AARP Bulletin*, November 1, 2009.

69. Frogameni, "Task Force Strikes Hard at Medicare Scams."

70. Remarks of Attorney General Eric Holder, Jr., National Health Care Fraud Summit, Bethesda, Maryland, January 28, 2010.

71. United States Department of Health and Human Services, "Attorney General Holder and Health and Human Services Secretary Sebelius Announce New Interagency Health Care Fraud Prevention and Enforcement Action Team," news release, May 20, 2009.

72. Remarks of Attorney General Eric Holder, Jr., National Health Care Fraud Summit, Bethesda, Maryland, January 28, 2010.

73. Remarks of Health and Human Services Secretary Kathleen Sebelius, National Health Care Fraud Summit, Bethesda, Maryland, January 28, 2010.

Index

access: free market and, 155–56; Medicaid and, 15–16; public option and, 156–59; single payer system and, 150–55; universal, 150; in U.S., 15

"Accidental Death and Disability: The Neglected Disease of Modern Society" (National Academy of Science), 122–23

Acquired Immune Deficiency Syndrome (AIDS), 141

advertising: campaign, 194–95; DTC, 43–45, 196–97, 206; physicians and, 82–83

Aetna, 32

AHA. *See* American Hospital Association

AIDS. *See* Acquired Immune Deficiency Syndrome

alcohol: statistics surrounding, 135–36; Sutterfield and, 136–37

alternative medicine, 168

AMA. *See* American Medical Association

ambulance-chasing tactics, 106

American Hospital Association (AHA), 54–55

American Medical Association (AMA): early history of, 22–23; education

guidelines, 100; fee for service model and, 24; tort reform and, 53–54

Angell, Marcia, 37–38, 45, 47

angina, 167

angioplasty, 81–82

Arizona, 173

artificial heart, 171–72

assembly line physicians, 79–80, 145

attorney bashing, 105, 118

automobile-related deaths, 184

Baby Boomers, 97–98

Babylonians, 21

bankruptcy, cause of, 17

Baucus, Max, 52, 53, 56, 57, 155

Bayh, Birch, 39

Bayh-Dole Act, 39–40

Baylor University Hospital, 23

bidder, lowest, 7

bimaristans (Muslim hospital), 66

Blankfein, Lloyd, 88

Blue Cross Blue Shield, history of, 23, 24, 31

Blue Shield of California, 160

Bodaken, Bruce, 160

Bono, Sonny, 186

Botox, 80

Brand, Michelle, 207–8

breast implants, 111–12

vs. Generation X and, 97–98; career dissatisfaction and, 102; causes of, 100–101; elderly population and, 98; fewer work hours impacting, 98; fields impacted by, 98–99; free agents and, 99–100; IMGs and, 102–4; managed care and, 100–101; new medical schools for, 199; physician extenders and, 200–201; primary care *vs.* specialists and, 200; retirement and, 101; specialty physicians and, 100–101; statistics on, 101, 104

Sick: The Untold Story of America's Health Care Crisis and the People Who Pay the Price (Cohn), 30

Sicko (Moore movie), 148–49

side effects, 197

silicone breast implants, 111–12

Silverman, Elaine, 71

single payer system: capitalism and, 152–53; chronic disease and, 152; cost-efficiency of, 152; database for, 151–52; device manufacturers and, 154; fundamentals of, 151–52; hospitals and, 154; insurance industry and, 153; as monopoly, 154; Patient Protection and Affordable Care Act and, 150–55; paying for, 152; pharmaceutical industry and, 153–54; physicians and, 154; politics and, 155; socialized medicine compared with, 150–51, 152–53

skiing helmet, 186

skylight story, 107–8

Small Smiles Centers, 206

smoking, 134–35

socialized medicine, 149; defined, 150–51; single payer system compared with, 150–51, 152–53

Sosa, Sammy, 91–92

specialists, 200

spinal fusion surgery, 81; smoking and, 135

spine surgery, 81, 135, 166–67, 178

Spitzer, Eliot, 118

stipends, 8, 125–26

Studdert, David, 117–18

subdural hematoma, 90

surgery: angina and, 167; bypass, 81–82; carotid artery, 167; centers, 128–29; cosmetic, 80–81, 111–12; elective, 178; neurosurgery, 108–10; spinal fusion, 81, 135; spine, 81, 135, 166–67, 178

Sutterfield, George, 136–37

Task Force for Effective Care, 176–77

Tauzin, Billy, 43, 51–52

tax breaks, 72–73

Tea Party, 215

technology, 209–11

Tenet Health Care, 64–65

term limits, 193–94

terrorism, 103–4

Tobey, George, 34

Torricelli, Robert, 48, 188

tort reform, 52–53; AMA and, 53–54; evidence-based medicine and, 179–80; honesty and, 180; judgment restrictions and, 181; lawyers' arguments against, 178–79; patients' arguments against, 179; physician silence and, 181; politics and, 179; problems leading to, 178; review council and, 180–81

translator services, 60–61

traumatic injuries: ER rerouting and, 119–20; lawsuits and, 112; malpractice and, 109–10, 112; related deaths in U.S., 13; trauma teams and, 123

Truman, Harry, 25–26, 76

The Truth About the Drug Companies: How They Deceive, Us and What to Do About It (Angell), 37–38

Tutton, Mark, 20

UCSF. *See* University of California, San Francisco Medical Center

UHG. *See* United Health Group

About the Author

Jeffrey M. Lobosky, M.D., was awarded his bachelor of science degree in preprofessional studies from the University of Notre Dame and his doctorate of medicine from the University of California, at Irvine, where he received the J. Gordon Hatfield Award for Outstanding Student in the field of surgery. As a surgical intern at UC Irvine Medical Center, he was named Resident of the Year. He completed his neurosurgical residency at the University of Iowa, where he was the recipient of the Department of Surgery's Outstanding Resident Research Award.

Dr. Lobosky currently serves as associate clinical professor in the Department of Neurological Surgery at the University of California, San Francisco, and is co-director of the Neurotrauma Intensive Care Unit at Enloe Medical Center in Chico, California. He has served on the board of directors for the Joint Section on Trauma and Critical Care for the American Association of Neurological Surgeons and the Congress of Neurological Surgeons. Dr. Lobosky recently completed his term as one of organized neurosurgery's representatives to the American College of Surgeons Committee on Trauma, which advises national policy makers on health care issues.

Dr. Lobosky has received national and international acclaim for his work on injury prevention, has been an invited lecturer throughout the United States and abroad, and is listed in *Who's Who in American Medicine*. He has served as chairman of the board of the National Injury Prevention Foundation and has written a variety of research articles published in national journals as well as several book chapters and articles on the health care crisis in America's trauma system. He has received numerous awards for his contributions to the field of trauma and injury prevention. In 2007, Dr. Lobosky was recognized for his distinguished teaching experience by the students and faculty of the University of California, San Francisco School of Medicine.

He and his wife, Diana, reside in Chico, California, where he continues an active practice as a founding member of Northstate Neurosurgical Associates.